Implementation Theory and Practice
Toward a Third Generation

Malcolm L. Goggin
University of Houston

Ann O'M. Bowman
University of South Carolina

James P. Lester
Colorado State University

Laurence J. O'Toole, Jr.
Auburn University

SCOTT, FORESMAN/LITTLE, BROWN HIGHER EDUCATION
A Division of Scott, Foresman and Company
Glenview, Illinois   London, England

This book is dedicated to our parents

Library of Congress Cataloging-in-Publication Data

Implementation theory and practice: toward a third generation
   Malcolm L. Goggin . . . [et al.].
      p.   cm.
   Includes bibliographical references (p. 208)
   ISBN 0-673-39692-4
   1. Policy sciences.   2. Bureaucracy—United States.
   I. Goggin, Malcolm L.
   H97.I49   1990
320'.6—dc20   90-8033
                                                          CIP

1 2 3 4 5 6—MUR—95 94 93 92 91 90

Preface

"If the study of theory and the study of fact do not fertilize each other, both will be barren."

William Glazer

Implementation Theory and Practice: Toward a Third Generation is about knowing and doing. It addresses two types of readers—those who wish to know more about how policy implementation is studied, and those who seek a better understanding of how implementation is practiced.

The book is meant to serve as a textbook, a monograph, and a practical guide. We have tried to combine what we think are the best features of an enlightening and stimulating educational tool with a thought-provoking professional report. With the student in mind, we have produced an original, theoretical account of policy implementation that simplifies, clarifies, and explains a very complex process—without distorting its true nature. With the scholar in mind, we have tried to raise and answer many thorny questions about how researchers conduct implementation research, questions that have not been fully addressed in the past. (For example, we discuss effective ways to develop and use operational indices and units of empirical measurement, the lack of which has hampered previous efforts to develop and test sound theory.) With the practitioner in mind, we have tried to synthesize a vast quantity of recent literature that shows how implementors have actually identified and tried to resolve implementation problems.

Like much social science research, this account is an accumulation of our own—and other researchers—theories and observations. It is premised on a firm belief that the study of theory and the study of fact are interdependent, as are inquiry and action. If social scientists can develop general theories that account for implementation's causal complexities, then they have a much better chance of solving specific implementation problems. If they systematically observe the regularities of actual implementation behavior, then they improve their chances of achieving a theoretical understanding of implementation. The payoff of joining principle and practice is usable knowledge. From knowledge comes better practices.

By joining a quest for better theory with a search for improved practices, we raise and address a number of questions:

- What are the problems confronting implementors in the field?
- How have implementors—implementing different policies in different states at different times—attempted to solve these problems?
- Which factors and which patterns of relationships among implementors are important predictors of identifiable styles of implementation?
- How might causal variables be manipulated to achieve improved results?
- What are the consequences of adopting alternative implementing strategies for programs that differ with respect to time, policy areas, units of government, organizations, communication patterns, and personnel?

In answering these and other questions about implementation, we synthesize and assess two decades of theoretical and empirical research and chart the way for the next generation—a third generation—of research.

We also report the results of three years of collaborative research that we have conducted on the implementation of three major U.S. policies. We draw on several comparative studies to address the first of these three policies, the Resource Conservation and Recovery Act (RCRA) of 1976. We address the Family Planning Services and Population Research Act of 1970 through a cross-sectional investigation of the implementation of several family planning laws in California in the late 1970s, as well as analyze very recent legislative and administrative attempts to redesign the act. A study of the role of state organizations, including those in the private sector, is the basis of our discussion of the third policy, the 1972 Amendments to the Federal Water Pollution Control Act, commonly known as the Clean Water Act.

The principal sources of data for this collaborative research project are many. The RCRA data were generated primarily from the responses of state administrators to a mail questionnaire administered by Lester and Bowman. (The data were gathered while Lester was a Visiting Scholar at the Council of State Governments and the University of Kentucky in 1987–88.) These data were supplemented by interviews of U.S. Environmental Protection Agency officials. The Clean Water Act data came from extensive interviews with local waste-water officials, and less structured interviews with state and federal clean-water regulators and legislative staff, representatives of private groups, and union officials. (The interviews were conducted in 1988 by O'Toole and his collaborators, John Heilman and Gerald Jackson, from Auburn

University.) The Family Planning data were derived from face-to-face interviews with elites in California, Washington-based administrators of the Title X family planning law, Congresspersons and staff who are members of the House Energy and Commerce Committee, and members of the family planning establishment in Washington, D.C. (Goggin conducted the California interviews when he was a lecturer and researcher at the Stanford University Medical School, and completed the Washington, D.C., interviews while he was a Guest Scholar at the Brookings Institution in 1988.) During all our research, we also relied on systematic analysis of federal, regional, state, and local public documents, as well as the records of corporations and nonprofit organizations.

We are indebted to all the people who agreed to talk with us during the course of our research. We are also grateful to Karen Baird, Janice Butler, Lucy Gee, John Hindera, and Steven Moody, graduate research assistants at the University of Houston and at the Brookings Institution, who helped with data collection and analysis. Jean England and Robert Gottesman, graduate research assistants at Auburn University, helped with data collection and analysis for the waste-water treatment portions of the work.

We also wish to thank several colleagues who read various parts of this book and shared their thoughts with us. These include Fran Berry, R. Steven Brown, Charles Davis, William Dunn, Richard Hofferbert, Helen Ingram, Hank Jenkins-Smith, Sheldon Kamieniecki, John Kingdon, Dean Mann, Daniel Mazmanian, Phillip Roeder, Paul Sabatier, Anne Schneider, John Scholz, Robert Stoker, Carl Van Horn, and four reviewers for Scott, Foresman/Little, Brown: George Edwards, David Lowery, Michael Reagan, and Bruce Williams. We have listened to their constructive criticisms and acted on much of their advice.

Several institutions supported this collaborative effort, in one form or another, during three years of research and writing. During the 1987–88 academic year, Malcolm Goggin was supported by a faculty development leave from the University of Houston, and was fortunate to be able to spend much of that time at the Brookings Institution as a Guest Scholar. He would like to thank Thomas Mann, Director of the Governmental Studies Program, and the scholars and staff at Brookings who created such a stimulating environment for research and writing. A portion of the research on policy redesign was also supported by a Limited Grant in Aid from the University of Houston Office of Sponsored Programs. There are no words that can express his gratitude for the love, patience, and sacrifice of Mary-Margaret, an understanding and supportive spouse.

Ann Bowman served as the 1986–87 Lincoln Government Fellow at the National League of Cities when this research project was conceived. Since then, she has benefited from a research release provided by the Department of Government and International Studies at the University of South Carolina.

During the 1987–88 academic year, James Lester was supported as a Visiting Scholar by the University of Kentucky's Martin School of Public Administration and the Council of State Governments.

Larry O'Toole owes a number of debts. Several scholars have helped over the years to clarify his thinking about implementation. Among these are Ken Hanf, Benny Hjern, Robert Montjoy, and David Porter. The U.S. Department of the Interior Geological Survey, Reston, Virginia, as authorized by the Water Resources Research Act of 1984 (P.L. 98-242), funded some of the clean water research reported here, through the Water Resources Research Institute of Auburn University, Auburn, Alabama. (The contents of this book do not necessarily reflect the views and policies of the U.S. Department of the Interior.) O'Toole's research was also supported somewhat more indirectly by the Geological Survey, through a grant to John Heilman and Gerald Johnson, two Auburn colleagues. To his wife Mary and to their children, Conor and Katie, he expresses great gratitude for inspiration, uplift, patience, and faith. To the memory of his dear brother Michael, who tolerated the intrusion of this project at a time of great personal travail, he offers a special expression of gratitude. On this occasion, as so often before, Michael served as the most unprepossessing of teachers.

Every book needs good editors, and for their support, guidance, and patience, we wish to thank John Covell, Richard Welna, Lynn Brown, Bob Olander, and the entire editorial staff of Scott, Foresman/Little Brown.

Malcolm L. Goggin
Ann O'M. Bowman
James P. Lester
Laurence J. O'Toole, Jr.

Contents

List of Figures and Tables

Introduction

In a December 6, 1986 radio broadcast to the American people, President Ronald Reagan admitted that the implementation of a U.S. policy to swap arms for American hostages and to improve relations with moderate forces in Iran had gone awry. Despite a specific Congressional prohibition in the form of the Boland amendment, the Administration's National Security Council used the profits from the sale of arms to Iran to provide military assistance to Contra forces opposed to the Sandinista government in Nicaragua. The problem, according to the president, was not with the initial policy, but rather with the way in which it was put into practice. For their role in the implementation of this failed policy, President Reagan dismissed one zealot at the National Security Council—Marine Corps Lieutenant Colonel Oliver L. North—and asked for the resignation of his boss, Admiral John M. Poindexter. (For an insider account of the Congressional Iran-Contra inquiry, see Cohen and Mitchell, 1988.)

Indeed, in attempting to give the American people an accounting of what went wrong at a November 25, 1986 press conference, Reagan frequently used the term, *implementation.* On the subject of implementation, the President said, "I am deeply troubled that the implementation of a policy aimed at resolving a truly tragic situation in the Middle East has resulted in such controversy. As I've stated previously, I believe our policy goals toward Iran are well-founded. However, the information brought to my attention yesterday convinced me that in one aspect, implementation of that policy was seriously flawed" (Reagan, 1986: 38-D).

THE IMPLEMENTATION ERA

In March 1988, North, Poindexter, and two others were indicted on charges of conspiring to defraud the government by illegally diverting millions of dollars in profits from U.S. weapons sale to Iran to help the Contras. After eleven months of delays and pretrial haggling, the

3

trial of Oliver North opened before Federal District Court Judge Gerhart Gesell. In his February 21, 1989 opening statement, John Keker, the associate independent prosecutor, presented a version of the facts of the Iran-Contra case that supported President Reagan's claim that he knew nothing of the unauthorized dealings of his underlings at the National Security Council. If one believes this version of the facts, then Iran-Contra is a classic case of a nonelected public official exercising bureaucratic discretion to make policy without having *specific* orders from his or her superiors and without having to account to the electorate.

Another version of the facts, however, came from Brendan Sullivan, North's defense lawyer. In his opening remarks, Sullivan characterized his client as a mid-level policy mechanic, faithful to his commander-in-chief, merely implementing official policy as he understood it. If one believes the facts as represented by North's attorney, then President Reagan, not North, was the zealot.

On May 4, the jury acquitted Oliver North of nine of the twelve counts for which he was charged. The jury found North guilty of three other charges—obstructing Congress, destroying documents, and accepting an illegal gratuity. The trial did not, however, resolve the question at issue here. Was the president guilty of directing North to circumvent the law that prohibited giving military aid to the Contras, or was he merely guilty of poor management because he neither monitored nor controlled the activities of his subordinates?

The North trial and an earlier report of a three-member presidential commission headed by former Texas Senator John Tower, joint House-Senate hearings, and revelations in the press about the circumstances of the arms-for-hostages deal and the diversion of funds to the Contras all focus on a potential Constitutional crisis. This crisis stems from the tensions that the Iran-Contra incident created between the executive and legislative branches of government. The investigations also highlight implementation problems of control, coordination, and competence associated with Reagan's management style, thus drawing national attention to implementation issues.[1]

In May 1988, the issues of control, competence, and especially coordination surfaced again over the Reagan Administration proposal that the U.S. drop drug charges against General Manuel Noriega, the chief of the Panamanian National Defense Forces (NDF), and negotiate with him over the terms of his departure from office. On the floor of the U.S. Senate, Senator Alfonse D'Amato urged his fellow Americans to let President Reagan know what they thought of the plea-bargaining offer to Noriega, which D'Amato described as a "legal golden parachute"—"our pleading and Noriega bargaining" (D'Amato, 1988: §5986).

The Republican Senator from New York charged that Latin American dictators and drug dealers would "laugh at the United States at our ineptitude, and at our incompetence." He placed the blame for the Reagan Administration's policy on implementation problems—on Defense Department advisors to the president who were "coming to set policy as opposed to carrying it out" (D'Amato, 1988: §5987). Commenting on Administration ineptitude in its handling of the Noriega affair in 1988, Senator D'Amato said that the Republican Administration "set its hair on fire and is trying to put it out with a hammer." The Bush Administration was also the target of severe criticism from both sides of the aisle for the way it missed an opportunity to take custody of Noriega in Panama during an abortive coup attempt on October 3, 1989. In answer to criticism that the administration's response to the attempted coup was ineffective, the White House ordered a thorough review of the way policy was made and implemented. Apparently, flaws were corrected by December 20, 1989, when President Bush ordered American troops to invade Panama for the purpose of protecting American lives; restoring democratic processes; preserving the integrity of the Panama Canal treaties; and, probably most important of all, ousting and capturing Noriega. The preplanned mission was a model of implementation efficiency: prompt implementation (within twenty-four hours), and implementation without modification by military leaders in the field, and satisfactory results—the downfall of Noreiga.

The implementation issues that are illustrated by the Iran-Contra and Noriega affairs have also recently received national attention because of other, no less dramatic events during the decade of the 1980s. Two of these developments are the huge budget deficit and a resurgence of the American states as important partners of the national government in the nation's federal system. Both have highlighted the importance of implementation.

Fighting the Budget Deficit?

During the Reagan era, the nation amassed a huge national debt, with annual deficits soaring above $200 billion on several occasions. During Reagan's two terms, nationally held debt increased by 160 percent—from $725 billion to approximately $2 trillion as George Bush entered the White House. As a percentage of national income, debt rose from 32 percent to 52 percent during the Reagan years (Economic Report of the President, 1988). In response to rising deficits, in December 1985 Congress passed the Balanced Budget and Emergency Deficit Control Act, better known as the Gramm-Rudman-Hollings deficit reduction plan. It forced Congress and the President to set limits on the budget deficit for each fiscal year between 1986 and 1991, at which time spending would not be allowed to exceed revenues.

Limitations on government spending that have been imposed by the deficit reduction plan and President George Bush's campaign promise of "no new taxes" make major, new "big-ticket" items virtually impossible to pass in the Congress. Already many new programs, like the abortive Medicare Catastrophic Coverage Act that was passed in time for the 1988 presidential election and repealed a year later, are typically self-financed. For catastrophic illnesses, the elderly who could afford it were to have paid a premium for the insurance, with the wealthiest of the elderly paying a maximum surtax of $800 in 1989, rising to $1050 in 1993. Led by their more affluent members who were obligated to pay for benefits they had already procured in the private sector, the elderly resisted this self-financing scheme, pressuring their representatives in Congress to repeal the program. Given the recent emphasis on austerity measures to reduce the budget deficit and the albatross of no new taxes, there is little likelihood that Congress will pass and the president will sign many bold, new programs in the near future.

If proposals do get through Congress, either those who benefit directly from these programs or the American states may be asked to foot much of the bill. Prime examples are President Bush's war on drugs and his proposals to improve the nation's public schools. According to Senator Joseph Biden, the federal mandates for fighting drug pushers and users could require states to spend $9 billion for new prisons and more police officers (Farney and Davidson, 1989: A20). New education initiatives that emerged as a result of a historic September 1989 summit conference between President Bush and the nation's governors provided few new resources from Washington. This is consistent with the typical pattern between 1980 and 1989, when actual federal expenditures for education declined by 30 percent.

The retrenchment that has characterized recent Republican administrations has created an emphasis on program efficiency and effectiveness. Indeed, in 1981 President Reagan promised "to limit government to its proper role and make it the servant, not the master, of the people" (Reagan, 1981). In his January 1989 Budget Message to Congress, as he reflected on his Administration's eight years, Reagan claimed improved program management as one of its major accomplishments. He took credit for returning the federal government to "its proper role," and for initiating "a major program to improve the management of the remaining programs" (Reagan, 1989).

Ronald Reagan skillfully used the budget as a statement of conservative principles—an instrument for implementing his campaign promises and his policy priorities. He also used the Office of Management and Budget (OMB)—at least during his first two-and-one-half years in office—as a tool for political control and for central coordination to ensure uniform implementation of policies. Loyal political appointees placed in strategic decision-making positions in the executive branch, doing the bidding of a popular president, also helped ensure consistency and political orthodoxy across agencies throughout Reagan's tenure in office.

Although in his first year in office President George Bush showed signs of a greater willingness than his predecessor to compromise with Congress, he also has used many of the same tools that made Reagan so successful in advancing his political agenda.

Promoting States' Rights

Another major Reagan initiative—a resurrection of states' rights and reliance on community autonomy as a means of advancing the individual American state's own interests—has also underscored the importance of implementation issues. States' rights issues were exemplified in "New Federalism" programs and their principal instrument, twelve block grants (as of 1989). This initiative reflected the conservative public philosophy that combined devolution of program responsibility with deregulation and a firm belief that the government that governs least governs best.

The states' rights era was ushered in with the passage of the Omnibus Budget Reconciliation Act of 1981 (OBRA) (Chubb, 1985). In 1981, when the majority of these block grants were created at the behest of the Reagan Administration, Congress also cut federal support for individual program operation, assuming that states would replace reductions with state funds. But several early studies of the effects of OBRA showed that states were slow in replacing the cutbacks with appropriations from state coffers (Bender and Stever, 1986; Goggin et al., 1985). In the environmental area, which is not covered by the block grants, some of the available evidence suggests that states have not replaced reductions in federal grants-in-aid to the states either (Lester, 1986; Davis and Lester, 1987).

Nonetheless, there are several recent examples where states have taken the initiative in regulation and enforcement. California, for example, decided to block a $2.5 billion merger of two supermarket chains (Labaton, 1989). Los Angeles devised its own sweeping three-tier plan to attack the regional air pollution problem, especially ozone pollution (Reinhold, 1989).

The policy of reducing the role of the *national* government in the federal system has had mixed results, however. For example, there are now fewer grants-in-aid but the number is rising again. Federal dollars as a proportion of federal-state outlays are down, but total federal spending is up, as is total spending by state and local governments (Walker, 1988: 11–14).

Nonetheless, the combination of a clear signal from Washington that the states must take more responsibility for their own destinies plus the states' own sustained efforts over the past twenty years to build managerial and technical competency have resulted in appreciably less hierarchical control from Washington and more discretion in the hands of state and local policy makers and managers in charge of intergovernmental implementation. This recent resurgence of the states in American federalism (ACIR, 1985; Bowman and Kearney, 1986; Harrigan, 1988) also contributes to the growing importance of implementation as a field of study.[2]

The Need for Increased Attention to Policy Management

The dramatic example of the National Security Council's implementation of the United States foreign policy toward Iran and Nicaragua and the more recent confusion over how the nation's foreign policy toward Panama should be implemented highlight a serious problem of governance. The problem is our collective ignorance about why the implementation, or carrying out, of public policies occurs as it does. Equally troubling is that out of ignorance about the *general* characteristics of the process, relatively little is known about how implementation can be made to work better.

Furthermore, as cases of national policies transformed into operational programs, the Iran-Contra initiative and the 1988 and October 1989 mishandling of U.S. policy to oust Panamanian dictator Noriega dramatize the potential disaster inherent in ignoring problems associated with management style, often manifested in poor implementation performance. The rising budget deficit; the demand for greater control, coordination, and competence; and the resurgence of states' autonomy in policy spheres also serve as a reminder that there is a pressing need for improved understanding of how and why implementation actually works the way it does.[3]

The line of argument pursued in this book holds that one of the most promising ways to make sense of the causal complexities of policy implementation is to adopt a more "scientific" search for the patterned regularities as well as the idiosyncrasies of implementation decisions and actions. This search extends across time, policies, and units of government. By comparing assertions about how implementation might ideally work with systematic observations of how implementation is actually working (or not working), we expect to be able to unravel several puzzling questions about implementation theory and practice. We call this a "third-generation" approach.

As a separate field of study, implementation is still in its infancy. As a set of activities that are analytically distinct from public administration, implementation received relatively little scholarly attention before the 1973 publication of Jeffrey Pressman and Aaron Wildavsky's *Implementation*. In the mid- to late-1960s, as the monumental social policies of the Great Society were enacted in the 89th and 90th Congresses and as Congressional scholars gained increased access to the national legislature, what excited students of politics was the legislative process—how a bill becomes a law. By the end of the decade, the term *public policy* had come to mean policy formation or adoption.

In the 1970s, amidst claims that the Great Society had failed to live up to expectations, scholarly attention shifted to answering questions of how a law becomes a program (Bardach, 1977) and why program performance falls short of legislative promises (Ingram and Mann, 1980; Jones, 1988; Mazmanian and Sabatier, 1981). The fascination with policy formation ebbed somewhat, nudged aside by a surge of applied—some would say "policy relevant"—research that was triggered, in part, by David Easton's (1969) call for a "post-behavioral revolution" in political science. Spurred by the widespread belief that the Great Society had failed and that its salvation resided in implementation and evaluation research, an interest in the implementation and evaluation phases of the policy cycle (Brewer, 1974; Lasswell, 1956) emerged simultaneously and developed in tandem (for the nexus between implementation and evaluation see Palumbo, 1981).

That there is keen interest in both implementation theory and implementation practice is widely accepted. This interest is likely to grow during the 1990s and continue well into the twenty-first century. In fact, the field of public policy in the next decade will very likely be defined by its focus on implementation. The nineties are likely to be the *implementation era*.

OVERCOMING IMPEDIMENTS TO FURTHER ADVANCES IN KNOWLEDGE

Despite widespread agreement that there is still much to be learned about how implementation actually works and how it can be made to work better, many skeptics doubt researchers' ability to more fully comprehend the causal complexities of the political and administrative phenomenon called public policy implementation. In fact, there are compelling reasons to agree with this assessment. Chief among them is that after more than twenty years of laboring in the implementation vineyards, the scholars who study implementation—and we count ourselves among them—have yet to come up with an agreed-upon theory that adequately explains why those who implement public policies behave as they do. Nor is there a theory capable of predicting the political and administrative behaviors of those at national and subnational levels of government who jointly put policy into effect throughout the American federal system.[4] ⌐

There are additional reasons to be skeptical. Besides the absence of a predictive or explanatory theory that commands general agreement, the major impediments to understanding this important aspect of the policy process are

- the problem of research that uses too many variables, but too few cases, or "overdetermination"
- the lack of attention to the development of measures
- a dearth of empirical research that is truly comparative, longitudinal, and synthetic (Goggin, 1986; Lester, et al., 1987; Linder and Peters, 1987; O'Toole, 1986; Sabatier, 1986; Wittrock and DeLeon, 1987)

The Cases/Variables Problem

The nature of the implementation process has forced many of those who practice the "craft" of implementation research (Yin, 1982) to eschew statistical or experimental methods in favor of the case study or small "N" comparative approach. Choosing these research methods has made it exceedingly difficult for investigators either to introduce the element of control for the effects of extraneous independent variables or to generalize from their findings (Goggin, 1986).

Essentially, previous investigators have been plagued by the problem of "many variables/small N" (Lijphart, 1971: 686), creating a situation where two or more variables might explain variations in a particular phenomenon equally well.[5] The complication for both the implementation scholar and the practicing implementor is that the typical research design does not permit her or him to rule out rival explanations for why implementation occurs as it does.

A more serious complication of the cases/variables problem, however, is the extent to which findings can be generalized. Another factor affecting generalization, or external validity, of findings about implementation is the selection of cases to be examined. In the past, many implementation scholars have either failed to identify or experienced difficulty in defining the policy universe and then effectively sampling from it. One underlying reason for the problem is that there is still no widespread agreement among those who do implementation research about what actually constitutes a case of implementation. There is still some confusion over when implementation begins, when it ends, and how many types of implementation there are (Goggin, 1986:

335–38). Questions about the size and other attributes of the universe from which cases are drawn for comparison are addressed more fully when the procedures for defining the universe of cases and the approach to case selection that has been adopted in this book are described and justified.

The Lack of Estimates

In addition, measures of implementation, an exceedingly dynamic and complex phenomenon, as well as measures of its antecedents and consequences, have yet to be adequately developed. In the place of operational definitions of concepts and precise measures of variables is what several critics have called a "checklist" or "how-to manual." Laurence O'Toole (1986) has criticized the literature for its plethora of "proverbs." Even the most sophisticated schemas have provided only a general map of the broad terrain of implementation behavior. What is needed is a topographical map that characterizes the terrain in precise terms, indicates quantitative measures, and specifies precise relationships among the various elements.

Neglect of the Role of the States

Despite an impressive growth in the quantity and quality of implementation research in recent years, surprisingly little attention has been paid to the role of the states during the process of a program's implementation. Typically, studies are either "bottom-up" or "top-down" investigations. A bottom-up study may show how local communities or school districts (including "street-level" bureaucrats) negotiate with federal, regional, and state agency personnel, elected representatives, and the environment to arrive at a mutually satisfying policy. Top-down studies show how a federal mandate (a public law or a Supreme Court decision, for example) structures choices at the level of state and local government. (For a recent review and synthesis of this literature, see Lester et al., 1987). We return to this subject in the context of an analysis of federal-level inducements and constraints in Chapter 3 and again in Chapter 5 of this book.

The bottom-up and top-down strategies typify implementation research. Top-down research focuses on implementation effects of national- or central government-controlled variables, to the exclusion or heavy deemphasis of other factors. Examples include Bullock, 1980; Gunn, 1978; Hogwood and Gunn, 1984; Mazmanian and Sabatier, 1981, 1983; Rosenbaum, 1980; and Sabatier and Mazmanian, 1979. Critics of this approach have correctly indicated how much of the implementation process, outputs, and outcomes are left unexplained by this kind of effort. These critics have noted that such studies are likely to lead primarily to conclusions that are quite impractical, because implementors themselves often cannot control some of these variables (Barrett and Fudge, 1981; Berman, 1978; Elmore, 1979; Hjern, 1982; Hjern and Hull, 1982, 1985; Hjern and Porter, 1982; Thompson, 1982; Weatherley and Lipsky, 1977).

The bottom-up response to this strategy has been not to investigate formal policies established by a central regime or even, sometimes, behavior of the officially prescribed implementation actors. Bottom-up studies start with action at the street level, so to speak, and determine through network-like analyses just what happens—what action emerges around a policy problem.

Both approaches can develop significant weaknesses. Each tends to ignore the portion of implementation reality explained by the other, and neither addresses the question of the relative influence of these different sorts of variables on policy as it is converted into action. More importantly, perhaps, neither conceptualizes the process in a fashion that is likely to explain clearly how these different factors interactively affect implementation in a dynamic fashion. The model developed in this volume is an effort to do just that.

Often neglected in these two approaches is the state as an actor caught between pressures from above *and* below. Although the state has occasionally been characterized as an "intermediary" or "gatekeeper" in the conversion of plans into actions (Thomas, 1981), only a handful of researchers have used the state as the primary unit of analysis (notably Aron, 1979; Goggin, 1987; Ingram, 1978; Lester and Bowman, 1989; Lester et al., 1983).

Finally, state-level variables are seldom examined in an intergovernmental context. For example, much of the comparative state policy literature has focused on the relative importance of socioeconomic versus political variables over time in explaining public policy outputs (Lewis-Beck, 1977). Absent from this approach is an expansion of these "ecological" variables (Riggs, 1980) to include *federal- and local-,* as well as state-level variables in influencing policy outputs (Hanson, 1983; Rose, 1973). This "levels of analysis" issue is reconsidered in Chapters 3, 4, and 6.

Treating Implementors as Autonomous Rational Actors

Much of the extant implementation research that does take the state into account conceptualizes state government as a unitary rational actor (Allison, 1971: 4–5). With the few notable exceptions mentioned earlier, research has not incorporated the important consideration suggested by Douglas Rose (1973: 1170) that states are areal collections of various subsystems of national and local politics. Taking a cue from the recent literature on national bureaucratic behavior (Bendor and Moe, 1985; Miller and Moe, 1983; and Scholz and Wei, 1986), state-level implementation decisions and actions need to be treated as the joint product of interactions among bureaucrats, politicians, and representatives of organized interests.

In our view, implementation cannot be comprehended fully without observing the continual exchange among these interdependent actors. In the approach adopted in this book, states are placed in the center and then examined in the context of the constraints that they face from below, horizontally, and from above. Because the states have increased their managerial and technical capacity and are increasingly the locus of policy action in the federal system, making the states the central focus of research makes a lot of sense.

TWO "GENERATIONS" OF RESEARCH ON IMPLEMENTATION

There are sound reasons to be skeptical about investigators' ability to comprehend implementation. Several formidable conceptual and methodological problems have, in fact, made it difficult to understand the complexities of the policy implementation process (Bowman et al., 1987; Lester et al., 1987). There is also reason to be optimistic about the future. Consider the progress that has been made in two "generations" of implementation research in the past two decades. (For a comprehensive review and assessment of implementation models, see O'Toole, 1986, and Lester et al., 1987.)

First-Generation Research

First-generation studies were, for the most part, detailed accounts of how a single authoritative decision was carried out, either at a single location or at multiple sites. Jeffrey Pressman's and Aaron Wildavsky's (1973) ground-breaking *Implementation* is typical of this genre of implementation research. First-generation studies have been criticized for being atheoretical, case-specific, and noncumulative. They have also been accused of being overly pessimistic.

Despite this criticism, they served several valuable purposes. They

- managed to shift the focus from how a bill becomes a law to how a law becomes a program

- demonstrated the complex and dynamic nature of implementation
- emphasized the importance of a policy subsystem and the difficulties that a subsystem creates for coordination and control
- identified a number of factors that seemed to account for programmatic results, which, with the exception of the Fleet Ballistics Missile Project (Sapolsky, 1972), usually fell short of expectations
- diagnosed several treatable pathologies that periodically plague implementing actors

Second-Generation Research

A second generation of studies built upon this earlier work. This later generation of scholarship's unique contribution was the development of analytical frameworks to guide research on the complex phenomenon of policy implementation. To a large extent, although the breakdown among broad categories of variables differed, all of these second-generation studies focused on the same predictor variables:

- *policy* form and content
- *organizations* and their resources
- *people*—their talents, motives, predispositions, and their interpersonal relationships, including patterns of communications (Edwards, 1980; Goggin, 1987; Nakamura and Smallwood, 1980; Sabatier and Mazmanian, 1979; Van Horn and Van Meter, 1976; Van Meter and Van Horn, 1975)

A few studies also singled out the decision-making environments in the states as conditioning, if not determining, implementation and its results (Van Horn, 1979a,b).

The positive contributions of books like Daniel Mazmanian and Paul Sabatier's *Implementation and Public Policy,* Randall Ripley and Grace Franklin's *Bureaucracy and Policy Implementation,* and Helen Ingram and Dean Mann's *Why Policies Succeed or Fail* were many. Chief among these framework-development studies' contributions to the field were

- recognition that implementation *does* vary over time, across policies, and from one state to the next
- identification of the likely candidates for explaining those variations
- confrontation of many difficult problems accompanying the process of systematic empirical research in this subfield of the discipline

Second-generation research also taught researchers the importance of time periods—at what point in history implementation occurs and over what period of time (Van Horn, 1987).

Second-generation scholars accomplished a great deal. Nonetheless, Mazmanian and Sabatier were only able to *illustrate* their framework with six nonstandardized case studies that could not be replicated. The investigators paid virtually no attention to interstate variations in implementation. Moreover, their model failed to tell us which variables are more important than others (Browne and Wildavsky, 1984; Hargrove, 1980; Wagner, 1986).

Ripley and Franklin's approach, which built on Lowi's "policy determines politics" hypothesis (1964), was limited in scope. The emphasis focused, again, on the national level of government. Moreover, they relied heavily on anecdotal, case-specific evidence to make their case.

Later frameworks attempted to synthesize what was essentially two levels of analysis in the implementation field: the federal and the local (Sabatier, 1986). No one, however, has been able to validate the propositions that have been derived from the earlier frameworks or from a synthesis of perspectives. Few subsequent researchers have conducted studies that could be replicated by other scholars. Clearly, the challenge for the next generation of scholarship is to develop and test explanatory and predictive implementation theories of the middle range. Such theories consist of minor working hypotheses that have applicability to a limited range of data. The largest challenge will be to transfer the practical implications of this new knowledge to professional implementors.

THIRD-GENERATION RESEARCH

Inspiration for writing this book certainly comes from the contributions of this congeries of first- and second-generation scholars. Yet we have also been inspired by our own confidence in the future: Improved understanding of implementation is not only possible but highly probable. It is this optimism about the future that has encouraged us to elaborate a theory of how and why we think implementors behave as they do and begin to probe the validity of these notions with systematic observations of how implementation is actually practiced.

In this context, then, it is important to indicate clearly the nature of the work embodied in this volume: its purpose, its contributions, and also its limitations. First, it should be noted that all four authors of this book have conducted implementation research that is clearly characteristic of second-generation research. Yet we have all recognized the limitations of that kind of effort and believe that research in this field must move beyond the constraints embodied therein. Further, we are convinced that for scholarship of a third generation to flourish, some crucial steps must first be undertaken.

This book is an effort to initiate those steps—to serve, in effect, as a bridge between second- and third-generation implementation research. If the volume adequately serves its purpose, it will serve not only as an up-to-date assessment of the field but also be used to launch a third-generation research agenda that allows for many possible varieties of creative development in the field.

Precisely what kind of contribution is intended by this effort? It may be most helpful to begin by indicating what is *not* intended or accomplished here. The succeeding chapters do not report the results of a full-blown, completed third-generation research project. The volume does contain findings, some of which have not been reported in print before. But even the most recent results included here find their origins in second-generation designs. The evidence adduced herein, both from our own continuing research and from the published work of others, seeks to explain variability in the implementation process and in the anticipated and unanticipated consequences of implementation. The task of explanation is also approached here comparatively and to some extent longitudinally.

Yet the findings share the validity and reliability shortcomings of previous research as well. One will not find a definitive test of a general theory of implementation in these pages. Instead, this book aims at the accomplishment of two related purposes, both of which are essential components of any advance to a third generation of implementation scholarship.

First, we have surveyed the range of research and theorizing in this field to date—and indeed beyond the conventionally conceived boundaries of the field, to such related matters as research on persuasive communications and studies of comparative state policy that have thus far played almost no role in influencing implementation research. As a result of this wide-ranging study of the field, we have developed a model of the implementation process that integrates the major concerns and variables of the top-down and bottom-up research traditions into a single framework.

This framework is specified clearly and is elaborated in a core set of chapters that spell out the elements of the model (Chapters 3–7). Hypotheses derived from the model are summarized in Chapter 8. Thus the book offers both a synthetic theory and an inventory of related propositions tied clearly to the overall perspective. Even more—and essential for the development of third-generation scholarship—this book addresses questions of conceptualization and measurement so often ignored or treated superficially in much of the literature of the first two generations.

We select three policy sectors; present some implementation data about them (see Chapter 2 on dependent variables); and explore if only suggestively how the variations that exist across settings, policies, and time may be linked to the independent and intervening variables that constitute the main focus of attention. Thereby we attempt to suggest in rather concrete form how large-scale third-generation research can be accomplished in practice. The design for such a theory-testing research project is developed in Chapter 8. Furthermore, to the extent that empirical findings from second-generation research seem to speak to the propositions developed here, the appropriate evidence from others' research is also tied directly to the theoretical exposition.

Overall, then, the book

1. integrates disparate theoretical and empirical work
2. proposes one perspective on how implementation takes place
3. discusses this perspective in conjunction with three discrete policies implemented over an extended period in all the American states
4. draws on communications theory to tie the perspective and the policy fields to a set of propositions
5. addresses an array of conceptual and measurement issues and thereby offers a bridge to a more sophisticated, more scientific study of the policy implementation process

In the integration of approaches, the cross-policy comparisons, the emphasis on the role of the states, and the reliance on systematic analysis, we believe this approach is distinctive. It is grounded in two complementary premises perhaps best stated by William Glazer more than a generation ago: "Fact-finding without theory produces a jumble," and "Theorizing without relevance to fact is a dilettantish hobby rather than a useful contribution" (Glazer, 1955: 291).

We would like to think that in our efforts to synthesize, to be cumulative, and to specify hypotheses for future testing, we can point the way toward the third generation of implementation research (Goggin, 1986). If this book does mark the beginning of a new generation of implementation scholarship, it is only a first step. No single investigator or team of investigators can achieve it, but accumulation of knowledge leading to a positive theory of implementation is conceivable, even likely.

A More Scientific Approach

What is third-generation research and how does it differ from previous research on implementation? The principal aim of third-generation research is to shed new light on implementation behavior by explaining why that behavior varies across time, policies, and units of government. The research generates a means of predicting the type of implementation behavior that is likely to occur in the future. Third-generation research is designed to overcome the conceptual and methodological problems that many scholars agree have impeded progress in this field. In a word, the aim of third-generation research is simply to be more *scientific* than the previous two in its approach to the study of implementation.

Scientific in this context has several meanings. First, throughout this book we have made a conscious attempt to *clarify key concepts.* For example, Chapter 2 defines implementation operationally in terms of a range of political and administrative behaviors directed toward putting a policy in place. This range of decisions and actions goes beyond the traditional definition, which divides implementation into that which is successful and that which is not. Our definition also takes into account the reality of implementation as a dynamic process that unfolds over time. Thus, we associate implementation behavior with a set of activities that take place during the life of a program—not just during its startup.

Second, we have provided a blueprint for examining enough cases of implementation to be able to specify various *causal paths* leading to this range of implementation behaviors, or styles. By adding case analyses, we also expect to be able to eventually specify *frequency distributions,* or the number of times the various types of implementation behavior and typical causal patterns that lead to each occur.

Furthermore, although we rely heavily on our own previous work and the research of others to identify the various factors that have been associated with different types of implementation, we *organize* those variables into a model of implementation and suggest *indicators and measures* that would permit future testing of hypotheses that are deduced from the model. These tests for veracity could be conducted by us or by others in the field. The payoff, in the form of *weighting* predictor variables, comes later, when the most appropriate statistical techniques are applied to a large data set. We see this book as the beginning of a dialogue among students, researchers, and practitioners of implementation about how to proceed to develop reliable theories and sound practices, but it is only a beginning.

Third-generation research, then, is a conscious attempt to confront directly the conceptual and measurement problems that have impeded further theoretical advance in this subfield of the discipline and the discovery of sound implementation practices. What is distinctive about our approach is that it takes factors that many investigators have found to be linked with implementation behavior in unspecified ways and organizes them in a theoretical model from which testable hypotheses can be derived. Where this research departs most radically from previous research, then, is not in the *variables* that are specified, but, rather, in the *approach* to operationalizing and measuring variables and in its plan for testing propositions.

Throughout, this book reports on what other investigators have written and what we have found out about federal-, state-, and local-level inducements and constraints on state preferences with respect to how and when to implement family planning, hazardous waste management, and waste-water treatment policies, as well as measures of the capacity of states to act on their preferences. In Chapter 8, we identify a variety of longitudinal designs that other scholars are currently using to test hypotheses, including our own ambitious comparative diachronic analysis of the fifty American states' implementation of three major national policies that were adopted at least a decade ago.

In summary, one operating premise of this brand of research is that a scientific approach to the study of implementation can lead to a better understanding of what implementation is and why the people and institutions who are involved in implementation behave as they do. It is not the selection of variables for examination, then, that characterizes third-generation implementation research and distinguishes it from earlier approaches. The unique trait of third-generation research is its research design—an explicit theoretical model; operational definitions of concepts; an exhaustive search for reliable indicators of implementation and predictor variables; and the specification of theoretically derived hypotheses, with analysis of data using appropriate qualitative and statistical procedures as well as case studies for testing them.[6]

IMPLEMENTATION THEORY AND PRACTICE

As the title of this book expresses, this book is about both theory and practice. The theoretical argument—which is only one of several ways that for heuristic purposes one might simplify the complexities of implementation—is explicated in Chapter 1 as a dynamic model of implementation. We call this the Communications Model of Intergovernmental Policy Implementation, or Communications Model for short. The practical aspects of implementation can be found throughout the book, but especially in Chapter 2, where the implementation of three major national policies is summarized in terms of the Communications Model. Subsequent chapters expand on these summaries by analyzing their key lessons about implementation.

Implementation in Theory

The dynamic framework of analysis that Chapter 1 presents in full is conceptualized as a "candidate" theory (Eckstein, 1975)—a tentative set of related propositions capable of predicting and explaining state-level implementation processes, outputs, and outcomes and specifying the conditions under which various state implementation behaviors are likely to occur.

In brief, the starting point is to envision the implementation process at the state level, as well as its product (in terms of process, outputs, and outcomes), as resulting from choices made by the state. These are decisions about whether to implement at all, the timing of implementation, and, if there are conflicting pressures, to whom the state will be responsive. State choices are in turn a function of inducements and constraints provided to or imposed on the state from elsewhere in the federal system—above, below, and horizontally—as well as the state's capacity to effectuate its preferences.

A central feature of our theoretical argument is the dynamic interaction of bureaucrats, legislators, and organized interests at both national and subnational levels in the federal system. The Communications Model focuses on individual differences in motives and interests, using these and other variables to predict and explain behavior and its effects. We argue that implementation behavior varies predictably with attributes of the policy, the implementors and their organizations, and the environment in which implementation decisions and actions take place. This, in summary, is our theoretical argument. But how does the practice of implementing public policy square with our theoretical understanding of the implementation process?

Implementation in Practice

Our approach to implementation in practice is two-fold. First, we summarize the most important empirical research of others to describe implementation practices. Second, we probe, in a very preliminary way, the plausibility of some of our propositions, with data that we have collected in three policy areas—hazardous waste management, family planning services, and waste-water treatment.

We show that, to a certain extent, there is conflicting evidence from the real world; based on the accounts of implementation scholars of how the real world works, there are rival explanations for similar implementation results. Part of our argument is that without reliable data and valid measures, it is virtually impossible to interpret these conflicting results. This difficulty can be laid at the feet of data that researchers find to be intersubjectively unreliable and the "degrees of freedom" problem that was discussed in connection with threats posed by conducting studies with too few cases and too many variables.

Criteria for Selecting Cases

We used four criteria in selecting the three cases examined in this book.

- Because we wanted variability across policies, we selected cases that represent a range of policy types—from the distributional aspect of clean water (the construction of purification plants), to regulatory characteristics of both waste-water treatment and hazardous waste management, to the redistributive family planning services grants (Lowi, 1964).
- We wanted to examine the implementation of these policies over a period of ten to fifteen years, so we selected issues that have been addressed by government for at least a decade.
- Because one of our primary aims is to observe a range of implementation styles, outputs, and outcomes across policies, over time, and by state, we have selected policies that exhibited variable implementation behavior.
- We wanted to include policies that were truly intergovernmental in their implementation, meaning that two or more levels of government were actively involved in putting the policy in place.

In this regard, two of the cases came from a short list of policies that the Advisory Commission on Intergovernmental Relations labels "partial preemption"—major federal statutes in which the federal government establishes basic policy and allows state and local governments discretionary power to decide how to achieve national objectives (ACIR, 1984, Chapter 1). The third policy—family planning—was chosen not only as a case of partial preemption but also as an example of another common form of intergovernmental implementation, the grant.

Before we describe these three policies in brief, a caveat is in order. Our use of what others have observed about the practice of implementation and what we will present as our preliminary but systematic analysis of how these three major domestic policies have been implemented in the American states does *not* constitute a test of the Communications Model. Rather, we use these cases to probe some of the propositions for plausibility in anticipation of a larger, more costly empirical test described in detail in Chapter 8.

In this regard, we urge others who are interested in doing basic (as opposed to applied) research on the implementation process to posit a set of theoretically driven testable hypotheses, reduce the components of the model to categories that theoretically ought to display different implementation behaviors, and then make systematic observations. If these predicted differences are, in fact, observed, then there is a general basis for understanding the causal complexities of policy implementation. Now we turn to a brief description of each of the three cases that are examined in this book. (For a brief chronology of important events related to each policy's implementation, see Appendix A.)

THREE CASES OF INTERGOVERNMENTAL IMPLEMENTATION

Case 1: Hazardous Waste Policy

The Resource Conservation and Recovery Act (RCRA) of 1976 (PL 94–580) was passed by Congress to deal with the problem of hazardous waste disposal. Subtitle C is the heart of the legislation and it has caused the most difficulty over the past few years in that it requires the U.S. Environmental Protection Agency (EPA) to establish design criteria for treatment, disposal, and storage facilities and to create a manifest system for tracking hazardous wastes from their manufacture to their disposal.

EPA was to develop the regulatory framework of RCRA by April 21, 1978, and to operate a hazardous waste regulatory program in each state. Each state could assume responsibility for its own state program if it developed and implemented a program equivalent to the federal plan. Subtitle C regulations were mandated for issuance eighteen months after RCRA passage; however, they were finalized only by November 1980 due to court-ordered deadlines imposed only after the agency had been sued for delay by environmentalists and others.

Section 3006 of RCRA provides guidelines describing conditions under which states can be authorized to carry out their own programs. Specifically, section 3006 provides for two stages in establishing state programs that would meet minimum federal requirements. The first stage is interim authorization (Phases I and II) under which states can operate their own less exacting programs for two years while upgrading them. The second phase is full (or final) authorization.

Phase I interim authorization gives states the authority to regulate generation and transportation of hazardous waste within the state and to regulate existing treatment, storage, and disposal facilities. Existing facilities were granted "interim status" in the program, which meant they were allowed to continue operating within existing guidelines but would be required to meet new national standards or close when new (Phase II) standards were issued by EPA.

The EPA determined that Phase II authorization should be further divided into three parts. Part II-A would authorize granting permits for existing storage and treatment facilities. Part II-B would authorize permitting for hazardous waste incinerators, and Part II-C would authorize permitting of new land disposal facilities. Full or final authorization, a more stringent stage, has three main criteria for state programs.

- They must be "equivalent" to federal programs.
- They must be consistent with federal or other state programs.
- They must provide for adequate enforcement.

As of January 1, 1990, 44 states had received final authorization from the EPA to run their own hazardous waste programs. In fact, the states have exhibited substantial variation during the period 1984–1990 in their authorizations.

Congress reauthorized and amended RCRA in the Hazardous and Solid Waste Amendments (HSWA) of 1984. The slow pace of RCRA implementation so frustrated Congress that HSWA contained numerous deadlines and "hammer" provisions designed to speed up and improve the process. EPA was given specific deadlines for promulgating regulations and setting standards. HSWA expanded the regulatory universe by including small-quantity waste generators and underground storage tanks, and HSWA addressed the land disposal issue by banning wastes from solvents and dioxin, among others. HSWA is generally credited with toughening RCRA provisions and stimulating renewed regulatory vigor.

Case 2: Family Planning Services

The Family Planning Services and Population Research Act of 1970 (PL 91–572) was the result of an amendment to Title X of the Public Health Service Act. Partly in response to a 1967 report that documented the unmet needs of 5 million women of childbearing age, the overall objective of the new federal law was to coordinate and expand the nation's family planning services effort.

To accomplish this goal, the law established an Office of Population Affairs, and, on the condition that the state adopt a comprehensive family planning plan for the state, authorized formula grants to state health agencies for the purpose of delivering family planning services other than abortion. Although there were no eligibility requirements for services, the law specified that low-income families should be given priority. Whereas other laws provided funds for family planning services in the states, Title X was to be the "primary focus" within the federal government.

Final regulations were approved in December 1972, with responsibility for implementation assigned to the Health Services Administration at what is now the Department of Health and Human Services. Between fiscal year (FY) 1970 and FY 1976, funds for family planning services increased from $30 million to $115 million. Funds were divided according to the size and demonstrated need of the population, so most states shared in these grants. But the states that complied with the law initially appeared to be those states with the existing capacity to deliver family planning services effectively. The ten regional offices of the Public Health Service awarded and then monitored project grants, which went to both public agencies and private nonprofit organizations like Planned Parenthood in the fifty states. The regional office, especially in the early years, provided technical assistance and staff training for the states. For example, in 1971, an amendment was proposed that would make grants available for the purpose of operational research in the area of program implementation.

In 1975, a Special Health Revenue Sharing Act (PL 94–63) to amend PL 91–572 was enacted, and it increased from 75 percent to 90 percent the federal share of funding for project costs. This undoubtedly helped those states that were having difficulty raising local funds to match the federal contribution. In 1977, regulations were revised to conform to the amendment. These regulations would permit "flexibility" in organizational and consultation arrangements.

Between 1980 and 1989, the Reagan Administration attempted, without success, to fold family planning services into a state-administered program, with many characteristics of a block grant. By the late 1980s, considerable controversy surrounded repeated attempts in both Congress and the executive branch to build a "wall of separation" between abortion and family planning. In Congress, what has resulted is a stalemate, whereby requests for reauthorization of Title X funding have not been put to a vote on the floor of either chamber for fear that antiabortion amendments would be attached.

In contrast, the Department of Health and Human Services has successfully promulgated a rule—often referred to as the "gag rule"—that prohibits federal funds from being allocated to clinics that advised their clients about the availability of abortion services, even if such procedures were performed at another, unrelated clinic.

Of late, the courts in several states have also been involved in implementation. As of March 1989, in at least six states—California, Connecticut, Massachusetts, Michigan, New Jersey, and Vermont—court decisions based on state constitutions successfully overturned state bans on public financing of abortions. And in July 1989, the U.S. Supreme Court ruled in *Webster v. Reproductive Health Services* that states should have greater freedom to restrict abortion services. Supreme Court justices continue to make rulings affecting parental consent and government restrictions on abortion.

Case 3: Municipal Waste-water Treatment

The Federal Water Pollution Control Act (FWPCA) was amended in 1972 through a series of provisions commonly known as the Clean Water Act of 1972 [PL 92–500, especially Title 1, Section 101(a)]. This policy provided for the creation and enforcement of nationally established effluent limitations on the discharge of pollutants into waterways in the United States. The intent of the policy is to require the use of the best available water pollution control technology in the shortest possible time in the interest of making the waterways "fishable and swimmable."

The 1972 legislation gave the nation's municipalities until 1977 to comply with requirements. Congress authorized the federal implementing agency, the Environmental Protection Agency (EPA), to extend the deadline to 1983 for some municipalities and then again until July 1, 1988. In 1981 the legislation was modified to relax some of the basic treatment requirements for certain types of facilities. In 1987 new legislation tightened regulatory constraints further and covered new pollution sources (such as nonpoint sources and additional toxic chemicals from industrial waste).

The basic structure, purpose, and regulatory implementation mechanisms, however, have remained in place to the present. What has changed significantly in the more recent past has been the policy mechanism for implementing the construction of the needed infrastructure facilities in this policy sector. This latter issue is addressed shortly, but first more detail is provided about the regulatory mechanism employed for pollution control.

Except as provided in the act, the discharge of "any pollutant by any person shall be unlawful" (to use the formulation in the mandate). The best available control technology is required, although legislation also allows modification of the requirements and schedule for certain pollutants or sources. The implementation mechanism is based on a nationwide permit system, the National Pollutant Discharge Elimination System (NPDES). This instrument requires permits for discharge of pollutants from any point source into U.S. waters. The EPA issues all permits unless discharge is to be made into waters of a state that has adopted its own permit program and has received EPA approval for its program.

Currently, thirty-eight states have adopted approved programs and thus issue permits. Permits are issued for a period not to exceed five years, and the permit requires the owner/operator of the facility to monitor effluent and to report results periodically to the issuing authority. Noncompliance must be acknowledged, and discharge of certain toxic substances must be reported within twenty-four hours.

The EPA mandates that all municipal treatment works meet the deadlines and achieve the statutory objectives regarding water quality. Yet there is substantial variation across facilities and across states in the degree of compliance achieved. Many plants are still not in compliance. The EPA works through its regional offices to "cooperate with their respective states to develop strategies that describe how they plan to bring noncomplying facilities into compliance" (*EPA Construction Grants*, 1985, p. D-1). States must help to develop plans to induce compliance as soon as possible. Overall monitoring of regions and states is performed by EPA headquarters; the regional offices and state agencies in turn monitor local facilities. The full-fledged effort to induce compliance by the July 1, 1988, deadline is referred to as the National Municipal Policy by the EPA.

Prior to 1986, another provision of the Clean Water Act authorized construction grants for treatment facilities. Allocations to localities were handled by the states based on a priority system that assigned funding to those recipient areas that experienced the most severe or the largest pollution problems. Regions and states "use[d] the annual state program grant negotiation process to reach agreement on the specific activities they [were to undertake] to carry out the plan" (*EPA Construction Grants*, 1985, p. D-1). Then the permitting authority (federal or state) required municipalities not in compliance to develop a compliance plan.

Thereafter, the permitting authority worked with the affected municipality to achieve compliance. More than $40 billion had been expended for this purpose by the mid-1980s, but as of 1987 then-current capital construction needs were estimated to total more than $76 before the end of the century (EPA, *1986 Needs Survey Report to Congress*, 1987). Nevertheless, the federal match was altered downward from 75 to 55 percent effective in 1984. In 1986 the grants program was ended legislatively, and a several-year phaseout was initiated. In place of the grants option was enacted a revolving loan program administered by the various states. This newly developed instrument is in the early stages of implementation but will likely mean both a larger role and greater costs for state and local governments.

THE PLAN OF THIS BOOK

Chapter 1 presents the details of the Communications Model, which we believe approximates a reality of implementation processes, institutions, and behavior. In this book the Communications Model serves as a framework for predicting implementation behavior and explaining its causes and consequences.

Chapters 2 through 7 are devoted to each of six components of the model. Collectively, these chapters illustrate how the elements of the Communications Model of implementation work. To support the hypotheses, we draw on the findings of the scores of empirical studies that have been reported elsewhere by us and others as well as results of original research we have conducted on the implementation of RCRA, clean-water, and family planning policies. Many of these case studies are based on field work, and are, therefore, rich in the kind of detail that brings alive the complexities, dynamics, and subtleties of implementation. These chapters meld theory and observations of practices. Thus, these chapters should interest not only those who wish to construct and validate implementation theory but also practitioners (or practitioners-in-training) who engage in policy or implementation analysis for the primary benefit of policy makers and managers.

Chapter 8 is aimed at people who are contemplating a research project on the implementation process. Here we lay out a plan for third-generation style research. The chapter provides a research design complete with variables, possible indicators, measurement strategies, sources of data, and a variety of methods for collecting data and manipulating them statistically. Also in Chapter 8 a number of suggestions are offered for advancing the state of knowledge in the field, and a number of research designs for further study are contemplated. The concluding chapter reassesses our dynamic model of implementation in light of the practice of implementation and encourages readers to design studies to test the theory.

Just what explains differences in the types of implementation behavior is examined throughout the book. The use of these data are limited, however, because they are not always intersubjectively reliable. Therefore, the findings are tentative until such time that a large, empirical study of implementation—one that meets the criteria for third-generation implementation research that was outlined earlier and one that can be replicated by other scholars—can be undertaken. With this book, we have tried to chart the way.

Notes for Introduction

1. These aspects of management style reduce to three questions: "Who is in charge?"; "Are the various branches and offices of government working together?"; and "Do public managers know what they are doing?" The issue of presidential management style was an important element in a number of "kiss and tell" books that began to appear during Reagan's last months in office. Revelations that the president was influenced by personal friends around him (including his wife Nancy), that he consulted an astrologer, and that he even allowed Press Secretary Larry Speakes to make up quotes for him added up to a picture of a disengaged president who was not in control of his subor-

dinates. Surprisingly, management style under the Republicans did not turn out to be a major campaign issue in the 1988 presidential election.

2. Among those who study federalism and intergovernmental relations, there is some disagreement, however, over the question of just how much power the states gained during Reagan's two terms in office.

3. Besides huge deficits, contractions in resources for even minor new initiatives, and a Congress skeptical of—if not downright hostile toward—a politicized executive branch, other developments during Ronald Reagan's tenure in office have implications for the practice of implementation. For example, Reagan's legacy (Jones, 1988) is likely to include a continued use of the budget as a statement of principle rather than as a legislative proposal; a continuing role for the Office of Management and Budget as an instrument of central coordination of policy formation and implementation, coupled with decentralized, delegated authority; increased reliance on experiments, and pilot and demonstration projects to try out reforms in existing programs; and a greater willingness to use the private sector to implement programs, especially in the service delivery sector.

4. This in itself is not unusual. There are few fields in political science that are not in need of good explanatory and predictive theory.

5. This is called "overdetermination." For a discussion of the problem of overdetermination in comparative research, see Przeworski, 1987: 38–39, 41; Przeworski and Teune, 1970: 34.

6. This is not to say that the approaches used in extant research have avoided longitudinal, comparative, or systematic analysis. To our knowledge, however, no study to date has combined all these elements *and* has had as its principal aim the development and testing of a general, or even "middle range," theory that explains and predicts implementation decisions and actions across time, policies, and states.

CHAPTER ONE

A Dynamic Model
of Implementation

❖
❖

The Early and Periodic Screening, Diagnosis, and Treatment (EPSDT) program exemplifies the typical process of intergovernmental public policy implementation. One might expect a program dealing with such an "apple pie" issue as preventive health services for poor children would be implemented swiftly and without alterations that make it more difficult to achieve program objectives. Available evidence, however, belies this expectation. A five-state analysis of the implementation of the EPSDT program uncovered four identifiably different policy implementation styles (Goggin, 1987).

Among the five states studied, only Oklahoma implemented EPSDT in the predicted manner: promptly and without modification. Texas represented the other extreme, delaying implementation of EPSDT and making substantial modifications in the program. Agents in Louisiana, too, dragged their feet, but eventually implemented an EPSDT program that has remained intact. In both Arkansas and New Mexico, the program was implemented swiftly but underwent extensive modification in the ensuing years. What explains the variation in how states reacted to EPSDT? Or, to pose the question in another way, why do implementation styles vary across the states?

The simple answer is that implementation styles vary because each state is different. Such a response is helpful but not very enlightening. In casting about for more satisfactory answers to the EPSDT case, one could point to Oklahoma's autonomous welfare agency and compare it to the extremely decentralized human-resource delivery system used by Texas. Perhaps agency structure accounts for the divergent implementation styles of these neighboring states. Structure is, in all likelihood, part of the answer. Consider Louisiana. In this state, agency structure is less important in explaining how EPSDT was implemented than is Louisiana's strong public health tradition. Thus, the way a federal enactment "fits" within the policy climate of a state also influences implementation.

An explanation for the implementation style exhibited by both Arkansas and New Mexico is different still. In these states, implementation appears to have been measurably affected by the involvement (or lack of involvement) of private physicians. Organized interests and their support for (or opposition to) a policy is another factor that affects state implementation behavior. As the EPSDT example demonstrates, intergovernmental policy implementation cannot be reduced to a unicausal explanation. A number of interacting factors create the implementation environment. Yet despite the diversity exhibited across states, patterns and regularities can be identified in policy implementation behavior. These commonalities make possible the construction of a model.

Analysis of intergovernmental policy implementation is aided by using a model that, while parsimonious, can accommodate explanations as diverse as those in the EPSDT example. The remainder of this chapter is devoted to the presentation of a "candidate" theory and complementary model. The model builds on and helps to integrate second-generation developments and research on comparative state policy. The theory and model position state decision makers at a communications crossroads—receiving, interpreting, and acting upon information flowing in from several directions. Components of the model—senders and receivers of messages along with their accompanying structures—are discussed briefly here and fully explained in the chapters that follow. Subsequent chapters also clarify the connections between our model, the research literature, and our findings.

UNDERSTANDING WHY IMPLEMENTORS BEHAVE AS THEY DO

One enduring challenge for democratic governance is that in the modern administrative state, considerable public action occurs far from the realm of elected officials and the electoral process; appointed officials exercise significant discretion by making policy in the course of implementing it (Lipsky, 1971; Long, 1949; Lowi, 1979). This matter is especially salient when intergovernmental policies—those necessitating the cooperation of at least two levels of government—are implemented in the American states. Despite the significance of this topic, until recently empirical studies of intergovernmental implementation have paid scant attention to the dynamics of how states collectively make choices about whether and how to respond to federal policy initiatives.[1] Even less is known about pressures that build from below— from the collections of interests that surround public policy. Nor has implementation research adequately addressed the issues of whether and how the use of administrative discretion during a state's implementation of a policy can comport with the requisites of democratic governance (Goggin and Laubacher, 1990; Hindera and Goggin, 1990).

To understand better the dynamics of intergovernmental implementation—the process by which state agents put intended federal policy into effect—several questions need to be addressed:

- Which state-level and local-level institutions are involved in making decisions about how the state should proceed with implementation?
- What are the patterns of influence among institutions and individuals?
- What are the interests and motives of the administrative and political elites who interpret federal directives and make them operative in each of the fifty American states?
- What incentives and constraints guide these agents in their efforts to implement? In other words, how is a state's decision about its own actions in the process of intergovernmental implementation actually made?
- How does the nature of the joint decision-making process affect ultimate state action with regard to implementation—its timing, and whether and how to modify policy during the course of its implementation?

The mid-range theory that we offer as a candidate for thinking about implementation offers some answers.

THE MODEL AND CANDIDATE THEORY

Figure 1.1 outlines our Communications Model of Intergovernmental Policy Implementation. It conceptualizes the implementation process at the state level, as well as its product (outputs and outcomes), as resulting from choices made by the state. State choices are not made in a vacuum, however. State policy decisions depend on external government influences as well as intrastate influences. State implementation behavior is a function of inducements and constraints provided to or imposed on the states from elsewhere in the federal system—above or below the state level—as well as of the state's own propensity to act and its capacity to effectuate its preferences. Inducements are factors—conditions and actions—that stimulate implementation; constraints have the opposite effect. Our approach is predicated upon the notion that no single factor can explain differences in implementation.

The national decision that triggers an implementation process affects by its form and content, to varying degrees, the choices and

Figure 1.1

The Communications Model of Intergovernmental Policy Implementation

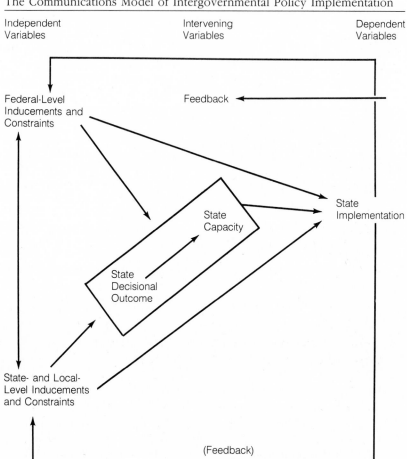

behaviors of agents charged with execution.[2] If this decision were the only factor, implementation would vary little from state to state. But states are discrete units, with their own policy agendas. State responses to federal inducements and constraints vary, depending on the nature and intensity of the preferences of key participants (including, importantly, local-level agents) in the state policy process. Finally, state responses are also influenced by the state's capacity to act.

This synthesizing approach yields the conceptual model displayed in Figure 1.1. Three clusters of variables affect state implementation:

inducements and constraints from the "top" (the federal level), inducements and constraints from the "bottom" (the state and local levels),
and state decisional outcomes and capacity. At a given point in time
in any state, the interaction of these three clusters determines the course
that implementation will take.

The implementation experience sets into motion a feedback process in which agents (subnational politicians and administrators) transmit messages to principals (federal-level policymakers). Policy redesign
may result. As noted in the Introduction, the lack of grand theory ob-
fuscates what implementation is and is not. In lieu of a paradigmatic
breakthrough, we have adapted a "middle range" communications theory to help link the pieces of the model (Merton, 1949). We use it here
because it helps to integrate a good portion of the extant implementation literature and a wide range of empirical findings.

Communications theory provides a means of understanding the relationships in intergovernmental policy implementation. State-level implementors form the nexus for the communications channels. These
implementors are the targets of implementation-related messages transmitted from both federal- and local-level senders. As recipients, state-
level implementors must interpret a barrage of messages. The potential for distortion exists. Structuring the interpretation process are the
form and content of the message and the legitimacy and reputation of
the sender.

Therein lies the key to implementation's variability. Interpretation
is a function of *context*. Therefore, a single message, such as a federal
statute, may be interpreted differently in different states. Even within
a single state, the pluralistic and interactive nature of local-level policy
adoption makes the probability of multiple, conflicting messages high.
State-level implementation is correctly conceptualized as the sorting and
interpreting of messages by recipients in contextually different settings.
The result is a decision that determines the style that implementation
takes.

Intergovernmental policy implementation is an exceedingly complex process that takes place in a complex environment. An implementation subsystem full of messages, messengers, channels, and targets
operates within a broader communications system. More specifically,
our conceptualization of implementation recognizes the joint nature of
decisions and actions of interdependent institutions at the subnational
level of government. It also incorporates consideration of the bargaining that takes place among the three levels of government. Given the
assumptions underpinning our Communications Model of Intergovernmental Policy Implementation, communications theory offers a means
of synthesizing the "top-down" and "bottom-up" approaches that dom-
inate (and divide) the implementation literature.[3]

MODEL COMPONENTS

This section introduces the components of the model that operate on federal, state, and local levels. Other aspects of the model, such as feedback and policy redesign, are also discussed.

State Implementation

State implementation is a *process,* a series of state decisions and actions directed toward putting an already-decided federal mandate into effect. State implementation is frequently equated with the state's compliance, or the timely satisfaction of procedural requirements of a law. Also implicit in the notion of compliance is the expectation that the law will be neither modified nor subverted in a way that is contrary to the lawmakers' intent. The essential characteristic of the state implementation process, then, is the timely and satisfactory performance of certain necessary tasks related to carrying out the intent of the law.

This orientation to implementation, which features a focus on the implementation process per se, is the most common in the literature. A conceptual problem arises, however, in the equation of implementation performance with implementation results. We argue that the two cannot be equated. For analytical purposes, it is imperative that the process of policy implementation be distinguished from the policy's results.

For example, a statute may include specific provisions that set up a timetable according to which certain services are delivered to certain clients. If those activities are carried out as specified by law, one could say that implementation has occurred; however, mere occurrence does not mean that the particular problem has been solved or that programmatic objectives have even been partially achieved. Therefore, in our Communications Model, state implementation is also defined in two other ways: outputs and outcomes. The term *outputs* refers to the extent to which programmatic goals have been satisfied. *Outcomes* are the changes in the larger societal problem that the program is intended to rectify. Thus, the object of our Communications Model is actually a trio of items: the implementation process, the outputs of the implemented program, and the outcomes that are eventually produced.

Given the dynamic nature of implementation, periodic evaluation of the three factors is the only means of accurately portraying implementation. Not only does the implementation process evolve but outputs and outcomes can change over time. Thus we reject a dichotomous conceptualization of implementation as simply success or failure. As the EPSDT example illustrates, at least four different implementation styles exist. Under different conditions, various timing strategies and approaches work differentially.[4] The model implicitly acknowledges this result.

Federal-Level Inducements and Constraints

The content and form of a national government decision, be that decision a statute, an executive order, a court decision, or an administrative regulation, affect the choices and behaviors of state-level implementors. Federal-level variables, through their objective provisions (such as when the statute contains a penalty for noncompliance) and their subjective impacts (the importance of a penalty to a specific state) influence implementation. The message and the sender matter to the recipients in the contextually different states. One set of variables concerns the substance of the message. The federal-level "content-of-the-decision" variables that are plausible candidates for inclusion in a model of intergovernmental policy implementation include the policy type, the ease with which the problem can be solved, the degree of certainty of effects, the provision for coercion, the arrangement for financing, the anticipated effects on existing power arrangements, and the existence of a provision for citizen participation.

For example, a federal law that provides funds so that a state can devise its own solution to a problem is received very differently than is a federal law that imposes new regulations that are unwanted by powerful state interests. Generally, states prefer a federal program like the General Revenue Sharing (GRS) Act of 1971, which from 1972 to 1980 allocated funds for state governments to use as they pleased. With GRS, there was no five-inch-thick set of rules and regulations, no federally determined remedy; consequently, the program created few messy implementation problems for state governments.

The "form-of-the-decision" variables also affect the way in which a message is received. These variables include items such as the clarity of the provisions of the decision, the consistency of the decision with other policy objectives, and the flexibility of goals and procedures. State governments react differently to federal enactments that are clear and consistent than the same governments respond to enactments that are garbled and irregular. The Highway Beautification Act of 1965, which encouraged the removal of billboards from along major roads, is an example of a mandate that was considered "one of the worst-drafted pieces of legislation" to come out of the U.S. Congress (ACIR, 1984: 116). The unclear, often ambiguous language of the statute complicated interpretation and delayed implementation.

Another set of variables involves the extent of agreement among senders. The federal-level factors likely to affect state implementation include the legitimacy and credibility of officials and agencies. A unanimous Supreme Court decision, a bill that passes Congress with a wide margin, and an executive order of a popular president are actions that, *ceteris paribus,* facilitate implementation. Messages transmitted in this manner carry more weight. Federal agencies that, for example, are under fire in the media are weaker claimants and are likely to find their directives less imposing to recipients. For instance, states inclined to delay implementing the rulings of the U.S. Office of Civil Rights could do so more successfully during the 1970s when the agency was widely acknowledged to be "extremely ill-managed" (ACIR, 1984: 110). The "standing" of a sender influences the treatment that a message will receive.

The most salient feature of the model in Figure 1.1 is that it is dynamic. The model considers important political and administrative behavioral changes that happen over time, and across policies and states. Amendments and the promulgation of revised rules can alter the content of a federal-level message. A change in form can result. Nor is the standing of the sender immutable. The potential magnitude of these kinds of changes complicates the task of state implementors as they proceed.

State- and Local-Level Inducements and Constraints

The inducements and limitations imposed at the state and local levels are a component of the model that emphasizes the importance of state and local politics (the organization of interests at these levels) in understanding how and why implementation occurs the way that it does. This component is oriented toward three interacting institutional clusters: interest groups, state and local elected officials and their associated political institutions, and the focal (implementing) state agency. These clusters, ranging from a simple structure to a complex, polynucleated structure, send messages to state implementors. These messages generate the "receptivity climate"—the context of laws, regulations, and support structure—that the federal enactment encounters in each state. It is not surprising, then, that implementation is seldom simple or automatic.

The essential elements of the state and local subsystem are

- one or more bureau chiefs in each state, who receive federal communications and act instrumentally to ensure agency survival and to enhance their own welfare
- one or more bureaucratic organizations in each state whose organizational structure (and whose quantity and quality of financial and human resources) impinges on individual agent behavior
- spokespersons for organized interests in each of the fifty states, whose main interest is in maximizing benefits for group members and who also communicate their preferences to state-level implementors
- two or more state legislative committee and subcommittee chairs and one governor in each state whose principal driving force is reelection

- a wide variety of local-level agents with significant levels of interlocal diversity in interest and motive, who also communicate
  their desires to state-level implementors
- fifty states, each with its own level of capacity to act on its collective preferences
- feedback loops that permit those affected by implementation decisions and actions and distributional consequences of the decisions and actions to communicate their reactions to authorities
  at both national and subnational levels in the federal system

The seven elements of the subnational system just sketched are interactive, interdependent, and multidimensional. In essence, the implementation decisions made and actions taken at this level in the federal
system are jointly produced individual judgments of managers in charge
of program operations, the preferences of state elected officials, and
the cross-pressures brought to the bargaining table by consumer and
provider advocates. These individual judgments are reached, at least
partly, as the result of bargaining among various interests. Each interest
has its own expectations, goals, resources, stakes, and power (Allison,
1971; Lowi, 1964). These joint decisions are also constrained by the
political, cultural, and economic environment, and the capacity of
focal organizations to act on the state's collective choices. As the
EPSDT example illustrates, these variables have a powerful impact on
implementation.

The interdependence of these actors—federal principals (the
policymakers with jurisdiction over the program), local interest groups,
the governor, state legislators, local elected and appointed officials, and
appointed officials in the state's bureaucracy—and their respective institutions is assumed (Bendor and Moe, 1985; Chubb, 1985; Moe, 1985).
Finally, individual actors in the Communications Model are constrained
by the nature of the decision-making process itself (Braybrooke and
Lindblom, 1963; Cyert and March, 1963; Simon, 1957). Each institution is assumed to deal with the problem of the cost, in time and money,
of acquiring information by specializing and by dividing tasks. Because
of specialization and division of labor, power is usually concentrated
in the hands of committee and subcommittee chairs in the legislature,
bureau chiefs in state administrative agencies, and the leadership of organizations for consumers and providers of services, as well as direct
beneficiaries and cost-bearers.

Decisional Outcomes and State Capacity

The Communications Model positions state decision makers in a
pivotal role. They are the receivers and evaluators of streams of information flowing from the federal and the state and local levels. Even

under optimal circumstances in which there is perfect congruence between information from the "top" and the "bottom," two other conditions must exist before implementation can occur. First, a decision to proceed (to implement) must be made. This is no small step. In other words, even though the objective conditions may be identical in state X and state Y, the implementation decision may vary. This variance is a function of the manner in which decision makers interpret the information that they are receiving. Interpretation is related to characteristics internal to the decision makers (such as their psychological predisposition) and external to them (such as interpersonal relations among politicians and representatives of organized interests). This is a little recognized but powerful part of the implementation process.[5] Without the decision to proceed, implementation stalls.

The decision to implement is linked to a second factor: the state's capacity to act. Our model takes into account the important distinction between decisions and actions, suggesting that variations in the capacity to act across states, across programs, or across time also affect the manner or style in which implementation occurs. State actions regarding implementation are influenced not only by federal level and state/local level preferences, but also by the organizational and ecological capacity of the state to act on those preferences.

Organizational capacity refers to an institution's ability to take purposeful action. It is a function of the structural, personnel, and resource characteristics of state agencies. *Ecological capacity* pertains to the contextual environment in which state government operates. It is determined by socioeconomic and political conditions in a state.

The setting for the implementation of a program within a state involves bureaucratic organizations. Information must be converted into action. State capacity, then, is a function of organizational capacity. A vast literature on administration and public organizations testifies to the possible importance of many features of the organizational setting in determining behavior. In our Communications Model, three elements of the setting are paramount: organizational structure, personnel, and financial resources.

Simple structures reduce coordination costs and ease the transmission of information, thus enhancing capacity to act. The implementation process is facilitated by these structures, but they may not improve output and outcomes, depending on the needs of the policy. Similarly, when relevant organizational actors are sufficiently numerous, qualified, and disposed to accept and undertake the course of action, the capacity to act is increased. Finally, agency capacity requires possession of the requisite financial resources to initiate the program successfully. These resources are of two kinds: ones targeted directly to clients and those spent in the process of implementation. Transforming a state preference into action requires both types of resources.

Ecological conditions in a state compose the other aspect of state capacity. The conventional wisdom is that variations in a state's socio-political and (especially) economic conditions are systematically related to state implementation behavior, whether it is measured in terms of processes, outputs, or outcomes. A state's capacity to act on its preferences is constrained by these factors. Ecological factors include general characteristics that are constant across policies, including state wealth, policy liberalism, economic conditions, political culture, and public opinion. Also included as ecological factors are specific characteristics that vary across policies, including partisan support, the salience of the problem to the state, and the media attention given to the issue.

In implementing the federal Medicaid program, for example, states make critical decisions about eligibility, benefit levels, and local government involvement (Schneider, 1988). A state's ecology strongly influences the direction of these decisions.

Whereas it is unlikely that massive shifts in a state's ecology occur repeatedly during policy implementation, there is the possibility of some movement. If, for example, a rash of violent crimes breaks out in a state, the salience of criminal justice policy is heightened. If election results produce a change in partisan control of a state legislature, the new party in power usually offers policy alternatives that affect the state's ecology.

Feedback and Policy Redesign

The constraints and inducements at the national and subnational levels of government are assumed to vary—from program to program and from state to state. Through a process of mutual adaptation and policy learning (Berman and McLaughlin, 1978; Sabatier, 1987; Sabatier and Brasher, 1986), the constraints and inducements also vary from one time period to the next. Individuals and their organizations possess both a capacity to learn and an ability to adapt to changing circumstances.

Dissatisfaction with an existing policy may lead to its eventual redesign. For redesign to occur, however, the following actions must unfold:

1. At the outset, elected and appointed state officials have to relay their dissatisfaction to federal-level officials. These state officials, in all likelihood, are transmitting the dissatisfaction of relevant organized interests, such as clients and attentive publics.
2. As they receive repeated messages expressing similar sentiment, federal officials in the legislative or executive branches may respond by redesigning the policy. This was demonstrated quite vividly in the congressional redesign of the Endangered Species Act of 1973 after construction of the Tennessee Valley Authority's massive Tellico Dam project was halted in order to

save the snail darter, a small fish (ACIR, 1984). The importance of redesign has also been underscored by the recent reforms in the welfare program and in Catastrophic Illness provisions for the elderly under Medicare.

A feedback loop is an essential component of an implementation model.

The policy redesign component of the model reflects the fluidity inherent in intergovernmental policy implementation. The complexity of joint action often necessitates coordination and cooperation (Pressman and Wildavsky, 1973). However, because of differences between national and subnational priorities—and differences among individuals, institutions, and constraints and inducements—conflict is common. The need for coordination and cooperation, on the other hand, means that those who implement public policy have a strong hand in redesigning it.

CONCLUSION

The theoretical argument and its corresponding model offer a vehicle for exploring what Elmore (1987: 278) has called "the disorder that is policy implementation." Our model attempts to make sense of important aspects of the political and administrative behavior associated with the intergovernmental implementation of public policy. The model uses communications theory as the glue that holds the pieces together. Messages, their senders, and the messages' recipients are the critical ingredients. Decoding these messages and absorbing them into agency routine is what implementation is all about.

The strong features of the model are its dynamism and its synthesis of actions by disparate actors. In recognizing that implementation is a dynamic process, the model incorporates policy learning and redesign. It resists the temptation to opt for either a top-down or bottom-up approach and instead synthesizes both approaches into a more comprehensive vision of intergovernmental policy implementation. Such a model facilitates testing propositions, regardless of policy type. In the final analysis, the use of communications theory meets the paramount criterion of a good model in that it approximates reality.

The remainder of the book fleshes out the model's bones. Chapter 2 pursues the topic of implementation styles and presents what can be learned about implementation from the Resource Conservation and Recovery Act, the Family Planning Services and Population Research Act, and the Federal Water Pollution Control Act.

Notes for Chapter 1

1. For a review of the implementation literature, see O'Toole (1986).

2. Admittedly, the model posits a federal enactment as triggering the implementation process. That in and of itself does not condemn the model to a hopelessly top-down fate. The local context is accorded equal footing in the model. In addition, the feedback-policy redesign loop is another point of bottom-up influence—one frequently neglected altogether in the implementation literature.

3. Very simply, top-down theorists examine legal relationships and the achievements of objectives under a federal mandate; bottom-up theorists focus upon the local-level policy network. The Introduction summarized these divergent approaches.

4. See the discussion in Goggin (1987: 14–22) regarding different types of implementation theories and their treatment of cause and effect.

5. Examples of scholarly work that treats implementation behavior as the joint product of relations among bureaucrats, politicians, and representatives of organized interests are Bendor and Moe (1985) and Scholz and Wei (1986).

CHAPTER TWO

Implementation Styles
and Their Consequences

❖
❖

In 1970, the Title X Family Planning Services and Population Research Act was enacted in order to lower access and cost barriers to family planning for individuals, especially low-income women,[1] so that they would be able to exercise personal choice in determining the number and spacing of children. California was slow in getting the program started. But soon after 1973, when a political bargain was struck between the Democratic leadership in the state legislature and conservative Republican Governor Ronald Reagan, California quickly became the biggest state spender for family planning services. By fiscal year (FY) 1987, the state was spending almost $13.3 million of the federal government's money annually for Title X services; to this it added more than $20 million of state money. When three other family planning services programs (Title V, Title XIX, and Title XX) are taken into account, California led the nation with expenditures of more than $50 million (Gold and Macias, 1986).

In contrast, Utah, which was prompt in getting started with Title X in the early 1970s, spent slightly more than $500,000 for Title X services in FY 1987. In total expenditures, Utah ranked near the bottom. In family planning program obligations for FY 1987, Utah exceeded the spending of only five other states, Alaska, North Dakota, Rhode Island, South Dakota, and Vermont (Department of Health and Human Services, n.d.). Moreover, not a single penny of state money was allocated for family planning services in Utah.

In the early 1980s, soon after Reagan appointees were in control of the Department of Health and Human Services and a new position of Assistant Secretary for Population Affairs had been created, Utah was one of the innovators in implementing demonstration and prevention projects under the newly passed Adolescent Family Life Act (AFLA), called the "chastity act" by some of its detractors (for example, see Donovan, 1984). Unlike the Title X program, which is a categorical project grant program for funding comprehensive family planning *services,* the Title XX Adolescent Family Life Act funds *research* projects. Its mission is to address the problems of adolescent sexuality and pregnancy by funding research and demonstration projects in various states. Items on the not-so-hidden agenda of those who pushed the Title XX program include the promotion of chastity, infertility, and adoption services at the expense of contraceptive services; parental consent; the transfer of authority for administration to the states; and prohibition of abortion referrals.

In initiating and operating programs for AFLA, Utah has been a leader, with two major demonstration projects and one large pregnancy prevention program involving more than 1000 adolescents in progress as of January of 1987. California, on the other hand, has been a laggard; there was only one project under way in the state, a demonstration project in the city of San Francisco (U.S. DH&HS, 1987). In the first two years of operation of the Title XX provisions of the Social Service Block Grant, California reported no expenditures; Utah reported it spent over $200,000 (Gold and Nestor, 1985; Nestor and Gold, 1984).

Ten years and $1.4 billion in federal spending after Title X's enactment and on the eve of the passage of the Title XX adolescent pregnancy law, pregnancy, birth, and abortion rates among women aged fifteen through nineteen were up throughout the nation (NICHD, personal communications). California, the biggest spender in terms of both federal Title X funds and money earmarked for family planning services from the state legislature, ranked second in the nation in terms of pregnancy rates of women in the fifteen- through nineteen-year-old age group, twenty-fifth in birth rate, and first with respect to the rate of abortion. Utah, on the other hand, held the thirty-seventh and thirteenth positions in pregnancy and birth rates, respectively. In terms of the abortion rate, Utah ranked last.

THE VARIABILITY OF IMPLEMENTATION

The comparison between these two Western states shows that implementation in the real world can vary considerably across states and time, and among policies—even when these policies are within the same substantive area. One lesson to be learned from this comparison is that states do not often respond to federal initiatives in unison; they neither have identical problems nor seek identical solutions to their problems. More than one investigator has shown empirically that some states do a better job than others in getting a program off the ground. As has been demonstrated in an earlier study of the implementation of intergovernmental child health policies in several states, moreover, a state can begin the implementation period (Goggin, 1987: 34–35) by dragging its feet. When a solution to a problem comes along that suits that state's fancy, or when a fizzling policy is redesigned to fit with its environment, the state may change its approach to program implementation from defiance to compliance (Goggin, 1987).

Comparisons like this underscore the point that there are observable differences in the manner in which states implement public policies. The comparisons also dramatize the important distinction between the implementation process and its consequences, that is, implementation outputs and outcomes (Easton, 1969).

This brief discussion of variability in implementation and programmatic performance provides the questions that will be addressed in this chapter:

- What are the essential characteristics of implementation style?
- How can these differences best be captured?
- At what points in time and place ought these differences to be measured?
- What kinds of results can we expect to observe as a consequence of implementing actors' choices about the type of implementation strategy to adopt?

This chapter describes a range of implementation styles and their consequences. It begins with an explanation of two principal dimensions of implementation behavior. An examination of the spatial and temporal dynamics of implementation follows. But the main theme of this chapter is one of how hazardous waste management, family planning, and waste-water treatment programs have actually been implemented in various states. The chapter ends with a description and analysis of the results of implementation.

DIMENSIONS OF
IMPLEMENTATION BEHAVIOR

Implementation behavior combines interpretative, goal-setting decisions—usually reached through political bargaining—with operational, administrative decisions about the most appropriate implementation strategies for achieving specified objectives—usually reached through analysis (March and Simon, 1958). Agents' decisions and actions are viewed as a complex calculus based on information as well as political considerations. In essence, a state's implementation decisions and actions are jointly made. They reflect not only the individual preferences of policy managers charged with the task of solving state problems within a given functional area but also the desires and wishes of state elected officials and organized interests. Agents' behavior can only be understood, then, within the context of dynamic interaction among bureaucrats, politicians, and interest groups (Bendor and Moe, 1985).

Spatial and Temporal Dynamics

As the Communications Model of Intergovernmental Policy Implementation outlined in Chapter 1 shows, state implementation is conceptualized as a process, or a series of state decisions and actions directed toward putting an authoritative decision into effect. State implementation is frequently equated with the state's timely satisfaction of procedural requirements of a law, court decision, or administrative rule, for example. It can also mean putting in place policies that conform to the wishes of clients—those interests aggregated and articulated by street-level officials. The essential characteristic of state implementation, then, is the timely and satisfactory performance of tasks related to carrying out the intent of an earlier decision by legislators; the president; the president's executives, judges, service providers; or an "attentive" public seeking a solution to a state or local problem.

State implementation is also defined in terms of outputs, which measure the extent to which program goals have been satisfied. Finally, at the highest level of abstraction, state implementation also means that there has been some measurable change in the larger problem that is addressed by the adopted policy. Keeping in mind the policies that have been chosen for comparison in this book, outcomes can range from improvements in a state's water quality to changes in the health status of women who are at risk of becoming pregnant.

Typically, extant research views implementation in terms of a success/failure dichotomy, frequently on the basis of a one-time determination during the "take-off" stage of the implementation period (Williams and Elmore, 1976: 3). In the Communications Model, this cross-sectional, dichotomous measure of implementation is rejected in favor of periodic assessments of the status of implementation over the life of a program. Periodic measurement of implementation behavior, or style, is the best way to capture accurately the changing nature of the dynamic implementation process.

It is clear from myriad field observations that most cases of implementation fall between the extremes of a self-executing order and no implementation at all; however, normative judgments about any given state's implementation style are avoided here. That is because under certain conditions—for example, where the underlying theory is invalid—delay or modification may be in the best interest of the state. (See Lester and Bowman, 1989, for a discussion of "strategic" delay.)

Under other circumstances, prompt and faithful execution may be indicated. For pragmatic reasons, researchers who study implementation dynamics require contingent generalizations that specify the conditions under which various timing strategies and approaches to policy redesign work best (Goggin, 1987). Determining whether implementation is a "success" or a "failure" or "good" or "bad" is best left to others. But if we should avoid these subjective evaluations, how *should* implementation be portrayed?

Each case of implementation can be categorized on the basis of answers to three questions:

1. Has the state carried out the intent of the policy?
2. If the intent has been carried out, at what point in time did the state put the federal policy into effect?
3. Has the state modified the policy in the course of implementation, and, if it has, have the modifications helped or hurt the state's chances of achieving programmatic goals or the chances of satisfying clients' demands?

Four Implementation Styles

With answers to these questions, any case of implementation can be classified as one of four implementation styles:

- defiance (delay with modifications that hurt the state's chances of achieving goals)
- delay (delay with no modifications)
- strategic delay (delay with modifications that help the state's chances of achieving goals)
- compliance (prompt implementation with or without modifications that help the state's chances of achieving its goals)

Implementation Activities

Within the context of the "take-off" and "capacity building" stages of the policy implementation process, five recurring activities or functions frequently occur (Goggin, 1987; Hanf, Hjern, and Porter, 1978; Henig, 1985; Hjern, 1987):

- State legislatures pass state-enabling laws and initiate the hearings process associated with such legislation.
- State agencies undertake administrative rule making and establish administrative routines.

- States appropriate resources, including the money and the human capital needed by the state to carry out the policy as intended.
- Legislators monitor and, through the application of sanctions and rewards, enforce local adherence.
- After some experience with its operations, lawmakers redesign policies in response to design flaws or to missed opportunities.

A separate chapter (Chapter 7) is devoted entirely to an analysis of the final activity, policy redesign.

Because all five of these implementation activities take place within the framework of a state's policy subgovernment or subsystem (Ripley and Franklin, 1982), interactions among the various state and local political and administrative officials and institutions mentioned earlier can occur at any stage of the implementation process. Briefly, each activity is an occasion for delay and/or modification; each provides a unique opportunity for leaders to make known their views about what the state should do with regard to implementation. These five implementation activities may occur either simultaneously or sequentially; some may not occur at all.

OBSERVATIONS OF IMPLEMENTATION DECISIONS AND ACTIONS

To develop a general theoretical perspective that clarifies political and administrative behaviors associated with the intergovernmental implementation of public policy and to recommend solutions to specific implementation problems, the best place to start is with observations of actual decisions and actions that constitute implementation. The most significant behaviors at the level of subnational government tend to cluster around the five implementation activities discussed earlier. At each of these stages of the implementation process, the types of decisions and actions that matter concern whether to implement a policy at all, the proper timing of implementation actions, and the nature and any degree of change in policy ends or means.

Decisions about timing and intent are jointly made. They reflect the supports and demands from above by members of the relevant Congressional committees, the president and presidential appointees, the courts, and the agency with jurisdiction. They are also influenced by pressure from local interests such as city mayors, as well as the interests and motivations of the state bureau chief, the state governor, and policy influentials such as "fixers" in the state legislature (Mazmanian and Sabatier, 1983: 33–34).

To categorize the style of implementation—a function of behavior having to do with both the timing of implementation and the nature and direction of change in program objectives and the tools and instruments adopted to achieve them (Peters, 1986; Schneider and Ingram, 1988)—this section reconstructs the experiences of several states relative to the implementation of the Resource Conservation and Recovery Act of 1976, the Clean Water Act of 1972, and the Family Planning Services and Population Research Act of 1970.

Sources of data for these case histories are face-to-face interviews, a mail questionnaire, and unpublished and published documents. These contacts were made with administrators in Washington, D.C., in regional offices of the Environmental Protection Agency (EPA), and in states and localities. A brief chronology for each case is presented in Appendix A. Now we turn to an overview of each of the three cases of implementation.

Hazardous Waste Management

State implementation of the Resource Conservation and Recovery Act (RCRA), enacted in 1976, was hampered by EPA's protracted regulations process. It took the agency four years to make decisions about acceptable RCRA standards and guidelines. Only in 1984 was the first state authorized (under RCRA) to operate its own hazardous waste program. Among the eleven states that received authorization during 1984 were many that faced comparatively less serious hazardous waste problems. Table 2.1 displays the timing of RCRA implementation.

By the end of 1985, 30 states had received RCRA authorization from EPA; by mid-1988, the number had grown to 42. Most of the states that implemented RCRA in 1984 adopted RCRA minimums as their policy. In other words, these states simply conformed to EPA-generated guidelines. Some of the later-implementing states made a greater effort to design and develop a hazardous waste management system that reflected state preferences and/or exceeded RCRA minimums.

Regardless of the motivation behind the delay, taking action other than simply implementing the EPA-prescribed system led to extended negotiation and bargaining between regional EPA agents and the states. One early analysis of state hazardous waste programs characterized nineteen states as "policy leaders" in that they had exceeded RCRA standards on three of four dimensions (Bowman and Lester, 1985). These leaders modified RCRA by making it more compatible with conditions in their states. None of the early implementors of RCRA (the 1984 group shown in Table 2.1) appears among the policy leaders. In implementa-

Table 2.1   The Timing of RCRA Implementation by State*

1984 (N = 11)	1985 (N = 19)		1986 (N = 10)	1987 (N = 1)	1988 (N = 1)
Delaware	New Hampshire	Oklahoma	Pennsylvania	Alabama	Maine
Mississippi	Vermont	Arkansas	Illinois		
Montana	New Mexico	Kentucky	Oregon		
Georgia	Tennessee	Massachusetts	Rhode Island		
North Dakota	Nebraska	Louisiana	Washington		
Utah	Maryland	Minnesota	Wisconsin		
Colorado	Florida	New Jersey	Indiana		
South Dakota	Kansas	Nevada	New York		
Virginia	South Carolina	Arizona	West Virginia		
Texas	Missouri		Michigan		
North Carolina					

States without authorization, as of March 1, 1989 (N = 8)

Alaska	California
Connecticut	Hawaii
Idaho	Iowa
Ohio	Wyoming

*This reflects the year in which a state received final authorization from U.S. EPA to operate its hazardous waste program.

SOURCE: U.S. Environmental Protection Agency, "States Granted Final Authorization for Pre-HWSA Program."

tion, speed and substance are separable entities. The policy leaders (Bowman and Lester, 1985: 158) are

Arizona	Missouri
California	New Hampshire
Connecticut	New Jersey
Delaware	Pennsylvania
Kansas	Rhode Island
Louisiana	South Carolina
Maine	Vermont
Massachusetts	Wisconsin
Minnesota	

Family Planning Services

In the years immediately following passage of the Title X family planning services law, states turned their attention to implementation. Because of delays in issuing federal guidelines, several states were reluctant to begin delivering family planning services in the early days following the enactment of the Family Planning Services and Population

Table 2.2   Timing of Implementation: Family Planning Percentage
of Counties Serviced by State as of June 30, 1972

Region/State	Counties Serviced (in %)
Region I	
Massachusetts	50
Connecticut	75
Maine	81
Rhode Island	100
New Hampshire	80
Vermont	64
Total	72
Region II	
New York	82
New Jersey	76
Puerto Rico	—
Virgin Islands	—
Total	81
Region III	
Pennsylvania	58
Virginia	96
West Virginia	89
Maryland	100
D.C.	100
Delaware	100
Total	85
Region IV	
North Carolina	94
Florida	100
Georgia	99
Tennessee	100
Alabama	100
Kentucky	87
Mississippi	100
South Carolina	100
Total	97
Region V	
Ohio	78
Illinois	36
Michigan	93

SOURCE: U.S. Congress, Senate Special Subcommittee on Human Resources, Committee on Labor and Public Welfare, *Progress Report on the Five-Year Plan for Family Planning Services and Population Research Programs*, March 1972, pp. 47–48.

Research Act of 1970. As Table 2.2 shows, some states entered the "start-up" period by dragging their feet; other states acted expeditiously to put services into the hands of those who needed them.

Some states acted more quickly than others. Thirteen states put the new program in place in all counties throughout the state, and seven others failed to reach even 50 percent of counties. Regional facts are also enlightening. Region IV got off to a quick start, serving 97 percent

Table 2.2 (continued)

Region/State	Counties Serviced (in %)
Indiana	47
Minnesota	79
Wisconsin	51
Total	63
Region VI	
Texas	72
Louisiana	100
Arkansas	100
Oklahoma	84
New Mexico	94
Total	83
Region VII	
Missouri	67
Iowa	64
Kansas	66
Nebraska	65
Total	66
Region VIII	
Colorado	70
South Dakota	69
Utah	100
North Dakota	49
Montana	29
Wyoming	46
Total	59
Region IX	
California	91
Arizona	86
Nevada	29
Hawaii	100
Guam	—
Total	80
Region X	
Washington	72
Oregon	58
Idaho	58
Alaska (Legislative districts)	36
Total	53

of all eligible counties, but Region X could only serve slightly more than 50 percent of the counties in its states.

State family planning program administrators always exercise some degree of discretion, especially in terms of the type of service delivery system each state employs. Many states use the state health department and county clinics around the state as the principal providers of services. This pattern of service delivery is typical of southern states. Other states rely heavily on Planned Parenthood clinics, private hospitals, or other types of freestanding health centers. Planned Parenthood clinics are most frequently used on the East and West Coasts.

Differences in the implementation strategy can also be found, for example, in the scope of services offered to clients, the location and number of clinic sites, and patient eligibility requirements. Based on a survey of state practices in the period immediately following 1981 cuts in federal funding for family planning services, the Alan Guttmacher Institute (1984: 142) concluded that "not only do states vary in the amount of funding received from each of four federal sources, but they also vary to some extent in using these funds to provide services."

Perhaps the best way to examine variations in the extent to which a state has modified the Title X statute is to compare what various states did when federal spending was cut by 22 percent for the FY 1982 funding cycle. How did states implement the changes necessitated by these dramatic cuts in program spending?

Several states redirected general state revenues to offset the shortfall in federal Title X money. Colorado, Maine, New York, and Washington, for example, appropriated state funds to offset part of the loss in federal spending (AGI, 1984: 177–83). Other states coped with revenue shortfalls by implementing improvements in program management. A few states initiated patient fees, with Wisconsin going so far as to make parents of dependent minors financially responsible, under certain circumstances, for the minor's offspring. As a general rule, most states tended to consolidate and centralize by administering programs through "umbrella" agencies. The most common change in program content was to reduce services—for example, by reducing the number of clinic sites and physician hours, by eliminating programs for men and adolescent mothers, and by reducing sterilization and venereal disease testing and treatment programs (Torres, 1983: 191).

Waste-Water Treatment

The national policy for regulating the discharge of pollutants into the nation's waterways allows states to assume permitting authority once they have demonstrated to the U.S. EPA that they are capable of handling the task. As Table 2.3 shows, the states have varied considerably in the speed with which they have entered into this implementation process. This fact is important because, as the Fund for Renewable Energy and the Environment—a pro-environment think tank and lobbying group—puts it, "State authority [can be] seen as a fundamental measure of state commitment to surface water protection and integration with federal programs" (Fund, 1988: 44).

The most important table column to examine is the first set of dates

Table 2.3 State NPDES Program Status

State	Approved State NPDES Permit Program	Approved to Regulate Federal Facilities	Approved State Pretreatment Program
Alabama	10/19/79	10/19/79	10/19/79
Alaska	not delegated		
Arizona	not delegated		
Arkansas	11/01/86	11/01/86	11/01/86
California	05/14/73	—	—
Colorado	03/27/75	—	—
Connecticut	09/26/73	—	06/03/81
Delaware	04/01/74	—	—
Florida	not delegated		
Georgia	06/28/74	12/08/80	03/12/81
Hawaii	11/28/74	06/01/79	08/12/83
Idaho	not delegated		
Illinois	10/23/77	08/20/79	—
Indiana	01/01/75	12/09/78	—
Iowa	08/10/78	08/10/78	06/03/81
Kansas	06/28/74	08/28/85	—
Kentucky	09/30/83	09/30/83	09/30/83
Louisiana	not delegated		
Maine	not delegated		
Maryland	09/05/74	—	09/30/85
Michigan	10/17/73	12/09/78	06/07/83
Minnesota	06/30/74	12/09/78	07/16/79
Mississippi	05/01/74	01/28/83	05/13/82
Missouri	10/30/74	06/26/79	06/03/81
Montana	06/10/74	06/23/81	—
Nebraska	06/12/74	11/02/79	09/07/84
Nevada	09/19/75	08/31/78	—
New Hampshire	not delegated		
New Jersey	04/13/82	04/13/82	04/13/82
New Mexico	not delegated		
New York	10/28/75	06/30/80	—
North Carolina	10/19/75	09/28/84	06/14/82
North Dakota	06/13/75	—	—
Ohio	03/11/74	01/28/83	07/27/83
Oklahoma	not delegated		
Oregon	09/26/73	03/02/79	03/12/81
Pennsylvania	06/30/78	06/30/78	—
Rhode Island	09/17/84	09/17/84	09/17/84
South Carolina	06/10/75	09/26/80	04/09/82
South Dakota	not delegated		
Tennessee	12/28/77	—	08/10/83
Texas	not delegated		
Utah	07/07/87	07/07/87	07/07/87
Vermont	03/11/74	—	03/16/82
Virginia	03/31/75	02/09/82	—
Washington	11/14/73		
West Virginia	05/10/82	05/10/82	05/10/82
Wisconsin	02/04/74	11/26/79	12/24/80
Wyoming	01/20/75	05/18/81	—
TOTALS	38	28	22

SOURCE: Regional Offices, U.S. Environmental Protection Agency.

Table 2.4 State Waste-water Treatment Construction Grant Program Variations During Implementation

State	State Authority over Grant Programs	Matching Grants	Grants to Communities Without EPA Help	Loans for Construction
Alabama				
Alaska		•	•	
Arizona				
Arkansas	•	•		•
California		•	•	•
Colorado	•		•	
Connecticut	•	•	•	
Delaware		•		
Florida		•	•	•
Georgia	•		•	•
Hawaii		•	•	•
Idaho		•	•	•
Illinois			•	
Indiana		•		
Iowa	•	•		
Kansas	•			
Kentucky				
Louisiana	•			
Maine		•	•	
Maryland		•	•	•
Massachusetts		•	•	
Michigan		•	•	
Minnesota		•	•	
Mississippi				•
Missouri	•	•	•	•
Montana	•			
Nebraska	•	•		
Nevada	•			•
New Hampshire	•	•		
New Jersey		•		•
New Mexico	•	•	•	

SOURCE: Data on state authority for construction grants program adapted from Fund for Renewable Energy and the Environment, *The State of the States 1988* (Washington, D.C.: the Fund, 1988), p. 8. Other data adapted from EPA, *Study of the Future Federal Role in Municipal Wastewater Treatment: Report to the Administrator* (December 1984), pp. 4-13 to 4-16.

(column 2), which indicates when states received approval for the National Pollution Discharge Elimination System (NPDES) permit program. Thus, the dates shown here are one good measure of implementation process for this policy sector. (The other columns show an additional dimension of variance, because they display information on the timing of implementation for less frequently used elements of the regulatory process. Currently, by this more detailed measure, only eighteen states have complete programs in place.) Some states, including Michigan and Oregon, assumed responsibility in the NPDES soon after passage of the

Table 2.4   (continued)

Use of State Revenues for Loans/Grants	Studies of New Financing Programs	Debt Management	Bond Pool	Revolving Funds
•				
	•			
•		•		
				•
•	•	•		
•		•		•
•				
•	•			
	•			
•		•		
•		•		
•	•			
•				•
	•	•		•
•		•		

1972 Clean Water Act. Their administrative operations are now well developed. Other states, including Arkansas and Utah, began full participation much later. Still other states, such as Arizona and Massachusetts, have not yet established permitting authority.

The states vary quite a bit in the extent to which they have adapted and/or supplemented the federal treatment plant construction grants program within their own jurisdictions. Table 2.4 arrays just a few of the options and modifications that states enacted.

By 1988—that is, by the time the phaseout of the grants program began—twenty-one states acquired authority over the construction grants program from EPA. And no matter which regulatory agency— federal or state—possessed administrative authority, the states have de-

Table 2.4 (continued)

State	State Authority over Grant Programs	Matching Grants	Grants to Communities Without EPA Help	Loans for Construction
New York	•	•		
North Carolina	•	•	•	
North Dakota	•			
Ohio				•
Oklahoma	•			
Oregon				•
Pennsylvania		•		
Rhode Island		•		
South Carolina			•	
South Dakota	•			
Tennessee				•
Texas	•			•
Utah	•			•
Vermont	•	•	•	
Virginia				
Washington		•	•	•
West Virginia	•	•	•	•
Wisconsin		•	•	
Wyoming		•		•

veloped all sorts of complex program possibilities. These range from the bare-bones federal grant program in Alabama to an intricate set of state supplementary efforts in states such as West Virginia—matching grants, loans, studies, technical assistance, innovative financing, and so forth. In a few years, great state-by-state differences in program assistance should emerge for construction, because the new state revolving loan programs seem to allow for even more discretion.

In assessing the timing of implementation of these three laws, one can discern groups of compliers, delayers, and defiers among the states. The map of the states displayed in Figure 2.1 shows the prompt implementors of hazardous waste management, Title X family planning services, and waste-water treatment policies. Delaware and Mississippi were the only states to implement all three policies promptly. Five other states—Hawaii, Georgia, Maryland, Montana, and Utah—met the implementation requirements in two out of three of the cases under study.

Figure 2.2 shows the laggards. For hazardous waste management, these states were without authorization as of March 1, 1989. For waste-water treatment, the laggards are those states in which, as of March 1, 1989, the NPDES permit program was not approved. Because most states distributed at least some Title X family planning project grants soon after the Family Planning and Population Research Act of 1970

Table 2.4   (continued)

Use of State Revenues for Loans/Grants	Studies of New Financing Programs	Debt Management	Bond Pool	Revolving Funds
	•	•		
		•		
•	•			
•		•		•
	•			
		•		
	•			
•	•		•	

was adopted, laggards in this policy area are states whose related family planning programs reached less than 50 percent of their counties within the first two years. To summarize, Figure 2.1 shows the states that moved quickly after a law was passed in an effort to comply. Figure 2.2 identifies states that either delayed implementation or turned to outright defiance. But, as noted earlier, speedy implementation does not necessarily mean "success," nor is delay or defiance necessarily "bad." This discussion merely documents state implementation behavior with respect to the early years of RCRA, Title X family planning, and clean-water policies. Any evaluation of implementation, as a process, must be tempered by an examination of implementation results.

THE RESULTS OF IMPLEMENTATION

In contrast to much implementation research, which equates implementation performance with programmatic results, the Communications Model of Intergovernmental Policy Implementation's design distinguishes between what happens during implementation and the effects of what happens. A key concept here is causal theory and its validity: if a state faithfully implements a policy (a process) but the causal

Figure 2.1
State Leaders in Policy Implementation
This figure reflects the speed with which states implemented federal poli-
cies on hazardous waste, family planning, and waste-water treatment.
States were considered leaders if the federal government authorized their
hazardous-waste-disposal policies and facilities by December 31, 1984,
under the guidelines of the Resource Conservation and Recovery Act of
1976; if they provided family planning services to 100 percent of their
counties by July 1, 1972, under the guidelines of the Family Planning Ser-
vices and Population Research Act of 1970; or if the federal government
approved their waste-water treatment program by December 31, 1974,
under the guidelines of the Clean Water Act of 1972.

SOURCE: Adapted from Tables 2.1, 2.2, and 2.3.

theory underlying the policy is flawed, then results (outputs and outcomes) are likely to fall short of expectations. In other words, goal satisfaction is a function of *both* inducing the implementation behavior
required to achieve program objectives *and* acting on the basis of a
sound causal theory.

Figure 2.2

State Laggards in Policy Implementation

*This figure reflects the speed with which states implemented federal poli-
cies on hazardous waste, family planning, and waste-water treatment.
States were considered laggards if the federal government had not authorized their hazardous waste–disposal policies and facilities by March 1,
1989, under the guidelines of the Resource Conservation and Recovery
Act of 1976; if they provided family planning services to less than 50 percent of their counties by July 1, 1972, under the guidelines of the Family
Planning Services and Population Research Act of 1970; or if the federal
government had not approved their waste-water treatment program by
March 1, 1989, under the guidelines of the Clean Water Act of 1972.*

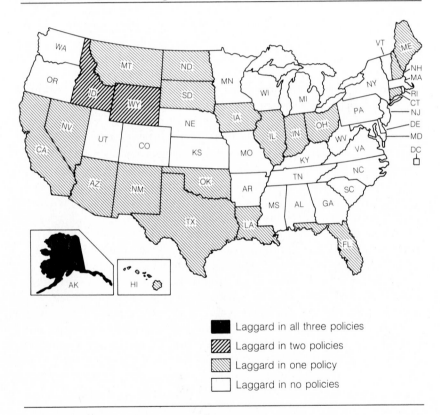

Laggard in all three policies

Laggard in two policies

Laggard in one policy

Laggard in no policies

SOURCE: Adapted from Tables 2.1, 2.2, and 2.3.

According to earlier research (Lester and Bowman, 1986: 13), however, the validity of causal theory may not be directly measurable. In
this regard, the *perception* of the validity of the theory (which is probably what matters in any joint state decision about when and how to
implement) is inferred from responses to questions in the face-to-face

interviews and our mail questionnaires conducted in the research. The measure of programmatic outputs and outcomes is peculiar to each policy. Thus, specific indicators vary among programs; although not identical, the indicators are functionally equivalent. The sources of data for the analysis in this section include agency records, annual statistical surveys, and *The Book of the States.*

Hazardous Waste Management

One common way of assessing implementation outputs is to look at the dollars being spent on programs. For hazardous waste management in 1986, those dollars ranged from a high of $61 million in California to a low of $107,161 in New Mexico. Table 2.5 reports annual hazardous waste management spending for the fifty states.

An examination of the list suggests a plausible explanation for the relative spending levels. States that have allocated substantial amounts for their hazardous waste programs tend to share two characteristics: people and pollution. Spending is related to objective conditions in a state—whether there is large population; the presence of waste-generating industries; and the existence of dangerous, abandoned waste sites. Low-spending states tend to be less populated and less industrialized. Yet, as with any comparative state listing, there are some anomalies: North Carolina is among the low-spending states, whereas Washington is counted among the big spenders.

It is difficult to separate outcomes produced by a government program from those that would have occurred without it and those that result from other factors. This is especially true for RCRA, which although enacted in 1976, was not administratively in place until 1980. It was 1984 before the first group of states received final RCRA authorization. Therefore, it is extremely risky to purport cause and effect. With such a limited time span, ostensible outcome measures could actually be indicators of problem severity. Here there simply is not enough of an "after" to compare to the "before."

RCRA implementation has generated a tightening of the hazardous waste management system. Safeguards created as a result include

- licensing and inspection of waste facilities
- use of reinforced, "fail-safe" landfills
- banning of particularly toxic wastes from land disposal
- imposition of standards for underground storage tanks
- inclusion of small quantity generators in the regulated universe, representing improvements over the previous (non)policy

What will these changes mean over the long haul? Will our land, water, and air be cleaner? Will RCRA adequately protect public health?

Table 2.5   State Expenditures for Hazardous Waste Management, FY 1986

State	Expenditures, FY 1986
1. Alabama	$ 2,118,251*
2. Alaska	1,420,000
3. Arizona	1,621,245
4. Arkansas	1,551,554
5. California	61,064,000
6. Colorado	2,271,261
7. Connecticut	4,474,000
8. Delaware	5,665,675
9. Florida	11,880,104
10. Georgia	1,563,887
11. Hawaii	2,055,761
12. Idaho	9,875,500*
13. Illinois	30,839,000
14. Indiana	5,669,169
15. Iowa	250,000
16. Kansas	1,221,528
17. Kentucky	6,358,850
18. Louisiana	2,981,588
19. Maine	975,637
20. Maryland	2,140,471
21. Massachusetts	6,566,141
22. Michigan	7,293,900
23. Minnesota	2,027,200
24. Mississippi	1,294,763
25. Missouri	11,605,094
26. Montana	2,356,980
27. Nebraska	483,670
28. Nevada	355,565
29. New Hampshire	404,885
30. New Jersey	14,795,000
31. New Mexico	107,161
32. New York	24,489,800
33. North Carolina	568,636
34. North Dakota	381,760
35. Ohio	8,137,948
36. Oklahoma	5,172,211
37. Oregon	1,777,455*
38. Pennsylvania	46,971,936
39. Rhode Island	1,996,602*
40. South Carolina	3,045,883
41. South Dakota	638,000*
42. Tennessee	1,668,000
43. Texas	10,490,808
44. Utah	2,324,400*
45. Vermont	1,892,095*
46. Virginia	2,142,000
47. Washington	20,687,732
48. West Virginia	1,380,831
49. Wisconsin	5,605,130*
50. Wyoming	261,040*

*Hazardous waste expenditures are included in solid waste, water quality, or air pollution expenditures for these states only.

SOURCE: R. Steven Brown and L. Edward Garner, *Resource Guide to State Environmental Management* (Lexington, Ky.: The Council of State Governments, 1988), pp. 83–92.

As yet, the pool of knowledge on these topics is fairly shallow. Discussion of RCRA outcomes at this juncture is premature.

Family Planning Services

For purposes of comparison, state expenditures per capita have been selected as the most important single indicator of a state's efforts in a particular policy area. Family planning practitioners have already noted a significant reduction in total federal spending for the Title X program. Title X funding peaked at $152.2 million in 1980, but was then cut drastically to $124 million. Since then funding has leveled off, but for the past several years Congress has failed to reauthorize the program. Funding has been granted through a continuing resolution. On the first legislative day of the first session of the 101st Congress, Senator Edward Kennedy and twenty-eight cosponsors introduced S. 110, a measure that would provide $163 million for family planning services in fiscal 1990. By June, the bill was voted out of the Senate Labor and Human Resources Committee, and by year end awaited full Senate action.

Although the family planning services programs that are operating in all fifty states and the District of Columbia are clearly aimed at making services more readily available (especially to teenagers and women on welfare) there is considerable confusion over the desired outcomes of the program and the extent to which anticipated and unanticipated outcomes have, in fact, resulted from the delivery of family planning services as part of the Title X program.

The confusion over what is the best indicator of program success lies in whether the goal of family planning services is to free women from unplanned *births* or reduce the number of unplanned *pregnancies* (see the Panel on Adolescent Pregnancy and Childbearing, National Research Council, 1987). Because of this difference in emphasis, one approach is to look at outcomes in terms of the number of live births, using readily available public health data. This measure has been criticized, however, because it does not take into account pregnancies that end in abortion or miscarriage.

Partly in response to this criticism, some investigators have chosen to examine the rate of abortion as a measure of outcomes. Still other researchers, who see the most desirable outcome as a reduction in the rate of pregnancies, have used the number of unintended pregnancies per 1000 women of child-bearing age as the best indicator of programmatic performance (Olsen and Weed, 1986; Weed and Olsen, 1986).

This debate over which outcomes measure to use has erupted into a contretemps of considerable policy significance. It prompted Senator Jesse Helms to deliver a scathing critique of the program in April 4, 1984, testimony before the Senate Labor and Human Resources Committee. Helms described the program as "one of the most misguided programs in the federal government." After questioning the appropriateness of *any* government involvement in decisions about who has children, the senator characterized the Title X grantees as "organizations which engage in abortion, promote abortion, lobby for abortion, litigate about abortion . . . I ask their support in building a wall of separation between family planning programs and the abortion business." Perhaps his most damaging criticism was leveled at the results of the program, charging that family planning programs were not only "totally ineffective in achieving their professional goals" but also "had actually contributed significantly toward making these problems worse" (Helms, as quoted in Rosoff and Kenney, 1984: 115).

This hyperbole triggered a response from Jeannie Rosoff, director of the Alan Guttmacher Institute (AGI), a private nonprofit research institute dedicated to analyzing reproductive health policy and educating the public about reproductive health. After emphasizing the voluntary nature of services, Rosoff and Asta Kenney, an associate for policy development at AGI, countered the Helms accusations with "the facts" about grantees and about program performance. On this last point, Rosoff and Kenney pointed out that compared to statistics for 1970, studies showed that many more teenagers became sexually active: "What is remarkable is that despite the two-thirds increase in the level of sexual activity in the 1970s, pregnancies had increased by only 12.5 percent by 1981." (Rosoff and Kenney, 1984: 111–16, 119).

The conventional wisdom—as reflected in the AGI position just articulated—is that the increase in the availability of family planning services since 1970 has reduced the rate of unwanted pregnancies, compared to its estimated rate if family planning services had been less accessible. According to John Anderson and Lisa Cope of the Alan Guttmacher Institute, "The family planning program has had an impact on aggregate fertility levels, as was intended" (Anderson and Cope, 1987: 156). Anderson and Cope conclude that this impact has been translated into "measurably lower fertility rates among women, including poor women and teenagers, across the entire country."

This conventional wisdom has been challenged of late by Stan Weed and Joseph Olsen, social scientists associated with The Institute for Research and Evaluation, a nonprofit organization in Salt Lake City, Utah. Writing in a journal called *Family Perspective* (not to be confused with *Family Planning Perspectives*), Olsen and Weed find, as a result of a multivariate analysis of the effects of family planning programs on pregnancies among 15- to 19-year-old women, that there has been a net *increase* of about 120 pregnancies for every 1000 teenage family planning clients (Olsen and Weed, 1986: 160). They write that "instead of the expected reduction in overall teenage pregnancy rates, greater teenage involvement in family planning programs appears to be associated with higher, rather than lower, teenage pregnancy rates." (Olsen and Weed, 1986: 167).

In another study published in the same issue of the journal, Olsen and Weed defend their measures and their approach. They stand by and extend their conclusions, which associate family planning program involvement with (1) lower teenage births; (2) higher abortion rates; and (3) no clear reduction in teenage pregnancy rates (Weed and Olsen, 1986: 190).

Our concern, however, lies primarily with interstate differences in program outputs and outcomes. As Tables 2.6 and 2.7 show, there is considerable variation across states and across time in annual expenditures for family planning per 1000 women in need. Moreover, the tables reveal that there is undoubtedly significant variance in the rates of teenage pregnancy, birth, and abortion among states, as well as from year to year.

The question is why this variability occurs across time and units of government? Our Communications Model posits a number of plausible explanations for variability, lumped broadly in the categories of national and subnational inducements and constraints, and organizational and ecological capacity. *Social* rather than *policy* factors are quite possibly better predictor variables for explaining interstate differences in teenage pregnancy, birth, and abortion levels, especially for whites (see Anderson and Cope, 1987: Appendix Table 1; Singh, 1986: 210). Any investigation of variance in family planning implementation would, therefore, have to introduce the element of control for the effects of social variables.

Waste-Water Treatment

Expenditures for Clean Water activities—both state agency funding and also support for plant construction—differ greatly on an absolute and a per capita basis across the states and over time. Of course, the major expenditure item in this policy area has been the construction grants program, which has allocated several billion dollars per year to deal with the treatment plant construction effort. States have had to match federal dollars for this program at rates fixed by formula.

There is opportunity for the states to supplement the required spending for this item with additional effort, but perhaps an even more revealing indicator of states' variation in their commitment to implementing water pollution control is the data from another, much smaller expenditure category—that authorized under Section 106 of the Clean Water Act. This intergovernmental category of support goes directly to state agencies to assist the monitoring and enforcement activities of the regulators. Table 2.8 displays some selected data on the topic.

Table 2.6 Annual Titles V, X, XIX, XX, and State Expenditures per 1000 Women Aged 15–44 in Need of Family Planning Services*

	FY 1980	FY 1981	FY 1982	FY 1983	FY 1985
Alabama	$23,777	$23,442	$21,987	$19,937	$28,187
Alaska	23,116	25,652	18,478	27,246	25,580
Arizona	36,771	36,719	28,109	35,266	39,394
Arkansas	26,552	26,843	24,253	23,272	16,973
California	74,656	78,057	74,618	64,403	59,593
Colorado	30,212	32,221	26,637	23,115	26,752
Connecticut	45,538	52,012	39,799	49,562	42,248
Delaware	45,466	56,991	48,686	62,458	60,339
D.C.	35,097	41,449	32,633	35,604	28,261
Florida	40,694	41,257	35,206	17,787	49,515
Hawaii	88,825	99,398	67,771	53,373	55,813
Idaho	23,520	26,403	22,245	24,184	29,770
Illinois	31,163	31,866	33,024	41,089	43,360
Indiana	35,952	37,600	13,042	27,429	38,970
Iowa	26,541	30,294	26,675	30,428	38,808
Kansas	19,728	20,834	15,454	17,207	18,894
Kentucky	27,866	26,372	18,990	24,095	28,324
Louisiana	29,132	31,332	33,271	44,367	40,554
Maine	39,071	40,483	46,896	70,874	73,364
Maryland	31,693	30,914	28,447	27,763	54,066
Massachusetts	34,899	38,586	36,447	35,717	41,937
Michigan	36,094	30,439	32,721	34,489	37,300
Minnesota	32,380	39,547	82,893	31,147	34,760
Mississippi	34,163	36,167	42,539	43,118	24,306
Missouri	27,419	28,015	20,643	17,930	27,161
Montana	42,000	36,320	33,040	33,493	31,893
Nebraska	18,697	18,725	17,241	18,473	20,112
Nevada	40,137	45,662	37,626	49,680	49,269
New Hampshire	34,197	43,508	39,410	37,410	42,951
New Jersey	54,917	50,751	39,703	55,744	50,751
New Mexico	35,887	32,554	28,701	36,811	39,538
New York	42,752	50,249	44,903	41,800	55,271
North Carolina	22,043	30,299	22,477	26,071	25,187
North Dakota	21,701	22,111	18,328	19,443	20,586
Ohio	30,904	37,399	26,585	25,826	20,586
Oklahoma	28,553	28,765	28,546	31,406	47,627
Oregon	22,688	20,762	29,873	29,503	34,656
Pennsylvania	33,402	35,360	34,871	35,044	40,899
Rhode Island	16,000	16,842	14,316	15,658	19,921
South Carolina	37,703	38,991	31,033	40,220	34,374
South Dakota	13,534	15,654	11,544	8,534	15,157
Tennessee	37,349	44,256	31,932	40,180	39,563
Texas	38,672	43,299	34,909	40,630	49,755
Utah	12,913	14,059	8,069	15,172	11,571
Vermont	47,220	45,112	24,215	39,282	47,937
Virginia	31,323	33,916	32,188	31,086	25,657
Washington	32,679	35,129	59,963	40,531	57,690
West Virginia	15,810	24,122	25,339	25,594	26,526
Wisconsin	32,715	41,430	37,476	32,560	72,518
Wyoming	34,110	28,159	30,184	29,264	28,344

*Number of low and marginal income women in need ($\leq$ 200% of poverty) in the state in 1974.

SOURCE: The Alan Guttmacher Institute.

Table 2.7   Annual State Title X Expenditures per 1000 Women
Aged 15–44 in Need of Family Planning Services*

	FY 1980	FY 1981	FY 1982	FY 1983	FY 1985
Alabama	$17,812	$16,674	$12,946	$12,692	$14,960
Alaska	20,217	22,464	18,478	18,188	25,580
Arizona	27,806	27,795	20,178	27,795	30,721
Arkansas	20,835	20,521	14,559	12,590	14,161
California	13,644	13,155	13,720	12,679	14,852
Colorado	13,549	13,885	9,469	9,186	12,513
Connecticut	16,390	15,408	13,467	13,988	14,899
Delaware	19,788	20,254	17,161	16,907	22,288
D.C.	23,599	30,555	9,952	10,966	13,478
Florida	15,269	15,869	11,732	11,709	11,669
Hawaii	31,747	32,349	23,042	26,325	25,000
Idaho	18,087	19,209	15,000	11,505	16,326
Illinois	17,082	15,897	8,126	9,724	10,266
Indiana	15,719	15,719	9,154	10,165	11,725
Iowa	16,860	17,061	11,310	11,335	14,097
Kansas	13,449	14,648	10,056	9,681	12,127
Kentucky	18,397	17,678	13,014	12,150	12,587
Louisiana	8,052	10,187	9,287	9,364	10,856
Maine	17,937	19,089	15,465	15,929	17,230
Maryland	19,235	17,231	13,781	13,495	15,837
Massachusetts	19,741	19,850	17,323	16,877	18,229
Michigan	21,230	18,984	16,094	13,766	13,967
Minnesota	11,680	12,767	9,360	7,440	11,100
Mississippi	18,662	19,614	14,928	14,655	18,413
Missouri	17,546	18,306	12,801	12,698	14,542
Montana	32,373	23,947	19,440	18,640	25,760
Nebraska	16,415	16,092	11,765	11,667	13,767
Nevada	32,420	33,379	37,626	38,447	38,219
New Hampshire	15,049	15,902	17,967	17,246	19,934
New Jersey	26,000	23,942	19,600	19,452	20,175
New Mexico	31,962	27,576	17,807	16,349	15,527
New York	13,883	14,537	11,712	11,279	11,781
North Carolina	13,403	15,338	11,495	12,162	13,840
North Dakota	18,035	17,067	11,818	11,320	11,847
Ohio	13,957	15,751	10,510	11,576	14,009
Oklahoma	16,776	16,509	13,793	13,539	14,575
Oregon	22,688	20,762	15,651	15,249	18,593
Pennsylvania	17,383	16,179	13,643	13,387	15,238
Rhode Island	10,763	10,287	7,710	7,947	8,184
South Carolina	25,145	22,884	15,875	15,579	17,745
South Dakota	13,534	15,654	8,770	8,534	11,963
Tennessee	19,073	19,114	14,318	14,040	15,441
Texas	15,041	14,807	11,289	11,716	13,571
Utah	11,407	11,964	7,086	7,954	9,378
Vermont	21,569	22,377	18,206	18,206	20,090
Virginia	13,367	11,680	10,365	10,426	11,626
Washington	19,690	20,052	13,934	14,908	26,081
West Virginia	6,290	13,199	10,569	10,726	11,276
Wisconsin	13,576	14,492	11,220	10,263	10,604
Wyoming	30,307	24,356	25,215	24,417	27,914

*Number of low and marginal income women in need (≤ 200% of poverty) in the state in 1974.

SOURCE: The Alan Guttmacher Institute.

Table 2.8   Federal and State Funding for Waste-water Treatment under the Section 106 Program, Selected Fiscal Years

| | FY 1971 | | FY 1979 | | FY 1983 | | FY 1985 | |
	S(tate)	F(ed)	S	F	S	F	S	F
Alabama	.17	.16	.33	1.40	.71	1.44	.41	1.44
Alaska	.10	.20	.11	.16	.08	.17	.10	.17
Arizona	.06	.07	.19	.55	.24	.45	.18	.45
Arkansas	.23	.12	.51	.73	.55	.80	.55	.82
California	3.31	.67	8.92	3.09	11.24	3.20	21.42	3.20
Colorado	.22	.09	1.04	.62	.51	.51	.50	.52
Connecticut	.44	.17	.80	.80	.80	.83	.85	.83
Delaware	.26	.09	.38	.51	.64	.46	.37	.46
Florida	1.15	.27	5.87	1.35	9.60	1.38	11.53	1.38
Georgia	.49	.22	1.06	1.63	1.60	1.70	2.10	1.70
Hawaii	.30	.07	.27	.37	.43	.38	.49	.38
Idaho	.27	.04	.67	.41	.58	.43	.52	.43
Illinois	1.76	.43	2.96	1.96	3.77	2.03	3.96	2.03
Indiana	.38	.23	2.28	1.17	1.94	1.13	2.32	1.13
Iowa	.13	.12	.44	1.63	.47	.78	.47	.78
Kansas	.45	.10	.84	.53	.84	.57	.45	.57
Kentucky	.35	.17	1.56	.74	1.60	.79	2.21	.79
Louisiana	.42	.19	.74	.92	1.33	.91	1.07	.93
Maine	.37	.06	.79	.58	1.09	.61	1.09	.61
Maryland	1.40	.18	3.41	.88	2.06	.91	3.49	.91
Massachusetts	1.01	.27	1.15	1.16	1.01	1.28	1.01	1.28
Michigan	.94	.36	3.17	1.88	1.68	1.94	1.50	1.94
Minnesota	.69	.16	2.53	.98	2.59	1.02	2.79	1.02
Mississippi	.15	.15	.61	.78	.78	.80	.79	.80
Missouri	.24	.20	.55	2.05	.44	.96	.44	.96
Montana	.06	.04	.07	.47	.07	.38	.08	.38
Nebraska	.14	.07	.38	1.00	.28	.62	.08	.38
Nevada	.04	.02	.21	.18	.20	.21	.27	.18
New Hampshire	.49	.06	1.80	.37	2.68	.38	1.76	.38
New Jersey	.68	.32	5.26	1.43	3.53	1.47	3.47	1.47
New Mexico	.17	.05	.36	.30	1.17	.32	.42	.32
New York	4.54	.66	4.95	2.89	5.01	2.99	7.56	2.99
North Carolina	.53	.27	2.37	1.92	2.10	1.99	3.17	1.99
North Dakota	.03	.04	.07	.24	.05	.24	.05	.24
Ohio	.87	.45	3.14	2.08	4.47	2.06	3.39	2.06
Oklahoma	.20	.12	.26	.66	1.17	.63	.30	.63
Oregon	.51	.10	.59	.86	.80	.88	1.56	.89
Pennsylvania	1.98	.49	6.03	1.32	4.96	2.42	4.96	2.42
Rhode Island	.15	.11	.66	.86	.38	.56	.48	.56
South Carolina	.44	.16	2.06	1.04	2.21	1.08	2.60	1.08
South Dakota	.06	.04	.07	.27	.07	.25	.07	.26
Tennessee	.28	.21	1.45	.95	1.40	.99	2.39	.99
Texas	3.06	.43	4.45	1.94	5.09	2.00	3.79	2.00
Utah	.10	.06	.53	.32	.57	.34	.50	.34
Vermont	.35	.04	.73	.26	1.85	.27	2.00	.27
Virginia	1.11	.21	6.62	.65	6.14	1.36	1.07	1.36
Washington	.98	.14	2.15	1.12	1.62	1.16	2.27	1.16
West Virginia	.21	.11	1.18	.67	.82	.69	.82	.69
Wisconsin	1.29	.20	3.02	1.55	3.02	1.53	2.99	1.53
Wyoming	.05	.02	.46	.18	.73	.17	.78	.17

($ millions)

SOURCE: Office of Water, U.S. Environmental Protection Agency.

Table 2.9 Implementation Output and Outcome Measures
for Waste-water Treatment Policy Among the States

| State | Output Measures | | | |
	% In Significant Noncompliance	$ Needed to Meet Stds. ($M)	Permit Backlog No.	Permit Backlog (%)
Alabama	19	181	11	(9)
Alaska	16	50	—	
Arizona	0	130	—	
Arkansas	33	244	5	(11)
California	8	926	9	(12)
Colorado	4	22	0	(28)
Connecticut	10	124	21	(9)
Delaware	7	0	7	(9)
Florida	20	not available	—	
Georgia	8	191	1	(2)
Hawaii	9	188	36	(5)
Idaho	25	21	—	
Illinois	10	985	8	(1)
Indiana	28	378	16	(9)
Iowa	2	not available	10	(6)
Kansas	2	55	0	(19)
Kentucky	7	33	11	(3)
Louisiana	31	not available	—	
Maine	10	90	—	
Maryland	28	1606	4	(14)
Massachusetts	13	625	—	
Michigan	16	1206	19	(11)
Minnesota	24	226	12	(4)
Mississippi	2	95	0	(25)
Missouri	11	344	19	(10)
Montana	0	12	8	(5)
Nebraska	12	43	5	(0)
Nevada	0	43	25	(67)
New Hampshire	5	361	—	
New Jersey	16	3159	14	(16)
New Mexico	14	121	—	
New York	6	1826	7	(15)
North Carolina	11	17	12	(9)
North Dakota	0	0	0	(0)
Ohio	26	1228	11	(17)
Oklahoma	7	202	—	
Oregon	9	34	11	(8)
Pennsylvania	12	not available	4	(5)
Rhode Island	20	92	20	(27)
South Carolina	10	166	7	(3)
South Dakota	12	61	—	
Tennessee	5	201	0	(4)
Texas	17	not available	—	
Utah	19	99	—	
Vermont	7	54	21	(40)
Virginia	3	217	0	(1)
Washington	24	1805	23	(11)
West Virginia	18	2591	0	(24)
Wisconsin	3	981	22	(71)
Wyoming	6	39	20	(0)

SOURCE: For second column of data: *Nation's Cities Weekly,* Feb. 2, 1987. For rest of data, Fund for Renewable Energy and the Environment, *The State of the States 1988* (Washington, D.C.: the Fund, 1988), p. 8.

Table 2.9 (continued)

	Outcome Measures	
State	% River Miles Meeting Stds.	% Lake Miles Meeting Stds.
Alabama	90	100
Alaska	53	53
Arizona	44	86
Arkansas	52	—
California	64	48
Colorado	—	—
Connecticut	68	95
Delaware	60	—
Florida	68	62
Georgia	95	87
Hawaii	—	—
Idaho	83	100
Illinois	55	7
Indiana	—	97
Iowa	2	73
Kansas	78	66
Kentucky	55	90
Louisiana	50	87
Maine	97	96
Maryland	92	76
Massachusetts	48	—
Michigan	98	—
Minnesota	—	—
Mississippi	90	96
Missouri	51	—
Montana	62	95
Nebraska	57	97
Nevada	—	—
New Hampshire	74	—
New Jersey	29	72
New Mexico	90	92
New York	78	80
North Carolina	67	97
North Dakota	—	—
Ohio	61	—
Oklahoma	—	—
Oregon	82	59
Pennsylvania	54	—
Rhode Island	90	97
South Carolina	87	99
South Dakota	47	87
Tennessee	66	80
Texas	94	—
Utah	—	—
Vermont	76	94
Virginia	20	91
Washington	—	—
West Virginia	56	89
Wisconsin	—	21
Wyoming	88	82

The table shows only absolute—not per capita—data. The differences in *federal* aid among the states are based on a calculation of the severity of the pollution problems in the various states; thus, these figures themselves are a kind of measure of problem severity. But it is even more interesting to examine the state figures and how they vary over time, especially between 1983 and 1985, when federal principals kept the overall level of program support constant.

For this program the states are not required to match the federal dollars at a set ratio, only to maintain the kind of effort they had made during several years of the 1970s. The states thus had an almost unhampered opportunity to adjust their own level of support for this activity without regard to intergovernmental aid formulae. During these years state variations reflect state decisions alone.

Some states, like New Mexico and Oklahoma, trimmed their spending drastically; others, like Pennsylvania, held theirs constant through the period. Additional states like Maryland and Oregon, however, used this period to increase substantially their level of commitment in dollar terms to the clean-water objectives. Another kind of comparison can be done with the same data: take, for instance, the states of Georgia and Alabama. Their support from the feds indicates roughly similar levels of pollution problems in the two states. Yet between 1983 and 1985, Georgia increased funding by approximately 31 percent. Alabama—which began with less than half the level of state funding provided in Georgia—cut its support for the state agency's activities by 42 percent. Clearly, the states differ in their spending for implementing clean-water policy.

Outputs and outcomes, too, vary significantly among the states. During the last two years, the EPA has mounted a great push through its "National Municipal Policy" to move all plants into compliance with standards by July 1, 1988. Data from earlier years document wide-ranging variations on such output measures as the percent of municipal facilities (that is, plants that are built to handle more than one million gallons per day) not in compliance with regulatory effluent standards. (See, for instance, SWIPSA, *America's Clean Water: The States' Evaluation of Progress, 1972–1982* [Washington, D.C., 1983].)

Despite the tremendous effort during the last couple of years, the first column of Table 2.9 shows some states, like Montana, to be in virtually complete compliance with the policy; the output is full adherence to the Clean Water Policy's mandate for no illegal point source discharges. Yet others, like New Jersey, face unfunded implementation prospects in the billions of dollars (note the second column, a slightly different measure of output—or gaps in output). The third column of figures in Table 2.9 provides another measure of the extent to which states, through their agencies, are addressing clean-water issues during implementation: the number (and percent) of permit requests that need to be processed. Again here, there is clear evidence of substantial differences among the states.

It is difficult to draw firm conclusions about implementation outcomes with regard to clean-water matters. In part this difficulty arises because of the extensive monitoring of the nation's waterways that would be required to derive the statistics, and in part it arises because the condition of those waterways is only partially dependent on the point source clean-water policy of federal and state governments. The EPA does have a vast collection of data that can be used to make such assessments for particular water systems (the STORET database), but it is difficult to develop a simple, reliable, and valid measure for states as a whole. As the federal regulators themselves have put the matter:

> What has been the actual water quality effect of these State, local, and Federal investments? . . . [T]he construction grants program is widely acknowledged to have led to a reduction in the loadings of pollutants from municipal sources; to have significantly reduced the number of untreated or undertreated sewage discharges; and to have improved water quality and biological conditions downstream of many new and upgraded facilities. However, efforts to quantify these improvements have lagged because of the extensive stream sampling and modeling efforts that are required. . . .
>
> Although such quantified results are rare, site-specific narrative information is available from the 1986 305(b) reports on water quality improvements due to the construction grants program (EPA, 1987).

The last two columns of Table 2.9, however, contain some rough measures: the percentage of river miles and lake miles that were meeting their designated use requirements during 1986. Once again, it is clear that the states vary greatly, in this case in implementation outcomes.

CONCLUSION

The major questions in this chapter revolve around the implementation process and its results—three policy implementation examples provide discrete measurable dimensions of implementation divided into five separate activities. A strategy for assigning values for the dependent variables for each state for each policy at each activity was discussed in general terms. Chapter 8 provides more details about measurement.

The findings presented here discount an earlier assessment of federal policy implementation as bound to fail, regardless of the circumstances (Bardach, 1977). Some states, in fact, do a faster job of implementation than others. Some states start out slowly but, after program redesign, change their style of implementation. Even within a single state or within the same policy arena, some of the programs examined in this chapter have performed differently—but not necessarily better or worse—than others.

This variability in process, outputs, and outcomes across policies, time, and units of government is well established. The balance of this book is devoted to a plausible explanation of this variability in these dimensions of implementation, and to outlining a strategy of research that permits investigators to advance from plausibility to predictability.[2] Because a number of the predictor variables that have been identified as theoretically promising are capable of manipulation, the results of this study should have practical utility as well. Chapter 3 begins to examine the first part of an explanation of why implementation processes, outputs, and outcomes vary as they do.

Notes for Chapter 2

1. Of the 9.5 million low-income women at risk of unintended pregnancy, about 44 percent obtained services from organized family planning clinics in 1983. There was considerable variation by state, however, with percentage of low-income women served ranging from 14 percent in Utah to 70 percent in Maryland (AGI, 1984: 32).

2. A plausible model is one that seems, on face value, reasonable. A *totally* predictive model is one that is capable of making a prediction about a specific case, given the facts about the values of the independent variables for that case (Blalock, 1971: 424).

CHAPTER THREE

Federal-Level Inducements
and Constraints

❖
❖

During the reign of Emperor Napoleon in 19th century France, the head of state sought extreme centralization for the process of policy implementation. Napoleon believed that the power and reputation of the empire would be directly linked with the ability of those on top to command nearly universal support for chosen courses of action. Regarding the policy sector of public education, for instance, he was heard to remark that he expected such predictable, uniform curricular efforts nationwide that, by looking at his watch at any time, he should be able to know exactly what every schoolchild in France was learning at that moment (Holtman, 1967: 143).

Much more recently—and across the Atlantic—Americans have been exposed to a very different set of descriptions and expectations about their own government. Whereas U.S. officials sometimes are heard to endorse bold new policy ideas, today's conventional wisdom is that one cannot really expect very much to happen when political leaders at the federal level create a program and funnel dollars into its execution. "Throwing money at problems is no answer" has become the catchphrase of the last decade.

Indeed, a significant portion of the professional literature produced by scholars of policy implementation does document the many fashions in which the best-laid plans can, and do, easily go awry. Whether the subject is federally supported economic development (Derthick, 1972; Pressman and Wildavsky, 1973, 1984) or education for the handicapped (Weatherley and Lipsky, 1977), students of implementation have been exposed to nationally sponsored failure and lassitude.

Neither Napoleon's machinelike vision nor the more recent, much messier reports ring true. If the American national government cannot (fortunately) expect to command perfect allegiance on the part of countless minions through administrative networks coast to coast, neither is it a toothless institution that can do simply nothing right. In short, it is unwise and empirically incorrect to treat the federal government either as an omnipotent central force or as an impotent, bumbling, and inept bureaucracy. Especially in any real effort to understand *intergovernmental* implementation—an activity involving multiple governments that may be ordered in no clear authority relationships—more careful descriptions certainly seem apropos.

It is a difficult matter to get an accurate picture of the national government's role. Because intergovernmental implementation varies by policy sector, across states, and over time, systematic study of federal-level inducements and constraints faces obstacles, and simple answers are elusive. Indeed, some large-scale research efforts will be necessary to address these matters satisfactorily. The material in this chapter does not report definitively on such a study but does provide the groundwork, and some evidence, for this kind of effort.

The chapter begins by orienting the discussion of federal-level inducements and constraints in terms of the implementation literature, especially the so-called top-down and bottom-up approaches to implementation analysis summarized in the Introduction. The chapter explores national policy decisions as messages—containing some mixture of inducements and constraints—intended for communication by federal policymakers to implementing actors at other levels. This way of thinking provides a useful approach for understanding how and why federal policies may have predictably varying effects on the implementation process. The following three sets of factors associated with these messages are considered in some detail:

- the *content* of the policy message
- the *form of the policy message* itself (several aspects of content and form seem important)
- the *reputations of the communicators* (that is, the national policymakers) among the implementors at other levels of government

For each set of factors, the chapter suggests propositions for testing. In addition, the connection between federal-level inducements and constraints, on the one hand, and policy implementation, on the other, is illuminated by a brief discussion of research results from both earlier studies of the implementation process and also preliminary findings from our current work.

NATIONAL POLICY AS FEDERAL MESSAGES

Earlier we noted that the top-down and bottom-up approaches to implementation analysis each provide helpful but incomplete perspectives. The Communications Model of Intergovernmental Policy Implementation in this book is an effort to combine the insights of both approaches to explain how diverse factors work dynamically to affect implementation. Because this chapter's subject is federal-level inducements and constraints, it is natural to emphasize some of the elements that are prominent in the top-down approach. Other portions of the volume, especially Chapter 4, link these to the additional segments of the Communications Model.

More specifically, in this book federal influence is conceptualized as a set of inducements and constraints communicated primarily to the states—at least for the kinds of policies we examine. Federal policy—whether contained in law, in regulation, or in a series of messages informally and sometimes even implicitly communicated to these other governments—consists of information, expectations, exhortations, often resources and sanctions intended to influence the actions of these others. That is, federal policy is a *political* message. Its goal is to affect action, to alter the distribution of values in (some portion of) society. Federal policy is, or can be, considerably more than bluster.

Such messages can vary considerably in their effectiveness, however. This kind of variation can be explained only partially by analyzing the message itself. Policy implementation is a dynamic and interactive process, one that simply cannot be understood by focusing exclusively on one level of action or another. What "the feds" can accomplish by sending a message is closely tied to how positively they are viewed in the eyes of potential implementors in state governments as well as elsewhere among the implementation participants. These general statements must be explored and explained more systematically.

Variations in federal-level communications—across states, programs, or time—ought to affect both the manner, or style, in which implementation occurs and the resulting outputs and outcomes. But how, exactly, is the process affected? State preferences (that is, outcomes of joint decisions among elected and appointed officials, as well as policy activists at the state level) are both induced and constrained by characteristics of the nationally generated message. These characteristics include both the content and the form of the policy message.

Of course, to simply refer to federal actors and federal messages begs several questions. The federal actors who affect the state's initial decision about what actions are required to implement a policy are the legislative committees in the Senate and the House of Representatives who have jurisdiction over the policy, and the executive agency or agencies that are responsible for putting that policy into practice. Additional policy actors, including the chief executive, individual members of Congress, and the federal courts, can also play important roles in constructing and transmitting policy messages. When President Bush "sends a message" about a war on drugs, as he did in his January 20, 1989, Inaugural Address when he said "Take my word: This scourge will stop,'' that effort influences the actions of at least some implementors.

For simplicity, this discussion focuses on legislative committees and especially administrative agencies. The primary interest of federal communicators is to see that the national legislative and executive will is not thwarted. All or only a few of the federal actors mentioned here may participate in the crafting of a particular policy message. Accordingly, the messages generated at the national level may be clear, vague, or even contradictory. Instruments usually accompany the message. These are designed to encourage attention to and often compliance with national policy on the part of states and localities. Federal principals use a combination of instruments, including appropriations, moral suasion (Peters, 1986: 9–10), technical assistance, loans, standard operating procedures, regulations, and penalties to advance their aims.

A comprehensive discussion of federal messages also raises the question, What should *count* as a policy message? Certainly, authoritative statements—laws, administrative regulations, court decisions, and executive orders—are examples of such policy messages.

Messages may be delivered through other channels and in additional, more subtle forms: in an accumulated stack of correspondence between a state and a federal agency's regional office; in a Congressional committee's interpretation of federal intent, as communicated when legislators grill administrators during appropriations hearings; and in certain items *not* said, as state officials look for cues as to ''real'' federal priorities and intent at intergovernmental bargaining sessions during implementation.

The practical problems involved in systematically studying *all* kinds of federal messages in an empirical fashion are especially daunting. In the discussion of evidence and the examples introduced later in the chapter, federal messages consist exclusively of law itself, with its accompanying regulations, as communicated by federal bureaucrats through their interaction with state officials. What national political and administrative elites have to say, how they communicate information, and how the actors who receive these messages in the fifty American states perceive the communications and the messengers have a bearing on state implementation behavior (Cobb and Elder, 1981; Edwards, 1980; McGuire, 1973; Nakamura and Smallwood, 1980).

Although the content and form of the message (such as a federal statute and subsequent federal regulations) vary across programs and over time, they are not likely to vary much across states.[1] Thus, even with a systematic research effort including data from all the states, it would be difficult to check carefully on how this part of our Communications Model squares with the real world. The implementation of *many* different federal messages differing from each other on the theoretically relevant dimensions must be studied before any firm conclusions can be established. Furthermore, much of the rest of this chapter shows how such important variables as policy form and content are themselves composed of a number of distinguishable elements.

When we find evidence in our own research of a relationship between an element of message content and some aspect of implementation style or output, there is no certainty about how to interpret the finding. This constraint on empirical testing is sometimes called "overdetermination" (see Goggin, 1986). Especially because of the limited number of policies we have been examining in the course of our empirical research, then, the portion of our Communications Model analyzed in this chapter should be seen as particularly tentative. Still, the Communications Model is largely consistent with findings developed in second-generation implementation research. A number of these studies are discussed as the Communications Model is developed here.

MESSAGE CONTENT

The basic idea regarding message content can be summarized as follows: If federally initiated messages are accompanied by resources and are credible as a viable solution to a salient problem for that state, the actors who make the joint decision for the state are more likely to opt for straightforward implementation. It should come as no surprise that the *content* of federally initiated messages affects what the states and other implementors actually do. After all, this proposition is the principal premise underlying top-down implementation research. And there has been some conceptual and empirical work aimed at examining how policy content affects implementation (see, for example, Baum, 1981; Goggin, 1987: 149–51; Hogwood and Gunn, 1984; Mazmanian and Sabatier, 1983; Montjoy and O'Toole, 1979). The major elements of the earlier work, plus some additional components of policy content, are explicated and integrated briefly here.

Resources

Money talks. People, time, and expertise matter, too. It should come as no surprise that one crucial element of policy content—the presence or absence of resources provided in connection with the message, as well as the form of the possible arrangements for financing and/or other resource provision—is prominent in the implementation literature. When the federal actors provide resources, especially in a relatively convenient and liquid form, the likelihood of straightforward implementation on the part of state and local implementors increases.[2]

When resources have been provided but are then removed or with-held, the likelihood of cooperative implementation declines—witness the reactions on the part of state and local officials to the recent growth in federal "mandates," or intergovernmental regulations without in-ducements (see ACIR, 1984). The same holds true for the impacts on state and local officials of Ronald Reagan's grant program devolution during the 1980s: Reagan increased state discretion in such important policy fields as housing, education, and transportation. But this shift was accompanied by substantial resource cutbacks. Implementation correspondingly was affected (Nathan, Doolittle, and associates, 1983, 1987).

It should be clear that this one aspect of policy content—resources—is related as well to other elements of the Communications Model. This point can best be seen by considering the impact of fed-eral cutbacks not only on implementation directly but also on the *credibility* both of the policy message and of the federal actors themselves. State officials are likely to view a reduction in support as a sign that national actors have their own doubts that a program is working. When messages are announced with fanfare, only to have resources withdrawn over time, hard feelings and suspicions can easily develop across gov-ernmental lines. Thus the links among the parts of our Communica-tions Model suggest some of the complexities of a dynamic intergovernmental implementation process.

It is important to note three facets of the resource question. First, a wide variety of resources may be necessary for implementing a policy message, and it is not always the case that resources provided by fed-eral principals can be exchanged easily for other kinds of resources. Even money, traditionally thought to be the most liquid, can be con-strained in subtle fashions in intergovernmental contexts. For instance, if a state budgets dollars and positions separately, and if hiring restric-tions prevent a sizable increase in the staff for the state's family plan-ning operation, no quantity of federal dollars can alter this resource constraint, at least in the short run.

For some policies, one way around constraints may be to contract out some aspects of implementation. It is no surprise that this sort of public-private activity, which has become increasingly popular in re-cent years, has been a frequent outlet for implementation processes in states and localities with various kinds of resource constraints. Joint public-private provision is an exceedingly complicated phenomenon and is beyond the scope of systematic discussion here. It should be noted, however, that contracting phases of programs to outside ser-vice firms entails problems as well as opportunities for the implement-ing agencies at the state or local level.

Second, the transmission of resources is almost always accompa-nied by administrative constraints, such as red tape. This phenomenon is understandable, because federal actors are reluctant to offer scarce resources without accompanying safeguards. But the result may be that proffered resources are much less of an actual than an apparent inducement. Both of these first two points are illustrated by examining the implementation of federal clean-water policy as it affects municipal waste-water treatment. Federal principals, especially administrators in the Environmental Protection Agency (EPA), made clear to the nation's states and local governments that the EPA intended to treat very seriously its policy of requiring compliance with federal clean-water regulations by July 1, 1988. This policy was accompanied by the inducement of resources—specifically, a construction grants program of which municipalities all over the country have been the direct beneficiaries.

Yet for a locality currently out of compliance, even a generous federal grant cannot be immediately converted into an on-line implementation process in a six-month or one-year period. There is simply no way that states like Louisiana or Ohio, where more than 25 percent of major facilities are in significant violation of standards, could have resolved this difficulty immediately, even had vast resources been devoted to the cause (see Table 2.9, described previously). Furthermore, some localities found that buying into the federal construction grants program for waste-water treatment means tolerating nationally imposed inspections, paperwork, delays, and design stipulations. Accordingly, even when the dollars were flowing fairly freely (the grants portion of the program was being phased out by 1988), some municipalities chose not to nibble on the fiscal carrot.

Third, it is important to note that policy messages may include resources in very different fashions. Of particular interest is whether resources are provided to help cover the costs of the output and/or outcome only, or whether federal principals include also some provision for the costs of the implementation process itself (GAO, 1976; Montjoy and O'Toole, 1979).

Obviously, some issues related to resource provision for policy implementation have not been addressed in this brief discussion. In particular, the administrative or organizational capacity of state and local implementors and a state's economic status are also directly tied to resource questions. For instance, resource-rich messages are likely to attract a disproportionate share of energetic administrative talent at the state level, as individuals on the make in state government move to where the action is, thus increasing administrative capacity (Downs, 1967). The analysis here has only been intended to highlight the impact of *federally* provided resources, via a policy message, on the likelihood of straightforward implementation. In that regard, then, it is possible to summarize by stating that the greater the quantity of resources provided with the federal message, the more likely it is for the state (and local) implementors to implement the policy expeditiously.

Credibility of the Message as a Viable Solution

The credibility, or believability, of a policy message among potential implementors is not a simple matter, but it is an important one. Messages that make no sense; seem unlikely to produce efficacious results; appear uncertain in their effects; reduce their certainty (in a technical sense, at least) by requiring mechanisms of citizen participation in the implementation process; or compound the implementors' potential political problems by the structure of benefits and costs likely to impact the target population are unlikely to provoke straightforward implementation. Discussion of each of these contingencies is worthwhile.

Policy Efficacy   All policies, save symbolic ones, are designed to address some public problem.[3] But some problems are more easily dealt with, either in a technical or political sense, than others; in short, these are more efficacious. States find it easy to distribute formula-provided state aid to localities (especially when the aid pie is growing). But developing innovative and effective family planning programs is another story, for technical (as well as political) reasons, because this policy problem is tough to solve (and many people believe that government should have nothing to do with it). Some messages may identify policy goals that are even technically *impossible* to achieve. Some critics argue that this description fits the combination of minimum wage and full-employment policies currently in force.

The policy message is more likely to induce prompt and cooperative implementation on the part of the states when, other things being equal, the substantive problem being addressed is easier or less controversial to solve than politically unpopular or controversial ones. Among the policies to which we gave special scrutiny, the waste-water treatment issue is a relatively easy one to solve in these senses, while family planning conveys a much more difficult message. Thus, in the measures of implementation output and outcome for waste-water treatment presented in Chapter 2, there were clear signs of progress in virtually all the states, despite variations across them. Family planning efforts have proven more inconsistent, as the parallel measures in Chapter 2 make clear.

Some policies are based on a set of cause-and-effect assertions that are extremely well-tested and thus provide the expectation of stable and certain effects. Policy messages vary considerably in the "validity of causal theory" underlying their injunctions (Sabatier and Mazmanian, 1979). Examples easily demonstrate this point: The technology of waste-water treatment to clean municipal sewage is generally well known. A significant portion of the implementation process for this policy has been reduced to an engineering problem, thereby providing ease and predictability to implementors involved in achieving this national goal.

Some private companies even market this service to cities as contractors, using as a selling point their guarantee to shoulder all regulatory obligations and to pay any fines resulting from noncompliance. In a policy field of lower efficacy—education is a prime example—virtually no public or private implementor promises certain and specific results. To take another illustration, the much-maligned Work Incentive Program (WIN), designed to equip and encourage welfare recipients to enter the work force, labored for years under a number of handicaps. Not the least of these was the fact that the United States as a nation does not know very much about how to move people from welfare to productive, responsible, and rewarding employment. Accordingly, as the certainty of effects to be induced by the policy message declines, the likelihood of prompt and predictable outputs and outcomes also declines.

This conclusion is hardly remarkable. Yet another related point is also significant. State-level actors, in responding to a federal message, inevitably make their *own* judgments and perceptions regarding the degree of certainty of the effects to be generated by straightforward compliance with a policy message. These perceptions themselves affect the style of state officials' implementation process. For instance, where state officials believe the Resource Conservation and Recovery Act (RCRA) of 1976 program to be an operation with uncertain and potentially dangerous consequences, there is less than wholehearted cooperation. The main point is that this result occurred even though the effects were actually quite knowable and easily understood. Therefore, as the perceived certainty of effects to be induced by the policy message declines among potential implementors, the likelihood of prompt and predictable implementation processes also declines.

Citizen Participation   A special set of considerations accompanies the issue of citizen participation. It often seems unfashionable today to consider citizen participation as a viable means of policy development. The heyday for federal experiments involving citizens directly in the making and implementing of policy was surely the 1960s, a time of dramatic and innovative efforts in this regard. These days, with voter turnout low, budget deficits high, cutbacks widespread in many domestic programs at all levels of government, and the considerable impact of two terms of Ronald Reagan's "new federalism" (an approach built upon the proposition that national government should withdraw from both the financial support and the regulation of state and local activities), one hears much less about either the uses of or the problems created by various forms of citizen participation in the implementation process—through direct administration, hearings, advisory mechanisms, and so on.

However, this appearance is deceptive. Whereas some of the most visible of such efforts have been scaled down, there remain many intergovernmental programs that include some sort of requirement for the involvement of private, often individual citizen, actors in the process of executing policy. It is virtually impossible to produce an exact tally of the number or proportion of federally initiated messages that include a provision for citizen participation as a part of their content. However, one survey of the content of formal federal policies during the preceding decade identified 155 such cases (ACIR, 1979).

The theory we have been developing leads to somewhat complex conclusions regarding this element of a federal policy message. On the one hand, this kind of provision is likely to make life more complex and less overtly "manageable" for state-level implementors. Provisions for citizen involvement may complicate administration, slow down agency processes, and politicize the implementation process. The more that additional actors are added to implementation networks, the greater the chance for blockages or pitfalls to develop as a program is converted into action. Such effects obviously vitiate in part the degree of certainty in the implementation process. One would thus expect the chances for implementation style to move from strategic delay or compliance toward delay or defiance to be greater, other things being equal, for messages with provisions or requirements for citizen participation.

Certainly the point of this proposition is a lesson taught by many of the case-study accounts of intergovernmental policy processes (for example, Moynihan, 1969), and it is an overt proposition of a number of studies of implementation. Pressman and Wildavsky assert that the chances for successful implementation are inversely related to the number of actors and decision points (1984: 87–124). Mazmanian and Sabatier, too, reach similar conclusions in their well-known theoretical and empirical work (1983: 27). This idea is a prominent component of the top-down conventional wisdom.

Among the policies to which we gave special consideration, RCRA contains provisions for citizen participation. Under this policy, the EPA initiated a national "Waste Alert" program in the late 1970s. The program involved a series of workshops to educate citizens about the hazardous waste issue and its attendant risks. EPA did not actually conduct the workshops; instead, the agency contracted out the responsibility to a broad coalition of environmental and public-interest groups (Rosenbaum, 1983).

The Waste Alert program was an eventual casualty of Reagan Administration budget cutting. The responsibility devolved to the states where fundamental questions about the intent of citizen participation (to inform the public *or* to solicit the public's opinion) hampered its implementation.

And yet this sort of analysis misses an important component of the implementation process. Although provisions for citizen participation are likely to complicate the process and may provoke some resistance among state officials, such requirements are not part of the policy message through accident or perversity. Involvement of some portion of the citizenry may be helpful, indeed sometimes essential, if the purposes behind a policy are to be brought to life in some meaningful way.

This point is one of the main themes of the bottom-up perspective. Especially for policy problems that demand for their successful execution that complex linkages and reciprocal patterns of interaction be worked out among a variety of public and private actors in an intricate arrangement, citizen participation provisions may be quite helpful.

Examples of such policies singled out for special scrutiny here include ones for family planning services, because a sizable proportion of the population objects to the federal government paying for contraceptive services. Policies that deal with social issues and/or that rely on a pattern of private and nonprofit providers, contractors, or "assistance structures" (Hull with Hjern, 1987) are especially important cases. In short, provision for participation by outside actors increases chances for an appropriate output and/or outcome from the implementation process by improving efficacy, even while decreasing the chances that strategic delay will be a state's implementation style.

Furthermore, citizen suits and right of private action can prod federal agencies to take their formal messages more seriously. The National Resources Defense Council has succeeded in numerous suits filed to require the EPA to act to enforce the law (see Shapiro, 1988).

This whole set of issues is also directly tied to the arrangement of organizational actors at the state (and local) level in an implementation structure. That is, citizens are not the only ones who may be related in a complicated fashion to implementation process and outcome; others, including implementing organizations inside and outside of government, also affect what happens in similar ways. As explained fully in Chapter 5, the evidence thus far produced by implementation researchers casts doubt on overly simple conclusions regarding organizational capacity, as it does for the matter of citizen participation.

Policy Type   Finally, the type of policy contained in the policy message can also be crucial for the pattern of implementation that is likely to emerge. The notion of policy type here has a particular sense—not to designate the substantive differences among, say, defense and housing and environmental and child welfare policies but rather to indicate the distribution of costs and benefits likely to flow from the policy in question. Policies that do not obviously portend a drastic redistribution of costs and benefits among the target group(s) likely to be affected by the message may hold little promise for solving major social problems.[4] However, such policies are likely to encounter less resistance during implementation. State and local implementors themselves have to rely on the support or at least sufferance of state and local elites if they are to achieve very much.

Although the implementation process provides opportunities to achieve subtle political goals, there are good reasons to expect that implementors are unlikely to affect major redistributions at that stage. One important reason is that the intricate processes of implementation often require a good deal of time, energy, expertise, and organizational capacity. These requirements effectively become filters affecting the type of influence likely to be exerted on the implementation process. Those in possession of such resources are likely to constitute an over-representation of the "haves" of society—those who are already favored by the social system (Schlozman, 1984). Even if there are millions of homeless Americans, a new intergovernmental program to subsidize low-income apartments is likely to attract more detailed attention from bankers and real estate companies than residents during implementation. The HUD scandals that were investigated by Congress during 1989 underscore the point. Implementors, sensitive to this distribution of interests, are likely to view a federal message as less credible the more it entails an overt redistribution of benefits and/or costs in society. A state, then, is more likely to make a joint decision to delay implementation and modify a policy message during the course of its implementation, if the message is redistributive.

On the other hand, waste-water treatment is a classic example of a policy that contains both regulatory and distributive components— the former in the clean-water standards, the latter via the construction grants program—but virtually no overtly redistributive features. The provision of federal aid even goes to provide infrastructure that is a "lumpy" and very public good. Thus, distributional questions virtually never arise within communities, and the program usually operates with low levels of conflict.

These last several pages have covered the aspects of message content that are important for purposes of the theory and have also summarized some of the evidence available on the issues. The task of *measuring* policy content, however, so as to test the Communications Model more carefully, can be a difficult one. A discussion of measurement and testing is reserved for Chapter 8.

MESSAGE FORM

State preferences in the implementation process (joint decisional outcomes) are constrained by the form as well as the content of the policy message. As with policy content, policy form refers to several attributes.

If federally initiated messages are clear, consistent, frequently repeated, and actually received, then the actors who make the joint decision for the state are more likely to opt for straightforward implementation.

Policy Clarity

Messages in ordinary life are more likely to be acted on expeditiously if they are communicated clearly. The same is true for policy messages from federal officials. Clarity can be defined in terms of at least two elements: means and ends. Messages that merely "prescribe . . . some desired future state of affairs or task . . . agencies with developing programs for some general problem" are vague with respect to both (Montjoy and O'Toole, 1979: 468). Messages that contain straightforward statements of their standards or targets—especially those without qualifying, contradictory, or ambiguous language—are specific and clear with respect to goals. Messages that "set forth specific particular procedures" (Montjoy and O'Toole, 1979: 468) to be followed by implementors, especially those with deadlines and/or instructions regarding the pattern of mandated interdependence and formal authority among the implementing actors (individuals or organizations), are specific and clear with respect to means. Policies embracing clarity with respect to both means and ends are to be considered clearer than those that are vague in one respect and clear in the other.[5]

The Federal Coal Mine and Safety Act of 1969 illustrates clarity in a policy message to national implementors. The law itself specifies procedures and schedules for reducing respirable dust in coal mines; achieving certain quantitative standards of dust concentration is clearly stated as the goal of the policy. This instance can be contrasted with the Mining and Minerals Policy Act of 1970, which was intended to encourage the development of a long-term government policy on nonfuel minerals. The Senate report accompanying this law explicitly states that the policy was deliberately drafted in very general terms (see Montjoy and O'Toole, 1979: 471–73).

Obviously, clarity encourages prompt implementation that is true to lawmakers' intent by reducing opportunities for misunderstanding, lack of coordination, or recalcitrance in the intergovernmental bargaining and negotiating process (Crotty, 1988). The clearer the policy message, the more straightforward the implementation process at the state and local level.

Policy Consistency

Messages can be, individually or cumulatively, clear but inconsistent. For if we conceive of policy as message, or as a stream of messages—perhaps emanating from several of the federal principals, perhaps flowing through time—we are alerted to the possibility, indeed the likelihood, that national policy on any topic may not be completely coherent and consistent.

Observers of the American policy process have long noticed the fragmented, somewhat incoherent nature of decision making there, as various interests, perspectives, committee jurisdictions, and swings of the electoral pendulum contend for policy-making prominence at any one time. In the classic example, then, the "same" federal government that warns the public not to smoke cigarettes also subsidizes the production of the offending tobacco crop.

In addition, policy problems are often complex, and tackling one aspect may interfere with another. The federal waste-water treatment plant construction grants program was intended to help localities cope with the financial burden of large capital construction costs for compliance with the Clean Water Act, but the program was also supposed to avoid subsidizing municipalities in their efforts to compete with each other to stimulate growth. Thus grants have been available to build "needed" facilities, but no federal support has been allowed for new facilities or expansions intended to deal with "anticipated increases" in plant load. While tensions within a policy such as this one can sometimes be controlled by detailed language and various regulatory mechanisms, the complexities of the message(s) may create at least a sense of inconsistency. In such circumstances, it may be difficult for potential state and local implementors, even those who clearly want to accede to national wishes, to execute the message on time and without substantial modification.

There may be another problem with policy consistency, as well. Clarity in policy messages may assist in the ease of implementation, but it may also render explicit the contradictory policy tendencies of the federal actors (Lindblom, 1980). Then, federal policymakers find themselves impaled upon the horns of a dilemma. Clarity, helpful in providing direction to actors at other levels, also increases the probability of inconsistency across the full range of federal messages. A familiar temptation, then, is to write laws that contain very little policy (Lowi, 1979), and then perhaps to attempt to follow this general policy message later—and quietly—with regulations and other administrative efforts to add clarity.[6] Of course, such a strategy can be criticized for sublimating rather than addressing the inconsistencies that so often emerge, and for shifting message creation to an arena where only the most well-organized and well-endowed interests have a full chance to exercise influence.

This discussion suggests a complex link between two relationships discussed earlier: how policy type and policy clarity affect implementation. Vague messages make redistributive policies seem like the less controversial, distributive ones. Thus we would expect an interactive effect: Clear messages are easier to understand and thus to implement, but they may be more difficult to swallow—or defend.

The findings of social science on the effects of messages with the characteristics just mentioned—complexity and ambiguity—are quite straightforward. Recipients of such messages are more prone to perceive messages selectively (Simon and Dearborn, 1958). Selective perception means that such policy messages are less likely to stimulate straightforward implementation in federally specified directions. The effect of a low level of consistency (or of its remedies, such as complicated or general messages) is likely to be a reduced level of implementation or a continuation of the *status quo ante* among the states.

An example of selective perception leading to this kind of implementation behavior within the federal bureaucratic structure itself is reported by Montjoy and O'Toole (1979). In the case of the Mining and Minerals Policy Act, discussed earlier, a GAO investigation of the program indicated that the message had produced virtually no effect in the implementing agency, the Department of the Interior. That department "maintain[ed] that all of its programs further the mineral policy. Interior also argue[d] that no specific change in departmental operations was or is required. . ." (GAO, 1976: 6; see Montjoy and O'Toole, 1979: 471).

Policy messages may also vary in consistency in another sense. As time goes on, even a fairly clear, consistent policy (at least with itself) may well be altered. Experience with the policy might provoke changes. Political pressures to tighten or loosen the constraints generated by the policy might generate alterations. Administrative shifts (centralization or decentralization within the major national agency) might put the message-sending or -interpreting authority in other hands, thus often stimulating changes. Deadlines and clear standards might be relaxed to accommodate technical or political resistance among the state and local officials and/or private organizations involved in the implementation network. In any of these contingencies, the result can well be policy inconsistencies across time. From the perspective of message recipients, these kinds of inconsistencies may signal a lack of resolve, or at least a confusion, about federal intentions. As one state program manager survey respondent commented on this issue regarding RCRA, "The . . . implementation process is characterized by a lack of EPA consistency, and the feeling of 'shooting at a moving target' has caused some serious difficulties." In other words, this kind of inconsistency can in turn lower federal credibility, another element of our Communications Model.

Whereas flexibility and accommodation during the implementation process itself can cement cooperative ties between governmental implementing units, actual changes in policy messages may have the unintended effect of blurring information, weakening wills, and impeding the efforts to convert the intention embedded in a policy message into action. For all of these reasons, then, the greater the federal message inconsistency in a particular policy domain—either across messages or over time—the more likely a state is to delay implementation and/or seek modification of the policy.

Evidence from others' studies of implementation as well as from our own research lends support to this positive relation between inconsistency at the federal level and delayed implementation. For instance, Crotty, using different measures than those proposed here, found states more likely to accept primacy for implementing environmental policies if federal messages are communicated more consistently from regional offices of EPA (Crotty, 1988: 645).

Table 3.1 displays the evaluations of state-level hazardous waste administrators to the RCRA message. The figures indicate that implementation style is facilitated by federal laws that are clear, consistent, and flexible. Mean scores are highest among those states that implemented RCRA quickly without modifications. In addition, actors in the compliant states felt that regional EPA representatives were most helpful in the implementation process. Overall, however, the comments of the respondents to our survey revealed a significant amount of frustration experienced by state implementors during RCRA implementation. Administrators in slow-to-implement states reported that "state/EPA relationships are poor," or that "the RCRA implementation process is characterized by a lack of EPA consistency."

A situation in which policy inconsistency has clearly affected the implementation styles of state and local governments is the shifting national policy on clean water and the related construction program for municipal waste-water treatment plants. For the years between 1972 and 1982, federally generated policy messages stressed the importance of clean water, encouraged the states to become actively involved in the regulatory scheme, and offered the financial assistance of the national treasury in helping to cover the construction costs by matching expenditures with 75 percent federal funds.

Since 1982, however, many factors have changed:

- The regulations clarifying just how clean the water has to be to meet federal requirements have changed, most recently in 1986. Each alteration has raised the standards and thereby increased the costs of satisfying them.
- Despite the raised standards, the national implementing bureaucracy, the Environmental Protection Agency, has delayed strict enforcement of these tightened standards (such as by post-

Table 3.1   Federal Level Inducements and Constraints
by Implementation Style (Means)

Variables	Compliance (n = 13)	Strategic Delay (n = 23)	Delay (n = 6)	Defiance (n = 1)
Clarity*	2.91	2.48	2.00	N.A.
Consistency	2.82	2.38	1.50	N.A.
Flexibility	1.82	1.81	1.25	N.A.
Regional Help†	3.62	2.86	3.00	1.00

*The scales for clarity, consistency, and flexibility range from 5 (very clear) to 1 (not very clear).
†The scale for regional help ranges from 4 (very helpful) to 0 (no help at all).
N.A. = Not available.

SOURCE: Survey by the authors.

poning the deadline for compliance from 1985 to 1988). As such delays have been sought by state and local officials in many cases, the effect has been to raise questions about EPA's willingness to press the matter eventually.

- In 1981, the construction grants program was reduced to approximately a 55 percent match.
- Federal tax law changes in 1982 created substantial incentives for private companies to become involved in the implementation process via privatisation, at least in some of those communities that had little prospect for benefiting from the grants program.
- In 1986, newer tax law revisions largely removed the incentives from the treasury for privatisation.
- The construction grants program was scheduled for elimination in the late 1980s by the Clean Water Act of 1986.

A summary of these policy changes is contained in Heilman and Johnson (1989). In the place of the original regulations was established a policy stimulating the establishment of State Revolving Funds from which loans can be made to assist with treatment plant construction. As of early 1989, when the nation had passed the "final" deadline for strict EPA enforcement of water pollution standards, few of these state revolving loan funds had begun to be implemented.

Our efforts to gather data from state and local officials have revealed attitudes toward this program ranging from skepticism to resentment and even some recalcitrance among state implementing officials, many of whom are generally attached to the values of the clean-water legislation. In this shifting set of messages, it is no wonder that currently hundreds of major treatment plants are not in compliance with federal and state standards.

Frequency of Repetition

Clarity and consistency assist in the process of communicating federal intent through a set of inducements and constraints to state and local actors. Communication theory suggests an additional factor: Messages transmitted frequently—when the content is consistent, that is—are more likely to be received and acted upon. This notion should hold for policy messages as well, especially because the communication channels between governments are complex, heavily used, and subject to competition—in terms of the priorities accorded to various messages—from many who want their preferences placed high on the policy agenda of the receiving unit. Accordingly, the more frequently repeated the policy message from the federal principals is, the easier is the implementation.

Policymakers at the national level, cognizant of the fact that repetition on important issues can make the difference between action and inaction, sometimes use their message-sending capacity to drive home important policy-relevant points.

Take the case of family planning and abortion in early 1989. In early January, the Supreme Court announced that it would consider the constitutionality of a state law in Missouri that prohibited the use of federal funds or buildings for abortion, or even abortion counseling. Within a few days of that announcement, and only one week before he was to depart from the White House, Ronald Reagan vowed that he would fight to reshape federal abortion policy "as long as there is breath in me" (J. Johnson, 1989).

On President Bush's first day on the job, he repeated the same message by telephone to pro-life demonstrators. One of Dan Quayle's first official acts as vice president was to meet with pro-life leaders on the anniversary of the 1973 Supreme Court decision legalizing abortion. This was Quayle's way of lending the Bush Administration's moral and political support to their cause. Repetition of the anti-abortion message did not stop here, however. During the January 1989 confirmation hearings of Louis Sullivan for the cabinet appointment of Secretary of Health and Human Services, the founder and former dean of Morehouse School of Medicine in Atlanta first equivocated on the issue of family planning and abortion. But by the time his confirmation hearings ended, he had set the record straight: he was unalterably in favor of overturning *Roe v. Wade*.

Receipt of Messages

The most brilliant policy in the world is meaningless in practice if it is shelved; left untranslated into administrative regulations that give some meaning to the policy outside the halls of Congress; or filtered out of the communications channels somewhere between federal actors and street-level, state and local bureaucrats. Thus, one reason why implementing actors at state or local levels may not view the policy message as do some of the federal principals is that not all messages are actually delivered.

In recent years, as the tenure in office of federal-level executive branch political appointees has decreased to eighteen months or less and departures from the top ranks of the permanent civil service have accelerated (largely in response to the political attacks mounted on the bureaucracy by Presidents Carter and Reagan), communication gaps have been magnified by personnel and organizational disarray. Ironically, some of the efforts in recent years to implement programmatic changes and cutbacks, especially in the Reagan era, seem to have foundered on communication blockages and lack of administrative capacity as federal program leaders have sought to deal with the states and locals. This seems to have been the fate of recent policy regarding the use and disposal of federal lands (Durant, 1987: 185–86).

To the extent that *private* individuals or organizations may also be required by a policy message to participate in an implementation process if it is to work, additional opportunities for mischief emerge. Private actors are less likely to be involved directly and regularly in the communication loops that can make all the difference in intergovernmental implementation, and messages sent haphazardly stand a good chance of never being received.[7]

It would take an extraordinarily systematic, careful, and rigorous research effort to explore all these possibilities. Furthermore, recalcitrant implementors have an incentive to claim ignorance of the policy once caught in noncompliant behavior—as the Internal Revenue Service learns with respect to individual and corporate taxpayers each year. Here we focus more narrowly on policy messages that are authored by federal principals but apparently (from the perspective of state and local actors) either never received or received considerably later than the message was established.

Numerous studies of implementation, of either the first- or the second-generation type, document instances in which messages from policymakers did not find their way to prime actors in the field. In one comparative cross-national study of implementation in the field of labor market training, locales with slower and weaker implementation responses evidenced lower levels of knowledge regarding national policy and the opportunities it afforded. This was especially true with respect to private firms in the Federal Republic of Germany; they were essential for the implementation process to work but operated largely in ignorance of policy messages emanating from Bonn or even from the field offices of the relevant national ministry (O'Toole, 1983).

In a recent empirical study of the impact of U.S. federal regional offices on the implementation of environmental policy in state and local governments, the importance of federal regional officials as message links between the federal actors and the message recipients is emphasized. The study notes quite properly that such officials can be crucial for communications in *both* directions when such reciprocal exchange of messages and information is necessary for implementation. EPA "regions take the national government's message that states should accept primacy and target it within each region. Regional officers also transmit to the national office messages from the states, such as requests for primacy, delays, and variances" (Crotty, 1988: 643). The feedback loop—the link between action in the field and the process of policy redesign—is another feature of our Communications Model and is treated in detail in Chapter 7.

The basic idea is thus that federally generated messages must actually be received by the states and localities if these governments are to participate effectively and appropriately in an implementation process. One might think that this point is so basic that no principals at the federal level would initiate a message without making sure that it is received by potential implementors. However, our field work on waste-water treatment implementation revealed that this is not the case.

Interview statements demonstrate that in 1989, for instance, federal policy on State Revolving Funds is simply unknown to many local public works and engineering officials in various parts of the United States. Some high-level administrators in the relevant state agencies profess ignorance about this development and have not begun to consider how their own agency might be involved in or affected by the shift in federal inducements and constraints.

To recapitulate, the discussion thus far has focused primarily on characteristics of the federally propagated policy message—specifically, on various aspects of message content and form. As indicated earlier, however, the impact of such messages is influenced by characteristics of the sender as well. We now turn briefly to this subject.

PERCEPTIONS ABOUT
THE FEDERAL PRINCIPALS

What federal principals say and do can affect state and local actors. But how those federal principals are *perceived* can be very important as well. To the extent that those who send policy messages are viewed as legitimate and credible, their messages are likely to have more impact in stimulating state and local efforts. The more legitimate and credible the federal principals are in the eyes of state officials, *ceteris paribus*, the more likely the state's implementation is to proceed promptly and without harmful modifications in program content.

Legitimacy

The way state and local governments view the legitimacy of federal officials is not an all-or-nothing affair. Rather, *some* national government actors are seen as authoritative in *certain* policy arenas or on certain issues. Even though nearly everyone supports the goal of preventing destructive fires in the nation's cities, involvement by various federal agencies in seeking to promote this goal has provoked resistance from state and local officials on the grounds of legitimacy. Federal agencies, many subnational governments believe, ought to have no official role on this subject of primarily local policy (ACIR, 1980). Chapter 2's data on family planning, including the example of virtually defiant Utah developed at the outset of the discussion, demonstrate this point clearly.

Credibility of the Federal Actors

Earlier, this chapter explored at some length the factors that enhance or impede credibility of a policy message. As shown there, the believability of a message is a complex matter. That analysis omitted coverage of one additional item that can affect the impact of a message on state and local implementors: the credibility of the sender. Those legislators or members of the executive branch whose word can be believed have an easier time converting their policy signals into action. As noted earlier, certain elements of policies can affect federal credibility. This element of our Communications Model can also be influenced by interaction itself. Because intergovernmental implementation frequently requires complex patterns of coordination over long periods of time, an absence of trust removes a key component that might otherwise induce cooperative action (O'Toole and Montjoy, 1984).

On the other hand, working with message recipients over an extended time and on many issues can both increase bargaining opportunities and, more important for present purposes, improve credibility. In certain states credibility may also be enhanced if the federal message is being advocated in Washington by representatives of the political party that is ascendant in the state political leadership.

Sometimes the presence of a "fixer" (Bardach, 1977), "reticulist" (Friend, Power, and Yewlett, 1974), or "facilitator" can assist in this process of building trust by helping to translate the perspective of one participant in the implementation chain into that of another, by holding parties accountable for their commitments, by bringing pressure to bear on those who seek to avoid their responsibility in the inter-governmental network, and by tying the complex pattern together long enough for trust to develop independently of the efforts of the facilitator (O'Toole, 1988). Whatever means is used to generate the policy, the point is that credibility can be a resource that federal principals can bring to an implementation context or can develop within that context, as the dynamics of the process unfold.

Credibility is not simply a matter of cooperative trust, however. Even the believability of *threats* can assist implementation in some situations by convincing potential implementors at other levels of government that sanctions are indeed likely to follow noncompliance. Federal policy initiators have faced problems in this regard on issues of civil rights and integration, following widespread delays during the implementation of federal court and legislative decisions (Ball, Krane, and Lauth, 1982). Visible and symbolic messages, communicated by such devices as the presence of federal troops on campuses and in city streets, finally convinced many states and localities that the renewed national message in the mid-1960s was credible.

Principals in the Environmental Protection Agency have recently faced problems of credibility in sanctioning violators of the Superfund (a trust fund set up in 1980 to clean up toxic contaminants spilled or dumped into the environment). Evidence exists that sweetheart deals characterized the Reagan Administration's response to the hazardous waste cleanup problem. In a careful empirical study of this general issue with respect to the EPA, credibility emerged as an important matter: "State officials may dislike national mandates and preemption, but they respond to national directives when a strong chance exists that they will be regulated by national standards. This indicates that, in dealing with states, a coercive approach is more effective than a conciliatory one" (Crotty, 1988: 646).[8]

One study by Deborah McFarlane (1989) supports our general contention that federal-level constraints and inducements are an important part of the implementation puzzle. Using family planning Titles X, V, XIX, and XX (McFarlane, Table 2) data for the years 1976 to 1981, she sets out to test the "statutory coherence" hypothesis—that statutory coherence is inversely related to state implementation. She calculated statutory coherence scores for each of four family planning laws, relying on measures of several of the federal-level inducements and constraints that were discussed earlier.

The most coherent statute was Title X, and, as predicted, it demonstrated significantly less variation in interstate per capita spending for family planning services. McFarlane concludes from her analysis that "the policy outputs of Title X—the most coherent statute—were much more evenly distributed among the states than were the policy outputs of Titles V, XIX, and XX" (McFarlane, 1989: 417).

McFarlane's analysis is a good beginning, but it is limited to a five-year period when funds for family planning were increasing and before major changes were instituted during Reagan's Administration. What she attempts to explain is cross-state variability in policy outputs and their distribution, not the variations in implementation process across states, policies, or time that our Communications Model envisions. Nevertheless, her effort to begin to test theories, or in this case a part of a theory, of implementation is laudable.

CONCLUSION

It is amply clear that the top-down tradition of implementation research does not provide an accurate picture of the process of how policy intention is converted into action. Furthermore, even if the top-down approach were accurate, questions could be raised about whether appropriate outputs and/or outcomes are likely to be produced by clear messages from Washington. This is especially true in certain policy fields, no matter what the pattern of federally generated inducements and constraints.

Nevertheless, this chapter has outlined the ways in which the top-down approach does indeed have value in an empirical theory of implementation. Messages initiated by the feds are neither worthless nor self-executing. Depending on their mix of characteristics and on how the feds themselves are perceived by those in the states, what happens in Washington can markedly affect what happens in other governments and in the world of action. The ideas advanced in this chapter spell out more specifically the kinds of predictions that can be made, and a variety of studies conducted by others provides some evidence suggesting the plausibility of the material integrated here.

Research findings on the three policies we investigated also lend support to these ideas. The detailed discussion through this chapter contains such evidence. For the reasons explained early in the chapter, one could not expect clear findings on the effect of federal-level inducements and constraints without examining the implementation of many more policies. Still, the programs analyzed in our implementation research lend plausibility to this part of the Communications Model.

Despite substantial state-by-state variations, some general tendencies can be discerned. Federal policy on clean water and waste-water treatment, a distributive and regulatory matter, has been backed by a heavy commitment of resources, high efficacy, and—despite shifting deadlines and instruments—considerable clarity. Of the three policies we have studied closely, this one has seen the most straightforward implementation, as indicated by the output measures reported in Chapter 2. RCRA, a representative of a more controversial policy type and a less credible mandate, has employed its considerable resources in the implementation process to more mixed results overall. Meanwhile, since 1981 family planning, which started off in many states as an alternative to abortion, has scored lower on most aspects of the inducements-constraints ledger. Since Reagan assumed office, the Title X program has been severely crippled and has been mired in controversy—especially in connection with building a "wall of separation" between family planning services, on the one hand, and abortion services and counseling.

Nevertheless, even these few general comments ignore the great variety in the implementation action occurring across the states. This is one of the weaknesses in any model that places emphasis solely on top-down elements. Accordingly, Chapter 4 shifts attention to other factors that cannot be ignored in any comprehensive study of inter-governmental implementation.

Notes for Chapter 3

1. Some variation is possible, for instance by virtue of different elaborations of the federal message as it wends its way through federal regional offices.

2. Examples from the multitude of studies that have documented the relationship between provision of resources in connection with a policy message and implementation behavior are Browne and Wildavsky, 1984; Hambleton, 1983; Mazmanian and Sabatier, 1981; Mead, 1977; Montjoy and O'Toole, 1979; O'Toole and Montjoy, 1984; Ross, 1984; Sapolsky, 1972; and Williams, 1980.

3. Even symbolic policies address problems, but for these policies the real aim is to solve the "problem" of pressure or demand placed upon government to deal with an issue.

4. For analyses of implementation processes based upon such policy typologies, see Ripley and Franklin (1982). Also, see Goggin (1987: 125–26) for coverage of policy type and its effect on implementation politics. The idea of policy types and their differential influence on policy making and politics is usually traced to Wildavsky (1962) and to Lowi (1964). Lowi has argued that implementation effects are likely as well (1972). Meier (1987) develops a parallel argument.

5. For an effort to detail the various dimensions of policy specificity, with measures, see Rosenbaum, 1980.

6. Clarity also holds the prospect of catalyzing rather than submerging political disagreement.

7. For a study exploring the importance of local communication and "reticulist" functions (Friend, Power, and Yewlett, 1974) in complex public-private implementation structures, see Hull with Hjern, 1987.

8. It should be noted that this finding refers only to the implementation process and not "whether primacy acceptance actually results in better policy delivery by the states" (p. 647). Thus, the point addresses process rather than output or outcome.

CHAPTER FOUR

State- and Local-Level
Inducements and Constraints

❖
❖

Truck drivers carrying a toxic cargo through North Carolina—31,000 gallons of polychlorinated biphenyl-laced waste oil—decided to dispose of it the easy (albeit illegal) way: They sprayed it along 200 miles of roadway. Their personal solution to a disposal problem became a public problem. Discovery of this hazardous waste presented the state of North Carolina with a monumental public health problem. The state had to implement a plan to remove and bury the contaminated soil. But where should it be buried? This question posed a different kind of problem for the state—that of a locally unwanted land use, or what is known in public policy as a LULU. Which isolated area of the state would be selected to serve as the dumping ground for dangerous poisons?

After consideration of a number of potential locations, the dubious distinction fell to Warren County, a poor, predominantly black, rural area. The county was to bear the costs, in a nonfinancial but no less significant way, of implementing the solution. As residents of the nearly one hundred rejected locations breathed a collective sigh of relief, the residents of Warren County mobilized in opposition to the dump. Extensive political protest ensued. Local residents, their ranks swelled by environmentalists and civil rights activists, attempted to block construction of the dumpsite. Hundreds of arrests resulted. The county government, in the grand tradition of horses and the locking of barn doors, adopted an ordinance prohibiting hazardous waste disposal in the area. Despite the best efforts of the opposition forces, the dump was built and the waste was buried.

The decision of the state was resistant to localized public demand, and toxic soil now lies beneath Warren County. The state of North Carolina was successful in implementing a solution to a trenchant public policy problem; Warren County residents, their local government, and sympathetic interlopers sought unsuccessfully to derail its implementation. Dump opponents were not regular participants in the policy subsystem, and the coalition that they formed had minimal impact (Bowman, 1983).[1]

The Warren County case is not unusual. Throughout the nation, communities are confronting serious problems regarding the disposal of hazardous wastes. Implementing a solution involves a variety of individuals and groups, each one striving to maximize its preferences.

For example, in Tampa, Florida, a corporate proposal to build a massive radioactive gypsum dump near an elementary school pitted representatives of the state's powerful phosphate and fertilizer industry against its growing health and environmental protection lobby (Stuart, 1983). In Brownsville, Texas, thousands of residents turned out at a U.S. Environmental Protection Agency (EPA) public hearing to oppose burning hazardous wastes in the Gulf of Mexico (Schneider, 1984). Marine scientists, the governor of Texas, and the seafood and tourist industries allied with the residents in expressing their disapproval of the plan.

These examples make one point crystal clear: government-sponsored solutions to public policy problems are not implemented in a vacuum. They are implemented in the raucous, rough-and-tumble world of politics in which individuals and groups have opinions, points of view, and preferences that they are more than willing to communicate. Conflict is inherent. Solutions that inspire policymakers inside Washington, D.C. may find quite a different reception beyond it. Some policy types—especially those that impose a cost—are more likely to provoke friction than are other types. Individual communities are collections of interests. The opportunities for delay and resistance are great. Consequently, implementation of intergovernmental policy, especially when it is complex and salient, is seldom smooth or easy (Gormley, 1986).

This chapter explores the subnational context of intergovernmental policy implementation. The context is presented as three interacting clusters: interest groups, state and local elected officials (and political institutions), and the implementing agency. As noted in Chapter 1, the nature and intensity of the preferences held by the groups within these clusters generate the "receptivity climate" that federal enactments encounter. The argument of this chapter is that a state's implementation style is greatly affected by *context*—the inducements and constraints found in communities that aggregate at the state level. Context is a characteristic that varies from state to state and, within a single state, from program to program, and from one time to another.

The chapter makes a special effort to distill the complexity of the subnational context. Intergovernmental implementation is dynamic: Interest groups become advocates, local officials mediate interests, implementing agencies adjust. For a given federal enactment, this process unfolds in fifty state capitals and in thousands of communities. The goal of the chapter is to provide an understanding of what the implementation environment "out there" is like.

The literature review presented in the following section sets the stage for the development of our theoretical argument regarding the inducements and constraints offered by the state and local levels. The theoretical argument is then made more concrete with the presentation of recent findings of other researchers, as well as initial findings from our own work.

THE IMPORTANCE OF THE SUBNATIONAL CONTEXT

Although there had been earlier studies of policy implementation (Stephen Bailey and Edith Mosher's 1968 study of the Elementary and Secondary Education Act), two analyses are generally credited as the first forays into the subnational implementation thicket. Martha Derthick (1972) examined the "new towns in-town" program of the Great Society. Jeffrey Pressman and Aaron Wildavsky (1973) analyzed a U.S. Economic Development Administration (EDA) program in Oakland, California. Both studies highlighted the manner in which the *local* community influences implementation. (Pressman and Wildavsky subtitled their book, *How Great Expectations in Washington Are Dashed in Oakland*.)

Derthick argued in her study that much of the opposition to the U.S. Housing and Urban Development's program to create new towns in existing urban centers came from local politicians (1972: 88). In a similar vein, the Pressman and Wildavsky volume identified the "shifting and volatile environment" (1973: 140) in Oakland as one of the great imponderables that the federal government encountered. Scholarly attention began to be focused on communities as something other than mere *places* where policy implementation occurs. What was it about the community that affected implementation?

The Local Community's Role: Bottom-Up Analysis

A primary reason that the new towns and EDA programs were less than successful was inadequate local support. The federal government, with its grandiose plans and free-flowing dollars, eventually came to realize that community interests and preferences can thwart the best of intentions and the most innovative of designs. Had federal officials been privy to some of the social science research that has ensued, they might have anticipated the inherent difficulties with externally developed remedies for local problems.

Implementation takes place in a turbulent environment (Palumbo, 1987). Certainly internal policy consistency, organizational capacity, ample resources, and political will affect implementation. But as Love and Sederberg (1987) point out in their study of Somali refugees, implementation very much depends on the compatibility of the policy with established dispositions and tendencies. These established dispositions and tendencies are reflected by organized interests and elected officials (and their political institutions).

Recognition of the importance of the local community to implementation eventually spawned a new research direction: "bottom-up" analysis. As noted in the Introduction, bottom-up theorists such as Hjern use a networking technique to identify the set of actors involved in delivering a service in a given area (Hjern, 1982). These actors form what is frequently called the *policy community* or *policy subsystem*. By focusing on their goals, strategies, activities, and contacts, the next "higher" level of actors can be identified. Eventually, the entire implementation system is mapped; hence the label "bottom-up." By applying this approach to a study of Swedish staff training programs, Hjern and his associates found that the local implementation structure did, in fact, play a major role in program success (Sabatier, 1986).[2]

Other contemporary research has validated the significance of the subnational context to intergovernmental policy implementation. For example, two Nebraska communities implementing the same federal program for the construction of scattered-site, low-income housing had widely divergent experiences (Mueller, 1984). The explanation for the divergence was found to be the existing direction of policy in each community. Where the federal program "fit" the local context, it worked. Where it did not, implementors sought to delay its implementation.

The Role of Coalitions

In another case, the effective implementation of youth employment programs in seven cities was attributed, in part, to the presence of "fixers" who could "repair" the implementation process (Levin and Ferman, 1986). The fixers worked to build coalitions in the community and to convert mild interest in the program into active support. Effective implementation did not occur serendipitously. It was the product of concerted, deliberate efforts by skilled implementors. In a pluralistic environment characterized by conflicting preferences, implementors must make strategic choices about the formation of alliances (Kessler, 1987).

Interest convergence must occur if implementation is to proceed without delay. An active support network or policy infrastructure is important (Levin and Ferman, 1986). Work on corrections policy has shown that the likelihood of program success increases when an assortment of actors who are involved in implementation (such as judges, prosecutors, sheriffs, probation officers, county commissioners, state legislators, counselors, halfway-house directors, and regional and county administrators) share a consensus about policy goals (Palumbo, 1986). In a pluralistic environment characterized by conflicting preferences, implementors must make strategic choices about alliance formation.

When interest convergence is absent, implementors frequently try to manufacture it. Cleaning up the extremely polluted Rouge River in southeastern Michigan is a case in point (GAO, 1988). Early attempts to restore the river under the provisions of the federal Clean Water Act failed markedly because few of the affected communities could agree on a common course of action. Their interests were community specific and converged only around the most general of goals—that the river should be made suitable for swimming and fishing.

Progress occurred only when representatives from forty-five local jurisdictions and from local interest groups and political parties joined with federal and state program officials to hammer out an acceptable action plan for the river's restoration. The creation of a committee provided a formal mechanism in which communication could occur and convergence could develop. Although individual priorities might differ, a common interest in the ultimate outcome is a first step in facilitating implementation.

In the words of Love and Sederberg (1987: 155), "Policy implementation is a polyvocal process." Extending the metaphor, they write that the voices sometimes harmonize to produce euphonious implementation. At other times they clash to generate a meaningless cacophony. An exploration of these "voices" and their many messages is the direction in which the chapter now turns.

MEMBERS OF THE SUBNATIONAL CONTEXT

Surrounding each policy problem are clusters of actors—people who have a potential interest in the problem and its resolution. These individuals are perceived as legitimate participants in a formal policy network. On any particular policy question, this network includes elected and appointed government officials, organized interest groups, and the state agency charged with the implementation task. These individuals work in concert with or in opposition to one another as alternative policy solutions are considered. They are all part of the same subsystem, however. These actors are specialists in the policy area; they frequently interact with one another, and they typically know where each other stands (Kingdon, 1984). They have established regularized channels of communication and have, in effect, formed a "community."[3]

As the hazardous waste problem described at the chapter's opening demonstrated, some individuals who are only loosely connected with the formal network have important impact on policy implementation. These people tend to be members of the general public who, because the solution to a policy problem will affect them negatively and immediately (as when an unwanted facility is to be located in their community), suddenly become interested in policy implementation.

These "loose connectors" are part of the large pool of potential participants. Their involvement in implementation is sporadic and relatively unpredictable. Lacking established communication channels, they frequently resort to unusual means to transmit their messages: attention-getting, often symbolic demonstrations. In most instances, however, implementation is confined to the following elements in the "professional" policy community:

- organized interests
- elected and appointed officials
- the focal state agency

This limit to the sphere of the policy community makes the implementation process more predictable. Each of these elements of the policy network will be examined in turn.

Interest Groups

There has been a virtual explosion in the number of interest groups active in subnational politics and a corresponding expansion in the range of interests represented (Thomas and Hrebnar, 1988). Some groups are continually active, others only intermittently so. It is fair to say, however, that policymakers are bombarded with communications from organized interests. One reason given for the increased incidence of groups is the formation-reaction phenomenon, which works this way. The formation of a group in support of a policy action frequently triggers the organization of a counter-group opposed to that policy action. As state governments move into new policy domains, groups multiply.

Spokespersons for organized interests seek maximum benefits from government for the people whom they represent. Depending on the anticipated effects of alternative courses of action, groups can be either proponents or opponents. Whether a group is a beneficiary or a cost-bearer undoubtedly has a bearing on that group's predisposition toward the policy (Chubb, 1983). If organized interests press for policies that benefit group members or, at a minimum, do not harm them, it may be in the group's interest to seek compliance or to maintain the status quo. If the latter option is preferred, it is likely that the group would favor delaying implementation until the law can be modified to conform to group preferences.

Interests vie with one another for the programmatic favors of policymakers and managers. Group influence is exercised in connection with the several implementation functions set out in Chapter 2.

Individual groups form alliances. For example, a state's "highway lobby" is typically composed of paving contractors, construction unions, equipment manufacturers, automobile clubs, and local business leaders (Hays, 1988). The weaker the group, the more important it becomes for that group to join with like-minded groups in an alliance. These alliances attract other members of the policy community such as government actors, journalists, and researchers into what has been called an *advocacy coalition* (Sabatier, 1986).

Factors Affecting Advocacy Coalitions   Influence is a function of three characteristics of each advocacy coalition (Sabatier, 1987; Sabatier and Brasher, 1986): skill, cohesiveness, and level of resources. Consequently, advocacy coalitions that are backed by ample resources and are cohesive and skillful are more likely to be influential than are less well-endowed advocacy coalitions.

Other factors affect advocacy coalitions and their relative impact. The size of the coalition, the intensity of its preferences, and the nature and scope of intergroup conflicts are also determinants of the influence the coalition will wield. Advocacy coalitions that are large and manifest dearly held preferences, confronting a situation in which intergroup conflict is low or confined to peripheral issues, are likely to be more influential than are less well-endowed advocacy coalitions.

Messages from Coalitions   Advocacy coalitions transmit their preferences to implementors. Implementors sort through the messages, decoding and evaluating them. Eventually an implementation decision is made. Quite probably, for a given policy, states with larger, stronger, and more cohesive supportive advocacy coalitions take the steps necessary to put the intended policy into effect than states lacking such a coalitional structure.

The detailed argument about the content and form of messages presented in Chapter 3 is apropos here. Members of advocacy coalitions constantly send messages to policymakers. Their messages reflect the coalition's policy preferences. How recipients react depends to some degree on whether the coalition is perceived as legitimate and its message credible. Legitimacy and credibility are instantly conferred on very few groups. (In most states, business interests have traditionally enjoyed this status.) For most clusters of interests, the effort to gain legitimacy and to produce automatically believable messages is part of a larger process of becoming a policy insider. The effort is worthwhile because the credible preferences of legitimate senders are more likely to be positively evaluated by recipients than are the messages of less well-situated senders. It should be reiterated that the issue here is less the objective features of the message than it is the message's perceived credibility.

State and Local Elected Officials

Elected officials are utility maximizers, driven by a desire to be re-elected (Mayhew, 1974). The fact remains that an incumbent who is unable to reflect the electorate's preferences in his or her district suffers at the polls (Glazer and Robbins, 1983; Johannes and McAdams, 1981; Kau, Keenan, and Rubin, 1982). Considerable evidence indicates that legislators may also be motivated by a desire to make good public policy or to enhance their reputations within the legislature (Fenno, 1973; Gurr and King, 1987). Peterson (1976; Greenstone and Peterson, 1976) adds to this the alternative aspirations of either reaching accommodation (pluralistic bargaining) or defeating opponents (ideological bargaining).

The interests and motives of individual state elected officials vary. Some legislators and governors take up the cause of a few powerful members of the "attentive" public (advocates). Others act on their own assessment of which policies are needed in the state (trustees). Still others try to gauge the majority preferences of all the voters (delegates). Several studies of legislative behavior have also stressed other important sources of cues, for example, party leaders, colleagues with similar constituencies, or lawmakers with expertise in the policy domain (Clausen, 1973; Kingdon, 1973; Matthews and Stimson, 1970).

Again, the *type* of legislator matters, with political behavior varying with role perception and issue context. For example, if the issue is salient or local interests are divided over the issue, a district representative is more likely to perceive accurately constituents' preferences (Erikson, Luttbeg, and Holloway, 1975; Kuklinski and McCrone, 1980; Miller and Stokes, 1963).

The legislative role in implementation is complex and uncertain. It is multidimensional (Ethridge, 1981), manifested in a large variety of modes of legislative participation, from committee rule review to other types of legislative oversight. The part the legislature plays in policy implementation is also a function of actions by the governor (Abney and Lauth, 1986; 1987) and the state bureaucracy (Hebert, Brudney and Wright, 1983; Wright, 1967).

Regardless of the type of gubernatorial and bureaucratic effects on legislative behavior, however, state legislatures are plagued with the same information processing problems that have hampered efficiency in the U.S. Congress. To cope with complexity, information overload, and a heavy workload, lawmaking bodies in the states have resorted to specialization and division of labor.

For these reasons, the Communications Model of Intergovernmental Policy Implementation requires scrutiny of the implementation activities of members of the state oversight and appropriation committees, especially committee chairs. The Communications Model portrays state legislative committee chairs as the pivotal actors within the legislative setting.

Now, suppose the federal level is pressuring the state to comply—promptly and with no change in program content—while a strong advocacy coalition is in favor of delaying program implementation until the policy can be redesigned to make it more favorable to the coalition's own interests. Recipient legislators are caught in a web of countervailing messages. What is the state's legislative committee leadership likely to do under these circumstances?

Fiorina and Noll (1978a, b) have an answer to this question. They argue that legislators, whose main desire is continued tenure in office, tend to increase the size of a bureaucracy while decreasing the amount of services provided. But the Communications Model constructed here assumes that a preference to either comply with the law (and presumably add to the scope of the state agency) or defy it (maintain the status quo), even temporarily, depends on the individual legislator and his or her interests and motives (that is, as an advocate, trustee, or delegate).

This accumulation of legislative preferences affects the style that implementation takes at a given point in time in a given state. In all likelihood, states with supportive state legislators are more likely to take the steps necessary to put the intended policy into effect than are states where legislators are lukewarm or, worse yet, hostile toward the policy.

The Focal State Agency

The agency charged with implementing the policy is the third component of the subnational system. Chapter 5 treats the agency (or agencies) in terms of its (their) resources and skills. (More than one agency may be involved, thus making for complex administrative patterns.) The focus is upon the agency's links to interest groups and state and local elected officials. As emphasized in Chapter 1, a state's implementation decisions are jointly made and are the result of a complex calculus. Although the individual preferences of policy managers who are charged with the task of solving state problems within a given functional area certainly matter, important too are the desires and wishes of state and local elected officials and organized interests.

Agents' behavior can only be understood within the context of dynamic interaction among bureaucrats, politicians, and interest groups (Bendor and Moe, 1985). An elaborate system of formal procedures structures the interaction, and it is supplemented by an array of informal contacts (Hays, 1988).

Implementors receive and process messages from the external environment (Brudney and Hebert, 1987). The state agency personnel are left to sort, interpret, and otherwise react to messages sent by the others. Even within a single state, the pluralistic and interactive nature of the local level makes the probability of multiple, conflicting messages high. This is the manner in which state- and local-level actors and institutions induce and constrain implementation. As a result, state-level implementors engage in a conscious process of receiving, interpreting, and reacting to messages sent by members of the policy subsystem.

This dynamic was in evidence in the U.S. General Accounting Office's (GAO) examination of focal state agency performance in enforcement of provisions in the Surface Mining Control and Reclamation Act (GAO, 1987). When GAO asked why state inspectors routinely failed to cite many mining violations, some of them potentially harmful to the environment, state program administrators frequently alluded to informal agency norms to "look the other way," to try to work informally with operators, to give small mining operations extra latitude in complying. Regulated mining interests had clearly communicated their feelings and preferences to agency personnel charged with implementing the act.[4] This is not a surprising finding.

As expected, states in which the messages from the policy subsystem clearly and consistently support implementation are more inclined to take the steps necessary to effect the intended policy than are states in which the messages are conflictual.

In an implementation-perfect world, unequivocal messages from harmonious advocacy coalitions and elected officials would be transmitted to the focal state agency. Given the pluralistic nature of subnational politics, the reality of implementation is quite different. The probability of multiple, conflicting messages is high. Add this intrastate diversity to existing interstate diversity and the situation is tailor-made for variable implementation. As Pressman and Wildavsky (1973: 161) note, the continuation of a federal system "means precisely that state and local organizations must be able to oppose, delay, and reject federal initiatives." It is the unusual case in which intergovernmental policy implementation is something other than slow and uneven.

THE SUBNATIONAL ENVIRONMENT:
RECENT RESULTS

Contemporary research sheds some light on the influence of the subnational environment in policy implementation. Subnational hazardous waste policy has been subjected to extensive analysis. For example, Kraft and Kraut (1985) examined the impact of citizen groups on the implementation decisions surrounding a hazardous waste disposal facility in an Ohio community. They found that over time, citizen strategies shifted from unfocused local protests to more sophisticated efforts at coalition building and legislative influence. The local group, Independent Citizens Associated for Reclaiming the Environment (I-CARE), teamed up with a statewide network of related groups, Voting Ohioans Initiating a Clean Environment (VOICE). The message did not change, but the vehicle transmitting it did. The result was increased receptivity of state legislators to the group's concerns and eventual legislative action.

The importance of community context or "established dispositions and tendencies" is demonstrated in a study of seven Massachusetts towns and their reactions to groundwater contamination (Powell, 1985). A primary explanation for why some towns implemented groundwater protection policies and others did not had to do with the relative cosmopolitanism or localism of power elites. Towns run by cosmopolitan officials took action; the localist-controlled communities delayed. Confronted with similar situations, different towns behaved differently.

Both of these examples highlight the subnational dimension of hazardous waste policy implementation. Bowman's (1984) study of Superfund implementation in South Carolina ties some of the subnational components together. Superfund is the federal law that structures and funds the cleanup of abandoned hazardous waste dumpsites. Bowman found that actual implementation of cleanups was marred by "multiactor tension." At one site, for example, tensions so escalated among local elected officials, the governor, environmental activists, nearby residents, the state court system, the state health and environment agency, EPA, and the cleanup contractor that implementation was substantially delayed. Such a case is not unusual. Lester (1988) called the Superfund implementation process an instance of "environmental gridlock" in which implementation is slow or nonexistent.[5]

Implementation of federal programs need not paralyze subnational governments, however. Consider the case of waste-water treatment under the Clean Water Act of 1972. Local policymakers confronted a situation characterized by incoherent national policy and shrinking resources. As pressure to take action accelerated, policymakers in some communities responded in an innovative fashion by considering the privatisation of their waste-water treatment works. An analysis of sixteen of these communities indicated that the decision to proceed with privatisation was a function of local leadership commitment and institutional characteristics (Johnson and Heilman, 1987). That is, the presence of an active city leader willing to lend his or her considerable prestige to the privatisation issue, combined with the absence of significant opposition forces, facilitated privatisation. Local conditions made the difference.

INITIAL FINDINGS FROM OUR RESEARCH

The initial focus of our research on Resource Conservation and Recovery Act (RCRA) of 1976 implementation has been aimed primarily at opening up the black box[6] in the center of the Communications Model (state decisional outcome and state capacity) and, to a lesser extent, at federal-level inducements and constraints. Consequently, the state- and local-level inducements and constraints aspect of the Communications Model has received only cursory attention thus far. Yet even at the surface level, it is evident that the state- and local-level context possesses vast explanatory power regarding RCRA implementation style.

The Central Actors in Implementation

In response to our survey, waste management program administrators in forty-three states indicated that the central actors in RCRA implementation were state environmental officials, state legislators, and the governor. More than half of the respondents indicated that this cluster of state-level actors was the influential implementing nexus. The influence of state bureaucratic officials and state legislators is not surprising; to qualify for authorization (primacy), each state must formulate its own enabling legislation that is consistent with federal standards and goals.

Thus, state bureaucrats and state legislators must work together to obtain RCRA authorization. Regional EPA personnel and local policy officials played important roles in selected states. States vary in the degree to which they encourage local involvement. A centralized process that provides limited local involvement facilitates implementation, but it carries the disadvantage of being perceived as heavy-handed and, possibly, illegitimate. Table 4.1 presents the influence scores for the various actors.

Table 4.1 Influence of Different Actors on RCRA Implementation

Actors	Influence Score*
State Environmental Officials	.98
State Legislators	.71
Governor	.52
Regional EPA Representatives	.41
Local Policy Officials	.29
Judicial Officials	.21

*The influence score is the percentage of respondents who indicated that these actors were influential in promoting RCRA implementation in the states.

SOURCE: Survey by the authors.

When the responses of the administrators were linked to their state's implementation style, the interesting pattern presented in Table 4.2 emerged. The degree of breadth in the advocacy coalition appears to influence implementation. States with an implementation style termed "compliant" and those categorized as "strategic delay" had a full complement of actors supporting implementation; "defiant" states had none. For compliant states, the coalition includes judicial and local-level officials. The advocacy coalition is more restricted in "strategic delay" states (compared to compliance or strategic delay states), and in defiant states, there is no such advocacy coalition at all.

Given that RCRA implementation is, at its core, an adversarial process with real costs incurred by regulated interests, countervailing pro-implementation pressures must be exerted or inertia results. A supportive mix of implementation officials is crucial to prompt and unmodified policy implementation.

Our work on the implementation of family planning services for the poor in California illustrates similar themes. California's style of implementation would certainly be described as strategic delay. In other words, California chose to wait four and one-half years after the passage of federal Title IV-A family planning legislation in 1968 before enacting state enabling legislation.

How can California's implementation style be explained? Five state-level actors were particularly important to implementation:

- Republican Governor Ronald Reagan, an opponent of the legislation
- Democratic State Senator Anthony Beilenson, chair of the Senate Committee on Health and Welfare and the Senate Finance Committee, a proponent of the legislation
- Dr. George Cunningham, chief of the Maternal and Child Health Unit in the California State Department of Health and the coordinator of family planning programs in California, a proponent

Table 4.2   The State and Local Context and Implementation Style (Means)

Variables	Compliance	Strategic Delay	Delay	Defiance
RCRA Difference*	3.77	3.46	3.17	2.00
Regime Support*	3.39	3.09	3.00	3.00
Governor's Help[†]	.69	.50	.33	.00
Legislators' Help[†]	.77	.77	.50	.00
Judicial Officials' Help[†]	.31	.18	.17	.00
Local Officials' Help[†]	.31	.27	.33	.00

*The higher the mean score above, the greater the belief that RCRA makes a significant difference in managing hazardous waste or the greater the support for the RCRA mandate.
[†]The percentage of respondents that indicated that these actors were helpful in promoting RCRA implementation.

SOURCE: Survey by the authors.

- the California Interagency Council on Family Planning, a supportive coalition of interests from the public and private sectors
- Planned Parenthood Affiliates of California, also a proponent

Two ideologically based factions emerged. One faction, represented by the governor's office, spoke for cost-bearers who may have initially opposed the law's implementation on the grounds that it would encourage promiscuity and the breakdown of the family. Governor Reagan was a "trustee," in that opposition to family planning squared with his own political beliefs. An unexpected ally of the governor was a segment of the black community that considered state-sponsored family planning programs a form of genocide. The other faction, led by Senator Beilenson (an "advocate") and Dr. Cunningham (who had a "local" orientation), responded to the unmet need of millions of American women, interpreting that need as popular demands for services. Included in this faction were the Interagency Council and Planned Parenthood, both of whom could be categorized as representing beneficiaries rather than cost-bearers.

Changes in Public Opinion

Apparently a gradual shift in public opinion contributed to breaking the political stalemate. An educational campaign by the state's Office of Family Planning (the focal state agency) demonstrated that it was in the state's economic self-interest to provide contraceptive services to Aid to Families with Dependent Children (AFDC) mothers. Short-term (first-year) savings in state welfare payments were estimated at two dollars for every dollar spent, and long-term savings were estimated to be $8.52 for every dollar spent on family planning services. The dissemination of this information helped persuade fiscal conservatives of the merits of the legislation.

In addition, among some groups, family planning emerged as a preferable alternative to abortion. Another factor that broke the deadlock was a compromise between Beilenson and Reagan. The powerful committee chair agreed to support a Reagan bill on welfare reform in exchange for the governor's support of the family planning services bill. Thus, California began its implementation "when the time was right," that is, when the supportive advocacy coalition prevailed.

Changes in Legislation

The story of what happened in California in the early 1970s is based on interviews conducted with the participants in the state's implementation of the family planning provisions in Title IV-A of the Social Security Act. In 1975, just before the interviews were conducted, Title IV-A was replaced with a new program, the Social Services Block Grant (Title XX). Like other block grants, this one was administered by the state. On the other hand, the family planning services grants portion of Title X of the Public Health Service Act has, since its inception, been administered by the federal government. That may be one of the reasons why, in the case of Title X, pressure from the bottom up has been directed at the federal, rather than state, government. A recent example illustrates the differences.

On September 1, 1987, the Department of Health & Human Services proposed in the *Federal Register* a rule that would prevent federally funded family planning clinic personnel from providing advice to pregnant patients about the availability of abortion services. After the customary public comment period provided for in the Administrative Procedure Act, a final rule was published on February 2, 1988. Before this new rule could go into effect, however, the National Family Planning and Reproductive Health Association (NFPRHA) and other interested parties challenged its constitutionality in the courts.

On March 2, 1988, a federal district court judge in Boston issued a permanent injunction against DH&HS on the grounds that the "gag rule" deprives clinic personnel of their constitutionally guaranteed right of free speech. The judge's permanent injunction has prevented DH&HS from implementing the final rule. A federal circuit court judge in Denver quickly followed suit. During the months that followed these injunctions, the Reagan Administration tried to implement the gag rule wherever injunctions were not in force. Encouraged by the July 3, 1989, Supreme Court decision, *Webster v. Reproductive Health Services,* the Bush Administration renewed its efforts to implement the gag rule by appealing the Federal District Court decisions that did not support the Administration's position. In early November of 1989, for example, the Bush Administration won a victory when the U.S. court of appeals for the second circuit upheld gag rule regulations that would forbid feder-

Table 4.3   Number and Type of Organizations Writing Letters to the Department of Health and Human Services

Type of Organization	Number and Percentage of Letters	
Religious	243	(38%)
Civic (including consumer)	33	(5%)
National Professional	16	(2.5%)
Subnational Professional	70	(11%)
Provider/Grantee	146	(22.8%)
Feminist	33	(5%)
State Government Agency	34	(5.3%)
Local Government Agency	55	(8.6%)
Other	9	(1.4%)
Total	639	(100%)

SOURCE: Content Analysis of Documents supplied to the authors by the Office of Family Planning, Department of Health and Human Services.

ally funded family planning clinics in New York from mentioning abortion.

The DH&HS's Office of Population Affairs received approximately 75,000 letters and postcards during the gag rule's public comment period. Most were one- or two-line postcards or letters that either opposed or supported the idea of the proposed rule; many were form letters. Among the several notebooks that were available to the public in the DH&HS library in Washington, D.C. were several hundred that contained substantive comments from clients, service providers, civic groups, and pro-life and pro-choice organizations.

Power of Advocacy Coalitions

By showing the number of letters by type of organizations mailing in their written comments, Table 4.3 illustrates the wide variety of public responses from those who were part of local advocacy coalitions either supporting or opposing the gag rule. Table 4.4 shows the principal protagonists—religious organizations, and providers or grantees. Of the 625 letters coded, 54 percent were opposed to the gag rule. Forty-five percent supported the Reagan Administration's attempts to provide counseling at family planning clinics. These numbers are not surprising, given the results of an October 1988 poll by the CBS television network and *The New York Times* that showed that 42 percent of the registered voters sampled favored keeping abortion legal as it is now, with 39 percent preferring legalized abortions only in the cases of rape and incest, or to save the life of the mother. Fourteen percent of respondents thought abortion should not be legal under any circumstances, and 6 percent had no opinion (Lewin, 1988).

Table 4.4 dramatizes the deep division at the local level between two factions of agents who are trying to influence principals in Washing-

Table 4.4   Overall Position on the Rule Change by Type of Organization

Type of Organization	Support N	Support (%)	Oppose N	Oppose (%)	Equivocal N	Equivocal (%)
Religious	209	(88%)	28	(12%)	0	(0%)
Civic (including consumer)	16	(50%)	16	(50%)	0	(0%)
National Professional	5	(31%)	11	(69%)	0	(0%)
Subnational Professional	26	(38%)	39	(57%)	3	(4%)
Provider/Grantee	16	(11%)	127	(88%)	1	(1%)
Feminist	2	(6%)	31	(94%)	0	(0%)
State Government Agency	2	(6%)	31	(94%)	0	(0%)
Local Government Agency	4	(8%)	49	(92%)	0	(0%)
Other	4	(44%)	5	(56%)	0	(0%)
	284	(45%)	337	(54%)	4	(1%)

SOURCE: Content Analysis by the authors.

ton. When these letters were coded for content, it was clear that spokespersons for organized religious interests, who strongly supported the proposed rule, spearheaded one faction. Service providers, along with feminist organizations, and state and local government agencies such as county health department heads, formed an opposing coalition of agents. More than three of every four letters were considered strong in intensity (see Table 4.5).

As the case of the gag rule proceeds through the courts, it clearly involves two strong advocacy coalitions, fairly equal in number of supporters, with each coalition possessing similar resources. Each is able to mobilize considerable public support. There is already mounting evidence that, thanks in part to NFPRHA and other interest groups who challenged the rule in the courts, implementation of the gag rule across the fifty states and the District of Columbia has been delayed, if not permanently stymied. Although it is quite different from the "pulling and hauling" associated with the implementation of Title IV-A family planning in California in the 1970s, this case also illustrates the power of advocacy coalitions. Both case studies certainly lend support to arguments about the importance of state- and local-level inducements and constraints.

INDUCEMENTS AND CONSTRAINTS FOR OTHER PROGRAMS

In the case of municipal waste-water treatment, state- and local-level inducements and constraints are especially compelling in implementation. Given the high degree of discretion accorded local officials by the state, implementation style runs the gamut. This is not an issue in which high-ranking state elected officials involve themselves; instead, implementation is a locally oriented process.

Table 4.5   Intensity of Overall Position by Type of Organization

Type of Organization	Weak N	Weak (%)	Strong N	Strong (%)	Neither N	Neither (%)
Religious	13	(5%)	152	(63%)	76	(32%)
Civic (including consumer)	1	(3%)	23	(72%)	8	(25%)
National Professional	0	(0%)	16	(100%)	0	(0%)
Subnational Professional	4	(6%)	57	(83%)	8	(12%)
Provider/Grantee	5	(3%)	128	(89%)	11	(8%)
Feminist	0	(0%)	29	(94%)	2	(6%)
State Government Agency	1	(3%)	29	(88%)	3	(9%)
Local Government Agency	2	(4%)	49	(92%)	2	(4%)
Other	0	(0%)	6	(75%)	2	(25%)
	26	(4%)	489	(78%)	112	(18%)

SOURCE: Content analysis by the authors.

Advocacy coalitions favoring implementation have often consisted of developers, real estate interests, and chambers of commerce more than environmental groups. This observation holds for all the communities visited in the course of our research. (Regulatory sanctions may mean a moratorium on building and also great difficulty in encouraging businesses to locate in a community.)

The threat by EPA or state regulators to stop growth and frighten away new industry by ordering moratoria on sewer connections or by issuing administrative or judicial orders has often been sufficient to mobilize a clean-water coalition locally where there has been only limited attention by state or local environmental groups. This point may explain why there appears to be essentially no statistically significant relationship between the sophistication of environmental policy development—a subject of great interest to environmental groups— and our measures of implementation outputs and outcomes for the states, as explored in Chapter 2.

Localities such as Key West, Florida, with independent politics and a history of run-ins with federal authorities dating from rum-running and pirating escapades, have been reluctant altogether to confront their clean-water problems. Other Florida cities, for which environmental concerns and organized interests are an important element of the local matrix, have been aggressively seeking solutions to their waste-water difficulties. In each policy area, our data show that inducements and constraints at the state and local level influenced the implementation of federal policy. Advocacy coalitions, as well as state and local elected and appointed officials, exchanged messages in vibrant communications networks. Points of view, preferences, and power affected decisions that were made by the recipients of the messages. Looking at implementation from this perspective recalls the words of research pioneers

Pressman and Wildavsky (1973: xiii) who said that, "Implementation, under the best of circumstances, is exceedingly difficult."

CONCLUSION

The state- and local-level governments play an important role in determining how intergovernmental policy implementation unfolds. If all of the state- and local-level ducks are in a row, implementation proceeds smoothly. If they are not, which is a more likely scenario, implementation becomes a series of fits and starts. In the fifty state capitals and thousands of communities across the nation, the true test of federal enactments occurs.

If one were to peer into the portion of Figure 1.1 labeled State- and Local-Level Inducements and Constraints, it would appear a tangled mass of lines extending from element to element. The state and local levels are a multiplicity of complex linkages. A federal enactment is enmeshed in this seeming dendroid. Its arrival sets off a communications buzz as messages surge through the lines. Each node in the subsystem evaluates the implications of the new policy and responds accordingly.

New programs require promoters and fixers. To achieve their objectives, promoters and fixers must build advocacy coalitions within the implementing environment. Implementation thus becomes a dynamic process as messages are designed, sent, received, interpreted, and responded to. This dynamism is what makes implementation a fairly messy process and, correspondingly, an elusive topic to study.

Implementation can only be understood as an interactive process. It centers on bargaining among competing interests, as in the California case of a consensus being forged, or as illustrated by the gag rule, deadlock resulting from ideological bargaining between uncompromising factions. An important factor in building a consensus for implementation (or breaking a deadlock) is organizational capacity. That is the subject that Chapter 5 addresses.

Notes for Chapter 4

1. Warren County did not emerge from the fray empty-handed. The following year, the North Carolina state legislature voted a special industrial-development package for the county as partial compensation for locating the toxic waste dump there.

2. The greatest contribution of the bottom-up approach has been to discredit research designs that are wholly top-down. Credible models of inter-governmental policy implementation contain a strong subnational component. They aim at providing the synthesis of the bottom-up and top-down approaches that many scholars, most notably Sabatier (1986), have called for.

3. The word *community* has multiple meanings. It refers not only to a formal settlement with geographical boundaries but also to like-minded individuals and interactive networks.

4. Evaluating the performance of the implementing agency can be a subjective process. A 1988 issue of the *Forum for Applied Research and Public Policy* confirmed this in a feature on the Surface Mining Control and Reclamation Act (SMCRA). An official with the National Coal Association wrote an article entitled "SMCRA: Ten Years of Solid Progress." A drastically different perspective was offered in a companion piece authored by a National Wildlife Federation official called "SMCRA's Implementation Is Flawed."

5. "Gridlock" characterizes many environmental programs. Southern California's effort to find replacement sites for closed hazardous waste landfills encountered opposition from a variety of state and local politicians and interest groups, especially environmentalists. Because the implications of having no disposal facilities were so dire (for example, illegal dumping would be likely to increase and industries might relocate), the replacement site issue was moved outside the conventional political arena and the gridlock was effectively broken. See the analysis in Mazmanian et al. (1988).

6. In systems models, inputs are converted into outputs through a "conversion process." Because the interaction of elements in the conversion process is frequently unknown and difficult to study, that portion of the model is typically referred to as a "black box."

CHAPTER FIVE

Organizational Capacity

❖
❖

Cleaning the nation's water involves a great deal of work, on a continuing basis and on a very grand scale. This mammoth task includes cleansing billions of gallons of polluted water each day and monitoring thousands of rivers, streams, and lakes. The job simply could not be accomplished without the efforts and capabilities provided by large organizations all over the continent. American policy on clean water is fundamentally intergovernmental, combining specialized units in Washington, the states, and thousands of local governments in an intricate and complex pattern.

In the states themselves, the crucial role in executing clean water policy mostly falls to agencies of natural resources or environmental affairs. The roles played by such units vary enormously.

In one state in the Northwest, for instance, the problem of wastewater treatment is monitored closely. The agency is structured to provide a coordinated, integrated approach to environmental issues, including those associated with clean water. Financial resources are considerable, and within the agency fifty staffpersons devote their efforts to implementation. The reputation of the agency in the state and region is nonpareil. The success of the implementation effort is seen in process, output, and outcome measures. In 1987, almost no municipal treatment plants were out of compliance with clean-water regulations.

At perhaps the other extreme, administratively speaking, are twelve states in various parts of the country. Here the relevant agency is not even authorized to conduct permit granting and monitoring. States are generally encouraged to handle this process themselves, with only some general supervision by the U.S. Environmental Protection Agency (EPA). But the states must first agree to accept a certain level of responsibility and provide a minimal amount of administrative support for the program. The states have good reason to want the National Pollution Discharge Elimination System (NPDES) program within their own jurisdiction. But in these dozen cases, the federal EPA itself acts as the permitting agency and administers the program on its own. The reason? The states in question have neither sufficient mandate nor administrative capacity to manage the program. Accordingly, they participate in no real intergovernmental regulatory process.

On the other hand, some state agencies *are* part of the clean-water structure but have not built organizational capacity that is nearly sufficient to their needs. For instance, another jurisdiction of roughly the same size, population, and problem-severity level (as measured by the size and complexity of the water systems in the two states and by the levels of industrial activity) as the one mentioned earlier does not have the benefit of the same degree of administrative or organizational capacity devoted to the policy issue. Here, eight staff in a low-stature office expend their energies on the implementation effort.

Financing for the process itself is miserly and has been cut drastically in recent years. Process, output, and outcome measures of the agency's clean-water activities (reported in Chapter 2) are consistent with this pattern. Agency officials report being overwhelmed with their workload. The efforts to anticipate policy developments and adapt implementation settings to them, for instance with respect to a new federal effort to entice them toward a revolving loan fund program, are minimal. Instead, management is passive, or reactive, and mostly uninformed of happenings at the local level. The agency is known as a "follower" rather than a leader in its region. Localities complain about lackadaisical state help on important regulatory questions and on the many issues requiring technical assistance. On the basis of measures reported in Chapter 2, this state is also much less successful in terms of implementation output and outcome.

 These vignettes provide a glimpse of how important organizational or administrative capacity can be. Here *organizational capacity* means simply the ability of a government to "get its act together," to institute the structure, the routines, and the coordinated efforts of talented people sufficient to convert a policy message into a set of real achievements. Of course, a state's administrative ability to deal with some policy issue may in turn be affected by other forces.

Indeed, this point indicates precisely why understanding implementation is a complicated and interesting affair. The model developed in this book takes into account this complexity. For instance, Chapter 6 explores state "ecological capacity," which can itself help to make a difference directly in state administration. States with a lower tax base simply have a tougher time patching together a first-class organizational apparatus for clean-water efforts. (Note in Table 2.8 what happened to state support for clean-water activities in Texas, Oklahoma, and Louisiana during the oil bust of the mid-1980s.) This chapter focuses on organizational capacity in its own right. Later, in Chapter 8, the discussion centers more directly on the question of how to measure and test for the complex interrelations sketched in the Communications Model of Intergovernmental Policy Implementation.

This chapter is structured around a set of ideas raised by the important notion of organizational capacity. The chapter considers what composes this kind of capacity and how we can expect its components to affect implementation. Both the top-down and bottom-up perspectives have something to contribute on this question of what composes capacity. Evidence from research efforts conducted by others as well as from our current work provides a check on the plausibility of the argument.

ORGANIZATIONAL CAPACITY:
A THEORETICAL OVERVIEW

In the Communications Model some factors exert influence between federal- and state-level inducements and constraints on the one hand and state implementation on the other. One additional element is state capacity, defined as the state's own ability to effectuate its preferences. One aspect of state capacity is ecological, both socioeconomic and political. This topic is the subject of Chapter 6. The other element that is important to discuss, and that has just been introduced, is *organizational capacity.*

States differ greatly in their organizational capacities to carry out their own preferences. Studies by the Advisory Commission on Intergovernmental Relations and others document steady improvements in state capacity over the years. Indeed, evidence since the outset of Ronald Reagan's New Federalism indicates that many states have coped quite innovatively with the cutbacks in federal aid and increases in state discretion of the 1980s because of such advances (Anton, 1989). Still, these developments have occurred unevenly across the country, and this variation can help to account for differences in implementation.

The overall political leadership structure in a state contributes to capacity. Factors of the structure include whether department heads are elected or appointed, how strong the governor's office is in setting direction for state government, and how professionalized the state legislature has become (Abney and Lauth, 1986). In this chapter, though, the emphasis is on organizational capacity in the administrative realm. Most implementation takes place in, through, and among large bureaucratic actors. These units must necessarily be included as part of any plausible explanation for the style, output, and outcome of the process (see O'Toole and Montjoy, 1984; Porter, 1976).

Indeed, virtually the whole subject of public administration has to do with how to amass organizational capacity, how to manage it, and how to direct it appropriately toward legitimate public goals. Public administration in its conventional sense does not speak to the implementation question as a whole, because many factors beyond the reach of state administrators can influence the course of action in a policy sector. Organizational and administrative matters are crucial to consider, however.

A sophisticated understanding of organizational capacity and its subtle influences on policy implementation would require descriptions of virtually the whole gamut of administration, from financial management to motivation, from information systems to affirmative action plans and their impact on the workplace. Obviously, these matters extend far beyond the scope of this volume. Mentioning them, however, highlights both the importance of organizational capacity and the extent to which it has received detailed treatment over the years. (For reviews of coverage in the implementation research literature, see Goggin, 1987; O'Toole, 1986.)

This chapter focuses particularly on the topic of organizational or administrative capacity and its link to intergovernmental policy implementation. Here organizational capacity is treated as a product of the structure, the personnel (or, in the jargon of the bureaucratic experts, "human resources"), and the financial characteristics of state agencies. Policy messages are more likely to trigger the anticipated large-scale responses when the established units are built well for the task with which they are charged. Furthermore, capacity is improved when the individuals hired to get the job done are sufficiently numerous, qualified, and favorably disposed toward the call to action. Agency capacity also requires possession of the requisite financial resources for the program.[1] These resources are sometimes of two kinds: those targeted directly to clients and those spent in the process of implementation. Transforming a state preference into action obviously requires both.

If organizational capacity is crucial for determining implementation, just what kind of administrative arrangement provides that capacity? It seems sensible to consider that improvements in any or all of these components—structure, people, and finances—constitute a strengthening of state capacity to deal with a particular problem. (How to measure and test for these items is addressed later, in Chapter 8.) One expects that the greater a state's capacity, other things being equal, the smoother the implementation process for a given program. Beyond this statement, each of the three underlying conceptual elements of organizational capacity can be discussed more carefully. The most complicated and perhaps interesting questions attend the issue of organizational structure. The chapter first addresses this topic, and thereafter discussion turns to the subjects of people and finances as components of a state's capacity to implement.

ORGANIZATIONAL STRUCTURE

Organizational structure sounds like a topic designed to cure insomnia, a subject that could be of interest only to paper shufflers or bureaucratic empire builders. Those experienced at government, however, know that organizing is a political act, and organization is an expression of political will.

Nasty fights in Washington over whether there should be a Department of Veterans Affairs or whether the Department of Education should lose its cabinet-level status are not just battles over symbols. The location and shape of administrative units strongly influence what happens to policy during implementation.

For example, pulling together the disparate offices that dealt with the nation's approach to air, water, and other categories of pollution problems to create the Environmental Protection Agency in 1970 did more than add a new box to the organization chart. This move created readier access for environmentally conscious interest groups in policy circles, gave sympathetic officials a permanent niche closer to the top policymakers, heightened morale among public experts working on solutions to our environmental problems, and pooled expertise to improve the quality of action during implementation.

What kinds of organizational structure improve a state's capacity to implement a program? The research literature on this subject and the investigations we have undertaken suggest that, in effect, it all depends. On what? It would seem that at least two factors are involved: what *aspect* of implementation is in question (style, on the one hand, or outputs and outcomes, on the other), and what type of policy problem is involved. Each of these issues can be clarified by drawing out contributions from the top-down and bottom-up approaches to implementation.

Conventional wisdom has long asserted that hierarchically integrated administrative structures ease the communication of policy messages and thus simplify and streamline implementation processes. Indeed, this is a sensible notion. Communicating a policy message through the intergovernmental system means creating some shared sense of implementation and some coordinated pattern of activities among many different individuals.

When these people are located in the same or closely clustered organizational units, the extent of coordinated action is likely to increase (for an empirical demonstration in German bureaucratic units, see

Scharpf, 1976). In short, other things being equal, intraorganizational implementation is easier to conduct than the interorganizational variant (for explicit discussion of this argument, see O'Toole, 1983; O'Toole and Montjoy, 1984).

In fact, a major point of the top-down approach is that implementation proceeds most expeditiously when the number of organizations involved is low and the administrative structure is well integrated from above, rather than being dispersed and fragmented into numerous offices and bureaus (O'Toole, 1986: 200). A few examples illustrate the point. Pressman and Wildavsky (1984) studied the implementation activities that occurred when the U.S. Economic Development Administration tried to generate jobs in Oakland, California by building a marine terminal and airline hangar. They found many actors and decision points, which in turn generated delays and roadblocks to implementation. Their analysis of the "complexity of joint action" concluded that as the number of units involved in the implementation process increases, the chance for action quickly decreases (see also Kelman, 1984).

Similar conclusions about organizational structures conducive to implementation success can be found in policy sectors like the intergovernmental regulation of occupational safety (Marvel, 1982), the implementation of equal education opportunity policy (Stewart and Bullock, 1981), and the execution of intergovernmental programs in child health care among the states (Goggin, 1987: 79, 124). More sweeping injunctions along these lines are offered by Mazmanian and Sabatier, who state that "one of the best-documented findings in implementation literature" is that the "degree of hierarchical integration" is a crucial determinant of implementation success (1983: 27; see also Bardach, 1977).

Yet the question may not be so simple. Several other studies, mostly conducted within the bottom-up tradition, cast doubt on such a straightforward conclusion. For instance, Hull and Hjern studied West German efforts to assist small private firms in economic growth. They concluded that policy effectiveness was improved where there were local intermediary units composing what they termed complex "assistance structures" (Hull with Hjern, 1987).

Other studies seem to confirm that complicated, multiunit structures may encourage success during implementation (see Durant, 1984; O'Toole and Montjoy, 1984). Intricate organizational patterns may carry benefits that are subtle but nonetheless real. These derive from such features as redundancy (overlaps among organizational units). These features reduce the chance that the issues or clientele of public programs will slip through the cracks in the system (Bendor, 1985; Bowen, 1982). Also, sometimes programs need many kinds of specialties and perspectives to be brought to bear during implementation. When some of these are already housed in separate administrative units, it may make sense to invoke a more complex organizational structure (O'Toole, 1983; Ostrom, 1985; Parks, 1985; Yewlett, 1985).

A useful example of this point is the Work Incentive Program (WIN), an intergovernmental effort of the last two decades that aimed at the training and placement of welfare recipients into positions of productive employment. At both federal and state levels (in most states, at least) the program required the participation of two agencies, the one charged with employment matters and the unit tasked with social services. Thus, at the national level, both the Department of Labor and the Department of Health and Human Services were heavily involved, with Labor as the lead agency.

In most states, both the employment service and the welfare department contributed staff and other resources. In fact, at the level of the street-level bureaucracy, employment placement workers and social services personnel have had to deal regularly with each other and coordinate in the referral, training, and placement of eligible individuals.

Furthermore, in many fields of social policy a vast network of private not-for-profit organizations operates. Without the cooperation of some of these units in the family planning field, carrying out any intergovernmental family planning policy would be next to impossible. Bottom-up researchers, then, are well aware of the need to take into account these kinds of elements of the implementation context.

It does seem sensible to conclude that implementation is indeed influenced by organizational structure, but how? The relationship does not seem to be simple and straightforward. Top-downers and bottom-uppers can *each* muster evidence and logic to buttress their position. For this portion of our model, conceptual clarification proves to be extremely useful in sorting out the apparent ambiguities.[2]

One ambiguity in much of the second-generation research literature is linked to an issue addressed in Chapter 1: What constitutes implementation "success"? In discussing the model used in this volume we have been careful to note that one can understand implementation process, or style, as distinct from the outputs and outcomes of the implementation process. These variables are not identical. "It is quite possible that utilizing hierarchically-controlled structures . . . might have different effects on process and output" (O'Toole, 1989a).

Implementation Style

Integrated structures should be easier to induce into action; there *are* fewer veto points and prospects for delay. Thus, one would expect that the greater the number of organizational units involved in the implementation process, other things being equal, the greater the chances that delay and difficulty will be exhibited in a state's implementation style.

Of course, a state may not always have an unencumbered choice about the number of administrative units it will involve in an implementation process. For intergovernmental policy, the national government may stipulate certain features of program structure as part of the "strings" attached to a grant program. To the extent that this kind of requirement has been imposed, however, it has often worked to simplify the structure.

The Single State Agency Requirement   For several decades, for instance, the federal actors imposed a "single state agency" requirement on many intergovernmental programs; in other words, a state involved in the program would have to manage its part of the operation through only one unit set up for the task. The effect of this kind of regulation was to force a simple and formally integrated structure on the states. The single state agency requirement is generally thought to have strengthened administration in a number of policy areas but has been dropped in recent years in an effort to provide more flexibility to the recipients of federal aid.

Inclusion of Nongovernmental Units   States may find that for either political or technical reasons they must involve nongovernmental units as part of the organizational apparatus during implementation. States typically find it impossible to run their Medicaid programs without regular involvement by the major health providers who actually deliver the care at the street level, so to speak; these include the state medical, hospital, and nursing home associations. Thus, actual program structures during implementation can become quite complex. The perspective developed here suggests that style difficulties are likely to accompany that complexity.

In two policy fields we have looked for evidence on this point. The Resource Conservation and Recovery Act (RCRA) of 1976 illustrates the plausibility of the idea. Preliminary research on the topic indicates that the presence of a single designated toxic substances agency in a state has facilitated timely implementation. In fact, research on both the RCRA and clean-water policy as they have been implemented over time shows that states have consolidated their environmental organizations since the 1970s. In part this move was made to adapt more effectively to such important intergovernmental programs.

An excellent illustration of how reducing the number of units can speed and ease the implementation process has occurred in recent years in the field of waste-water treatment. Following tax changes in 1982, privatisation in this sector became considerably more attractive. This adaptation had the effect of simplifying the interorganizational pattern. The EPA grants process had involved a larger number of public and private organizational units. None of these units had an incentive to submerge its own interests and perspectives in pursuit of the overall project. Under privatisation, however, an arrangement in which all design and building activities as well as the operations of the plant are handled under one roof, the process proceeded much more rapidly. This occurred despite the fact that EPA and state regulators are still heavily involved in setting effluent standards, permitting the facility, and monitoring it for compliance (Heilman and Johnson, 1989; O'Toole, 1989a, b).

The Lead Agency   The theoretical argument would also suggest that for a given program, states that designate a "lead agency" for implementation exhibit a more trouble-free and more rapid implementation style than those that do not. Implementation processes can be simplified by providing one of the units with some authority to induce a degree of integration. In the research we are currently conducting, there is insufficient variation among the states on this issue within particular policy fields to draw any firm conclusions about how this expectation stacks up in practice. Overall, however, the argument and the evidence seem to suggest that the top-downers have a valid point regarding the relationship between organizational structure and implementation style.

Implementation Output and Outcome

This book has examined the connection between organizational structure and the implementation process and demonstrated that simple and integrated structures are likely to smooth the style of action. As shown in earlier chapters, however, it is important to consider that prompt implementation does not always lead to optimal outcomes and outputs. Administrative capacity to produce *action* is not necessarily the same as administrative capacity to achieve *results*.

Theory grounded in a bottom-up perspective focuses on the importance of matching implementation structure to the real, practical nature of the policy problem to be dealt with if implementation outputs and eventually outcomes are to be satisfactorily achieved. Sometimes substantial discretion (often referred to as an "adaptive" implementation style, as in Berman, 1978) is required in the field to effectively address some policy problem. When such is the case, the issue may well stubbornly resist resolution if the implementation network is too tightly integrated, centralized, or simple (Porter, 1976). In this situation, implementation processes that are prompt, with no significant modification, may well score relatively low on effectiveness.

This point is perhaps the major theme of the bottom-up critique. It is also consistent with our Communications Model framework. If they are intense and detailed, regular communications at the operating level are required to address a policy problem; simpler structures may provoke compliance even as they squeeze out valuable information and reduce policy-related learning during the continuing cycles of implementation.

Therefore, when the policy problem at hand does not technically require lots of state or local freedom to adapt or adjust to changing conditions, simple integrated organizational structures should work well for output and outcome, as well as for style. For policies technically requiring an adaptive implementation style, however, states with more complex and variegated implementation structures should in the long run be more successful at achieving satisfactory outputs and outcomes than states with simpler structures.

Determining the technical requirements of a policy, and specifically whether a policy really "needs" a particular kind of implementation interaction if the policy is to be executed effectively, can be a tricky matter. Certainly some intuitive differences are fairly obvious. Setting effluent standards for a waste-water treatment facility can be handled centrally, so long as there is adequate information about the water systems in the area. RCRA would seem to require more complex channels of information and thus more intricate patterns of state-local interaction for ultimate success. And finally, there must be substantial and continuing local discretion in adapting family planning services to the particular character and context of a local community or target population.

Evidence gathered in our research supports the general argument here. In waste-water treatment, privatised structures not only induce prompt implementation with few programmatic modifications, but they do so at no sacrifice to clean-water output. (Treatment plants built under *all* implementation options produce consistently clean water. Technology in this field is sufficiently well developed that a great deal of local discretion on policy is not necessary. For evidence, see O'Toole, 1989b.)

For RCRA, which is a somewhat more technically contestable policy problem, the group of states that have done best in output terms has *not* been the group that proceeded with the quickest implementation style (see data in Chapter 2). Instead, the "strategic delayers" first built their more complex organizational structure and then began to address the policy problem (see Bowman and Lester, 1987).

In the family planning field, the evidence is spottier. As a result of increased pressure since 1980 for changes in the law and regulations that have been triggered by a perception on the part of some pro-life organizations that many clinic workers are engaged in "directive counseling,"[3] however, implementation has become a major issue. Many groups opposed to abortion view service providers as implementing the law in ways not originally intended. The pro-life groups, therefore, seek organizational and procedural changes as a remedy. Because this is a complex and contested issue, it has taken more time to develop new implementation patterns.

The discussion here has referred to state implementation in the "long run," which may vary from policy to policy. It is a failing of most implementation research that studies examining implementation over a considerable period, at least a five- to ten-year period, have not been conducted (see Sabatier, 1986). Our model, and the kinds of research it is designed to elicit, is aimed at correcting this defect.

The current discussion has shown, then, that clarifying concepts like administrative integration and implementation success can illuminate the strengths of both the top-down and the bottom-up perspectives as they support organizational capacity.

Goals, Structure, and Organizational Capacity

One final element of organizational structure should be addressed. Implementing organizations have goals, and the program being implemented may or may not fit neatly with these goals. Agencies are more likely to have communication and coordination problems with each other when the units do not see eye to eye on the program. Such organizations are more likely to screen out important elements of the policy message and to perform in a less-than-ideal fashion when the policy message deals with goals that are not of particular concern to the implementors. Therefore, the greater the compatibility among the goals of the implementing agencies and the concerns of the implementors, the greater the success of a program within a state. Also, the greater the compatibility of the goals of the implementing agencies with those expressed in the policy message, the greater the success of a program within a state.

The Early and Periodic Screening, Diagnosis, and Treatment (EPSDT) Program—an intergovernmental effort to help treat and prevent health problems in poor children who have potentially handicapping disabilities—illustrates this point. At both national and state levels, the program was plagued with "goal inconsistency," as it was shuffled around from the welfare to the health department and suffered in terms of output. On the other hand, the implementation of the Child Health and Disability Prevention (CHDP) Act, California's redesigned version of EPSDT, improved over time as "the various actors in CHDP's implementation odyssey moved closer to consensus" in support of the program's purpose (Goggin, 1987: 127–28).

One well-known method of reducing the effectiveness and efficiency of an unpalatable program consists of delegating it to an unsympathetic agency or requiring a lead agency to involve a variety of other, less-enthusiastic actors in the implementation process. Evidence on this notion is documented in a couple of second-generation studies of the implementation of intergovernmental health programs (Goggin, 1986; 1987), and has long been a staple of the literature on policy and administration (Downs, 1967).[4]

PERSONNEL

Another important element of organizational capacity concerns human resources, or personnel. An initial expectation is that the more personnel per capita that a state devotes to implementing a program (other things being equal), the more direct the implementation style and the more effective the program in producing its outputs and outcomes. An additional expectation, somewhat more sensitive to the quality as well as quantity of the entire mix of human resources targeted at an implementation process, is that as the number of *professional* staff per capita increases, implementation is more straightforward and more productive.

Thus far, systematic studies have not been performed to test these notions, despite their obvious nature and plausibility. Our own work has developed some evidence in this regard. The data suggest some interesting conclusions.

The RCRA Example

Consider the case of RCRA implementation. When a study is controlled for other variables, the absolute number of agency full-time personnel devoted to hazardous waste management appears to be less related to effective implementation and more related to ultimate goal achievement. True, states that were moving in the direction of compliance with RCRA had more hazardous waste personnel than did strategic delay or defiant states. The strategic delay states, however, had even more full-time employees.

A plausible explanation for this finding derives from the analysis in the previous section on organizational capacity: Strategic delayers seem to emphasize goal achievement over timeliness, and outcomes over style. Understanding the personnel aspect of capacity, as well as the structural component, thus may require a clear conceptualization of the different aspects of implementation itself.

Apparently, personnel characteristics in a state implementation system are linked in turn to the state's overall ecological capacity. There are vastly varying salary levels and degrees of professionalization (or patronage ties) across state administrative apparatuses. Some jurisdictions, such as Minnesota, run many programs with human resources at or above the level of the national government. Others, like Arkansas, have great difficulty attracting minimally qualified talent in several program fields.

Generally speaking, states with higher levels of ecological capacity (see Chapter 6) also support a more qualified and professional personnel force. Once again the complex links in the Communications Model are illuminated.[5]

Fitting Goals of Personnel with the Policy Message

One other element of personnel characteristics *has* received attention by implementation researchers and merits brief discussion. The coverage of the characteristics of organizational structure in previous chapters examined the matter of agency goals, their congruence among implementing units, and their fit with the purposes expressed in the policy message.

These items were conceptualized as characteristics of organizational structure, although they could have been considered features of agency personnel. (Considering goals or objectives of an agency as something entirely apart from the shared goals of agency personnel inappropriately treats administrative units themselves as living entities.)

Relation of Personnel Skills and Commitment to Implementation Success

Additionally, another pair of characteristics of *key* implementing personnel deserves separate notice here. These are the level of commitment (motivation) and the competency, or skill, of the important state-level administrative actor(s) in the implementation scheme. Both motivation and competency are staples of first- and second-generation research (for example, Mazmanian and Sabatier, 1983: 34–35; Ball, 1976; Berman, 1978; Rawson, 1981; Ross, 1984; Thompson, 1982). Goggin (1987: 187–88) summarizes the argument succinctly:

> The personnel capability model posits that a manager's conduct on the job is subject not only to the constraints imposed by factors internal and external to the manager's organization, but also to the limitations of his or her own capabilities, level of commitment, and attitudes and beliefs. This model explains variations in performance in terms of the individual talents and drive, as well as the motivations

and feelings that an individual brings to each situation—in other words, that person's contribution.

The first essential characteristic of contribution is competency, or skill, which is a function of the individual's capacity to interact effectively with his or her environment. The second ingredient is motivation, or will. In the implementation literature, both skill and will have been associated with program success.

No matter how clear the policy message, no matter the level of capacity of a given state, and despite an appropriate formal organizational structure, skillful and committed program management seems important for implementation success.[6] Evidence supporting this conclusion has been a staple of the research literature on public administration for years—even before the study of implementation per se attracted widespread attention.

Therefore, it is reasonable to conclude that the more skillful a program manager within a particular state, the prompter the implementation style and the greater the success in producing outputs and outcomes, other things being equal. The more committed a program manager to implementation success, the smoother the implementation style and the greater the success in producing outputs and outcomes.

These ideas are examined empirically in the studies referenced earlier, although in these cases such evidence was usually not carefully and systematically gathered. Goggin tested for the impact of managerial qualifications on a health program's outputs and outcomes in five states. Although the study was not designed to sort out clearly the competing explanations for program results, some of the findings are suggestive. There was evidence that "skill at bureaucratic politics" on the part of administrators contributed to implementation success; and "the most successful programs [were] managed by the more experienced, more senior, and more educated managers" (1987: 197).

Further instances of such administrative skill and commitment having a decisive impact have been reported in other second-generation studies. For instance, a comparative analysis of differential implementation styles and outputs in the labor market training field—programs to implement human resource development policy—shows that a major reason for the observed differences seems to be the skill and commitment of the managers strategically placed in regional implementation patterns (O'Toole, 1983).

Evidence consistent with this point is available in the clean-water/waste-water treatment field. Even in states where organizational capacity is limited at the state level, local implementors may have options. Some cities, in possession of managerial resources of their own, have found ways to implement the policy despite a lack of state assistance. A comparison of several grant-funded locales shows those with a skilled local manager active in maintaining the implementation net-work have experienced smoother implementation than those without (O'Toole, 1989a).

In one such city of approximately 50,000, for instance, clean-water activities are organized into an integrated, well-run engineering depart-ment. The head of this unit is an individual technically skilled and also administratively adept. He has slowly recruited a highly competent and motivated staff—one with the "will and skill" (Goggin, 1987) to do great deeds in the name of clean water. This unit has cemented ties with lo-cal political leaders to such an extent that the department has no budget problems to speak of.

Whereas in many locales the political leaders have a hand in day-to-day policy matters for clean-water programs, in this unit the detailed but troublesome administrative matters—like handling the red tape as-sociated with change orders on construction projects—are left to the discretion of the department head. He in turn has developed an infor-mal network of relationships with state and federal monitors, and these representatives of other governmental units have largely ceded juris-diction to him on monitoring and construction issues. The federal EPA has even been willing to allow the city to stand in violation of some technical staffing and administrative guidelines in the local treatment plants' operations because of the overall confidence the regulators have in this department's functioning.

FINANCIAL RESOURCES

It should come as no surprise that financial resources are deemed essential to prompt implementation with few programmatic changes. First, this topic was addressed in Chapter 3 in connection with resources provided as accompaniments or features of federal policy messages. Here the point is simply a reminder that financial resources for inter-governmental policy flow not solely from national coffers but from state (and sometimes local) sources as well. In complex or innovative pro-grams (privatised waste-water treatment is an example), there may be equity contributions from the private sector as well. Finally, certain pro-grams generate some operating revenue from user fees, such as is the case with urban mass transportation. All these revenue sources need to be considered.

Second, the literature on policy implementation has maintained the consistent theme that funding resources provided for implementation are crucial for success. A number of citations and illustrations were provided in Chapter 3 as well, so it should be unnecessary to repeat this evidence here. The assertion, then, is as follows: The larger the program budget on a per-capita basis, *ceteris paribus*, the more straight-forward is a state's implementation, and the more successful is the program in terms of outputs and outcomes.

The effects of providing financial resources can be demonstrated from some of our research findings on this question. State per-capita spending is higher in the more successful implementation cases in both family planning and clean-water policy when results are examined by the measures explained in Chapter 2. Our work on RCRA shows that resources as resources may not be the issue. The *target* of the spending is what matters. For example, states that implemented RCRA in a timely manner were not necessarily the wealthiest states in the country (see the data for RCRA presented in Chapter 2), but they did devote a higher proportion of their budgets to environmental protection than did nonimplementors.

Data on this issue are available in other policy sectors as well. State funding for AIDS is not fully explained either by the incidence of the problem (for example, as measured by the number of cases) or by the wealth of the jurisdiction. Alabama, for instance, spends more than Texas on this problem, despite heavy AIDS caseloads in cities like Houston and despite Alabama's relatively low wealth (Smith, 1989: 54). Although not without problems of its own, Alabama has responded correspondingly better in terms of certain significant outputs—including completing the first mandatory statewide AIDS education program in the country in its schools.

CONCLUSION

Organizational capacity can contribute to implementation. On the other hand, even well-designed policy messages, with all the appropriate encouragements for straightforward implementation, can be defeated by organizational or administrative glitches or weaknesses in the system. Organizational capacity consists of appropriate administrative structure, personnel, and financial resources and can vary considerably across programs and across the states.

Selecting or designing the appropriate structure for policy implementation is not such an easy matter; indeed, scholars of implementation have disagreed among themselves about the most important injunctions on this score. According to the theory sketched here, however, both the top-down and the bottom-up theorists have useful contributions to make on the issue. Indeed, some of the apparently competing claims can be reconciled.

Tight, centralized structures encourage compliance, but they may or may not assist in achieving policy goals. The result, other things being equal, seems to depend on characteristics of the policy tasks themselves. Plentiful, skillful, and motivated administrative actors can more easily convert a policy message into action—and the process can be streamlined by thoughtful and generous allocation of financial resources. Evidence from previous efforts at implementation research as well as our own current studies supports these generalizations.

It would be a mistake, however, to conclude that organizational capacity is all-important or that it exists in isolation from a host of other contextual variables. Chapter 6 shifts attention to this broader context by examining the impact of state ecological capacity on the activities of implementation.

Notes for Chapter 5

1. Personnel, mentioned earlier, require the expenditure of financial resources. Personnel, however, may be budgeted separately from dollars. Thus, it is important to consider each as an element of capacity.

2. This clarification of conceptual matters draws from a more detailed analysis and empirical investigation of the subject. (See O'Toole 1989b.)

3. Directive counseling is where workers in family planning clinics not only offer pregnant women who request it a range of options—from putting a baby up for adoption to an abortion—but also suggest an alternative.

4. Note Durant's analysis (1984: 312), however, for a challenge to and refinement of this idea.

5. For an analysis of the increasing professionalization of state and local administration, see Abney and Lauth, 1986.

6. This conclusion follows despite the fact that leadership skill can be an overrated component of administrative effectiveness (Pfeffer and Salancik, 1978: 9–10).

CHAPTER SIX

State Ecological Capacity

Receiving final authorization from the U.S. Environmental Protection Agency (EPA) is a major step for the states in the implementation of the Resource Conservation and Recovery Act (RCRA) of 1976. To receive final authorization, a state's program must

- be "equivalent" to the federal program
- be "consistent" with federal or other state programs
- provide for "adequate" enforcement

The EPA has defined *equivalence* as requiring state programs to include the following elements: a manifest tracking system, criteria standards, adequate resources and legal authority, a designated lead agency, and a public participation effort. It interprets *consistency* as preventing a state from imposing importation bans on hazardous waste from other states. *Adequate* enforcement means that a state must have the resources—both fiscal and staffing—to enforce the RCRA mandate.

Although the authorization process has proceeded slowly, all but seven states have received final authorization as of January 1, 1990; Idaho was on the verge of gaining EPA approval. Only Alaska, California, Connecticut, Hawaii, Idaho, and Wyoming had not received final authorization as of year-end 1989. Substantial variation exists, however, in implementation style, especially the length of time states took to receive authorization. Mississippi, for example, was one of the first states to receive authorization (on June 27, 1984). California, normally an innovative state, still does not have authorization, principally because this state is proceeding slowly and carefully in designing its regulatory regime and because of the state's public notice requirements. In addition, Pennsylvania received authorization after a significant delay due, to some extent, to the scope of the hazardous waste problem in that state. Finally, Wyoming does not intend to seek authorization, because this state has decided that achieving it is not in the state's best interests.

Rather, because the state has a relatively minor hazardous waste problem, Wyoming has decided that it is simply more cost-effective for the EPA to manage the state's program.

Using the implementation categories developed throughout this book, the Mississippi case is an example of "compliance" (prompt implementation with no modifications). The California case is an example of "strategic delay" (delay with modifications that help the state's chances of implementation). The Pennsylvania case is an example of "delay" (delay with no modifications). The Wyoming case is an example of "defiance" (delay with or without modifications that inhibit a state's chances of implementation). These four cases illustrate an important point in state implementation behavior: The states adopt various implementation styles, and these styles may be influenced by the internal conditions of the states themselves.

More specifically, the cases just described suggest a number of important questions:

- Does the availability of fiscal resources within the state provide the basis for a prompt response to a federal directive?
- Are institutional capabilities in the states an important inducement to or constraint on implementation behavior?
- Are characteristics of the states' situational milieu key factors influencing state implementation behavior?
- Does salience of the problem or media attention to the problem provoke a more prompt response than low salience or lack of media attention?

Thus, one plausible explanation for state implementation is the variability in states' *ecological capacity*. This term encompasses state wealth, state institutional capabilities, and state situational contexts (that is, the salience of the problem in the state or the media attention given, here to hazardous waste). In addition, the extant literature on comparative state policy has suggested the importance of these kinds of variables on state policy outputs. (For reviews of this literature, see Lester and Lombard, 1987; Savage, 1976; Treadway, 1985.)

This chapter examines the relationship between a state's ecological capacity and state implementation of public policies. A state's ecological capacity is defined by three dimensions: state economic capacity, state political capacity, and state situational capacity. A state's ecological capacity sets limits on, or provides opportunities for, the extent of policy implementation by the fifty states. State ecological capacity is a characteristic that varies from state to state and, within a state, from program to program.

This chapter strives to describe what state ecological capacity means and why it is important to understanding public policy implementation by states. In addition, some research propositions are suggested for testing either by us or by others. Finally, the chapter illustrates the links between state ecological capacity and policy implementation by drawing on the research of others, as well as our own findings, that shed light on the proposition that state ecological variables are valid predictors of state policy implementation.

THE IMPORTANCE OF STATE ECOLOGICAL CAPACITY

An element missing from earlier implementation research is the recognition that the state ecology (or environment) influences individual and organizational behavior (Perrow, 1972; Thompson, 1967). In other words, there are state limitations besides the constraints imposed by formal and informal organizational structures and resources such as money and managerial talent (as discussed within previous chapters). Individuals in the implementation subsystem contend with limitations imposed by the state's political, economic, and social context.

Moreover, the comparative state politics and policy literature has long recognized the importance of state context on public policy outputs as measured by expenditures and legislative enactments. Thus, this chapter's argument assumes that a state's ecological capacity is a crucial determinant of state implementation of federal programs.

One of the first comparative studies of the importance of state context (or ecological capacity) on state policy was a classic analysis of the effects of socioeconomic variables (such as state wealth) and political variables (for example, states' degree of interparty competition) on state welfare spending (Dawson and Robinson, 1963). This study emphasized the important constraints imposed on state spending by the availability of fiscal resources within the states. Later work by Thomas Dye (1966) stimulated research into the relative importance of socioeconomic and political variables to state policy that continues up to the present time (Tucker and Herzik, 1986).

In the seventies and eighties, a major debate ensued in the comparative state policy literature, which was founded on assessing the relative influence of socioeconomic development and political process variables on state policy outputs. (For an initial assessment of this work, see Fenton and Chamberlayne, 1969; Jacob and Lipsky, 1968.) This literature has received a great deal of criticism for its atheoretical nature; its endogenic nature (such as too great a reliance on state-level, as opposed to federal- or local-level, explanations of state-level behavior);

its time-bound nature (a reliance on cross-sectional versus diachronic analysis); and its methodological shortcomings. The research nevertheless occupies a central place in the state politics subfield. (For careful critiques of this literature, see Hofferbert, 1972; Savage, 1976.) Indeed, the research assumes that state context is the primary determinant of state policy behavior.

In the eighties, state ecology emerged from the shadows to occupy a more prominent place in implementation research. One comprehensive study examined the relationships between several state-level contextual variables, such as

- state wealth (personal income, per-capita spending, median family income, and percentage poor)
- problem severity (industrialization, pollution potential, chemical waste generation, and hazardous waste sites)
- political conditions (interparty competition and Democratic strength)
- administrative-organizational factors (bureaucratic consolidation and legislative professionalism)

The study reviewed state implementation of the Resource Conservation and Recovery Act (RCRA) of 1976 (Lester et al., 1983). Problem severity and administrative-organizational capabilities were found to exert significant influence on state implementation of a federal directive. Later research on state environmental spending (or implementation of state environmental programs) determined that such behavior by the states was strongly related to the severity of the pollution problem and the level of fiscal resources available (Lester and Keptner, 1984). A state's commitment to environmental quality was largely explained by the economic resource base of the state itself.

Such findings carried rather significant implications for future state efforts to implement federal programs. More specifically, as the states faced the prospect of federal budget cuts in the 1980s (and undertook cutbacks of their own), the amount of state expenditures given to implementation declined as well.[1]

In yet another state implementation study, Thompson and Scicchitano (1985) stressed such state-level contextual factors as wealth (for example, measures of per-capita income), interest group pressures (such as percent union members), and organizational factors (such as injury and illness ratio and complaints per employees) as key determinants of state implementation of the Occupational Safety and Health Act (OSHA) of 1970. The authors caution, however, that these findings may apply primarily to protective regulatory policies where broad agreement often exists both on how to interpret a problem and on the appropriate response to the problem. Subsequent research concluded that other state-level factors, such as business dominance (including items such as manufacturing employees), pro-regulatory pressures (such as number of complaints), and state enforcement vigor, were key determinants of state implementation of OSHA (Thompson and Scicchitano, 1987).

Thus, two previous decades of comparative state policy research, as well as contemporary research on the determinants of state implementation behavior, have provided credible support for the argument that state ecological capacity is a key determinant of state policy implementation. The following section further defines the key components of state ecological capacity and presents in greater depth the rationale behind the selection of these factors.

DEFINING STATE ECOLOGICAL CAPACITY: KEY COMPONENTS AND FINDINGS

The Communications Model of Intergovernmental Policy Implementation, shown in Figure 1.1, makes an important distinction between decisions and actions. An optimal solution to a problem is often beyond the state's immediate capabilities to provide it (Jones, 1975: 211–75). The model recognizes that states also have various levels of capacity that place limits on the ability of individuals to act on their decisions (Hansen, 1983; Jewell, 1982). In this instance, states are treated as bundles of assorted subsystems of national, state, and local politics (Rose, 1973). Hence to fully comprehend the dynamics of implementation of any given program requires consideration of state ecological capacities as well as national and local forces. What is the meaning of "state ecological capacity," and what are the construct's empirical referents?

The ecological setting includes environmental conditions surrounding implementation that have a recognizable impact on the implementation process (Love and Sederberg, 1987: 169). That is, public policies are thrust into an already structured social and physical environment that may either resist or facilitate those policies being carried out. Thus, state ecological capacity refers to the contextual environment within states that acts as an inducement or constraint on the freedom of action of state governments. It is a set of conditions that sets limits on (or provides opportunities for) what the states can do (or cannot do).

Among the types of environmental conditions that restrict state governments (Harrigan, 1988; Dye, 1988) are

- their constitutional and cultural environments
- the nature of intergovernmental relations at any given point in history
- the availability of financial resources
- the level of industrialization within the state
- the level of urbanization
- the level of education of the populace

In this book, state ecological capacity is defined by a number of contextual, state-level characteristics. Specifically, these characteristics include

- state economic capacity
- state political capacity
- state situational capacity

In the following sections, each of these factors is described and a rationale is provided for their inclusion in the Communications Model.

State Economic Capacity

Surrounding each policy problem is also a set of conditions—environmental constraints—that have an effect on state implementation. Some conditions are financial. That is, the availability of fiscal resources at the state level obviously affects state implementation behavior.

A relevant example is the implementation of a recent federal law intended to ensure that mentally ill and retarded people receive specialized health treatment. The legislation, an amendment to the Federal Budget Act of 1987, would require that states provide services for certain classes of patients in community-based mental health centers—halfway houses or group homes—rather than in psychiatric hospitals or nursing homes.

In effect, the law would require nursing homes to turn away people who seek admission solely because they are retarded or mentally ill. It would also require nursing homes to release the mentally ill if they have been in the nursing home less than thirty months. According to one of the bill's supporters, "This will force the states to make appropriate payments" (Tolchin, 1989).

The real problem, then, is fiscal. Large, wealthy states, such as California, New York, and Illinois, have the capacity to provide the community-based services that the law requires. Other states simply lack the resources to create a new services delivery system. In fact, Georgia, Indiana, and Oklahoma are stalling on a technicality. Texas and Louisiana, two oil-patch states that have suffered an economic setback of late, have filed a suit asking for a temporary restraining order that would prevent the law's implementation. Idaho has already won a temporary restraining order.

Relation of State Wealth to Implementation Speed   This specific mental health and mental retardation example illustrates a more general point: Governmental entities with greater financial resources tend to implement programs faster and with fewer modifications (Edwards, 1980; Sabatier and Mazmanian, 1980; Van Meter and Van Horn, 1975). In fact, the availability of fiscal resources is one of the most commonly mentioned variables believed to affect policy implementation.

In an examination of over one hundred studies of policy implementation, O'Toole (1986) found that roughly half of the published studies on implementation claim that resources (financial and other) are crucial to effective implementation. Moreover, as Sabatier and Mazmanian (1980: 546) argue, "A threshold level of funding is necessary for there to be any possibility of achieving statutory objectives, and the level of funding above this threshold (up to some saturation point) is proportional to the probability of achieving those objectives."

Similarly, Edwards suggests that even though implementation orders may be accurately transmitted, if implementors lack the resources to carry out policies, implementation is likely to be ineffective (Edwards, 1980: 53). For example, the federal Superfund bill (officially named the Comprehensive, Environmental Response, Compensation, and Liability Act of 1980, or CERCLA) requires the states to clean up abandoned hazardous waste sites. If the states are left to their own financial resources and receive little federal aid to help them, however, the poorest states are not as likely to comply with this federal mandate as are wealthier states.

In addition, the comparative state policy literature suggests that the amount of state economic resources (especially state wealth in terms of per-capita income levels) is the single most important determinant of state policy outputs (Dye, 1988; Treadway, 1985). In fact, the relationship between state wealth and state policy outputs (as measured by expenditures) has been found to hold consistently across time as well as within specific time periods (Tucker, 1982). Thus, it is expected that state economic capacity will strongly affect state policy implementation such that states with larger budgetary resources will implement programs faster and with fewer modifications than states with much fewer resources.

There is additional evidence to support the notion that state wealth affects state policy implementation. In an early study of state air pollution control expenditures, Game (1979) found that state wealth was strongly related to state spending for air quality. In 1983, Lester et al. found that greater resources—such as per-capita personal income, per-capita spending, median family income, and a lower percentage of poor persons in a state—were related to implementation of hazardous waste policy. This relation applied especially to those states with a more severe hazardous waste problem. The finding was confirmed in a separate study in which state wealth (especially median income) was the best predictor of state spending for environmental protection in the period 1975–1979 (Lester and Keptner, 1984).

Other Factors   State wealth matters, but it does not explain everything. For example, a state's fiscal capacity has been shown to affect state spending for clean land and water (Williams and Matheny, 1984). In that same study, however, when controls for overall state expenditures were introduced, environmental group activity and problem severity became the best predictors of public expenditures. Moreover, although state wealth (with indicators such as per-capita income and percentage of population below the poverty level) was initially found to be significantly related to OSHA enforcement, later work led the researchers to conclude that wealth "appears to play a modest role in shaping enforcement priorities" (Thompson and Scicchitano, 1985; 1987: 115).

All of these previous studies highlight the role of state economic capacity in facilitating or inhibiting state implementation of federal programs. Indeed, most of the extant research on this point suggests that state wealth is positively associated with state policy implementation, especially when the measure of state implementation is based on expenditure data. When state policy implementation is measured in nonexpenditure indicators (Thompson and Scicchitano, 1985; 1987) or compliance (Lester and Bowman, 1989), the findings suggest the importance of other factors, such as state political conditions or problem severity.

State Political Capacity

It is often argued that the political milieu makes the implementation of certain directives problematic (Ingram and Mann, 1980; Peterson, Rabe, and Wong, 1986). In some instances, an open, liberal, innovative, and progressive political milieu facilitates policy implementation; in others, the reverse is true. That is, a conservative, noninnovative, and generally nonprogressive political environment is more compatible with state policy implementation.

For example, the implementation of certain welfare proposals by the federal government (such as a guaranteed minimum income) would probably fare much better in a liberal political environment. The implementation of very different welfare proposals (such as workfare, or tying aid to gainful employment) would probably fare much better in a conservative political environment.

Partisanship and Public Opinion   In addition, political conditions such as public opinion, partisanship, and interest group mobilization affect states' policy implementation in a profound way (Van Meter and Van Horn, 1975). Similarly, Sabatier and Mazmanian (1980: 550) suggest that "Variation among political jurisdictions in support for a particular program is likely to result in pressures for ambiguous regulation and considerable discretion to local officials—both of which probably make behavioral change more difficult to achieve." The current public opinion, for example, can strongly affect the political agenda, because legislators are influenced by their constituents. This holds particularly true when opinion within the districts is relatively homogeneous. Moreover, public opinion polls are often employed by administrators to support particular policy positions (Sabatier and Mazmanian, 1980).

A state's partisan and ideological preferences strongly affect state politics and policy (Wright, Erikson, and McIver, 1985). More specifically, partisan and ideological differences strongly affect the behavior of state electorates, and they are differentially important depending on the nature of the choices offered to the voters.

Openness and Innovation in the State   The degree of "openness" in a state to citizen participation and other types of behavior is also a factor in facilitating state policy (Herzik, 1985). Open political systems facilitate the mobilization of voters, which in turn undoubtedly affects state policy outputs. It may be argued, then, that when voters are favorably predisposed, openness facilitates the implementation of state programs by encouraging supportive mass participation and interest in policy outcomes.

Related to the political milieu is the state's tendency toward innovation in state policy (Gray, 1973; Walker, 1969). The greater the tendency toward innovation, the greater the administrative capacity to apply the law in a more sophisticated and, perhaps, more equitable fashion.

Political Culture   Finally, a great deal of research has been devoted to the proposition that a state's "political culture" sets limits on (or provides opportunities for) what states may do (Elazar, 1984; Johnson, 1976; Lowery and Sigelman, 1982). Besides their fiscal resource limits, states are also affected by their citizens' attitudes, beliefs, and expectations about what governments should do, who should participate, and what rules should govern the political system (Harrigan, 1988: 23).

For example, Daniel Elazar argued that states may be categorized into three distinct subcultures: the individualistic, the traditionalistic, and the moralistic. The individualistic culture is associated with government as a "business"; the traditionalistic culture is associated with an "elitist" conception of government; and the moralistic culture sees government activity as the pursuit of a "commonwealth." Each of these cultures provides a different implementation environment. Thus, programs may fail not because resources and commitment are lacking, but because the cultural environment works against them (Love and Sederberg, 1987: 171).

This discussion suggests that states' political and policy environment affect eventual policy implementation. This argument leads to the proposition that the more conducive the political milieu to the program being implemented, the greater the tendency to implement a program quickly and with few, if any, program modifications.

A state's political characteristics have been linked to state policy implementation. For example, Lester et al. (1983) showed that partisanship, legislative professionalism, and bureaucratic consolidation were positively related to implementation of the states' hazardous waste regulatory policy. A subsequent study of RCRA implementation confirmed that bureaucratic consolidation was a strong predictor of the speed of compliance (Lester and Bowman, 1989).

In the area of OSHA implementation, however, Thompson and Scicchitano (1985) found interest group pressures (that is, percentage of voters who are union members, existing right to work laws, and perception of union strength) to be strongly related to OSHA enforcement, whereas partisanship was of limited utility in explaining state implementation in this area. The more recent work of Thompson and Scicchitano (1987) indicates that business dominance (that is, percentage of employees in manufacturing, value added by manufacturing, and the manufacturing index) is strongly related to health enforcement vigor in the American states, whereas wealth and problem severity were of limited importance. Business dominance variables were also found to be related to state implementation of hazardous waste policy, as measured by expenditures on land and water quality (Williams and Matheny, 1984).

Variables in the Research   Thus, in the area of state political
capacity, findings conflict about the relative importance of several political variables purported to affect state policy implementation. The
weight that partisanship, legislative professionalism, bureaucratic consolidation, interest group pressures, business dominance, political culture, and (to a lesser extent) region carry must be ascertained in future
work on state policy implementation. The findings thus far may be,
to a large extent, a function of the measures of state policy implementation adopted by particular investigators.

Each of the investigators cited here employed very different measures of their dependent variable. For example, Lester et al. (1983) used
a summated score of hazardous waste policy implementation collected
by the National Wildlife Federation (1979). Williams and Matheny (1984)
relied on expenditures on land and water quality control for the states.
In their later work, Lester and Bowman (1989) used a dichotomous measure of RCRA compliance that concerned the speed of authorization,
a nonfiscal measure. Thompson and Scicchitano (1985; 1987) used the
number of health inspectors, health inspections, and health citations
as measures of state policy implementation in the OSHA area.

Thus, noncomparability of research results stems from the fact that
various authors have used different measures of implementation. Until
researchers are able to develop more theoretically satisfying measures
of state policy implementation over the life of the program or, at the
very least, adopt similar measures of the same concept, the findings must
remain tentative. Results, therefore, are subject to additional testing by
these and other investigators.

State Situational Capacity

Situational variables—those that are peculiar to a policy, time, or
state—are important determinants of the success of policy implementation. Two apparently important situational components for state capacity are the salience of the problem to the state (problem severity)
and the amount of media attention given to the problem in the state
where the policy is to be delivered.

For example, both Van Meter and Van Horn (1975) and Sabatier
and Mazmanian (1980) stress the importance of salience of the policy
issue as a crucial determinant of policy implementation. Sabatier and
Mazmanian (1980: 549) note that successful implementation is rendered
more difficult by local variation in the seriousness of the problem being
addressed. Such variation produces enormous pressures for "flexible"
regulations and considerable administrative discretion to local units.

Other scholars, such as William Gormley, have emphasized the importance of problem salience as a key determinant of policy behavior.
He argues that regulatory politics vary systematically across issue areas

depending on the salience and complexity of issues. That is, each combination of salience and complexity produces a different kind of regulatory issue network (Gormley, 1986: 598). Thus, issue salience is related to the behavior of politicians, citizens, journalists, interest groups, judges, bureaucrats, and professionals and, by implication, the implementation of public policy.

Role of the Media   Mass media are important in the implementation process for at least two reasons (Mazmanian and Sabatier, 1980). First, mass media are generally a crucial intervening variable between changes in socioeconomic conditions and the perceptions of those changes by the general public and, to a lesser extent, political elites. Second, the tendency for most television networks and newspapers to play an issue to the hilt and then go on to something else is a real obstacle to the infusion of political support from diffuse beneficiaries of most programs (Sabatier and Mazmanian, 1980: 550).

Thus, it is argued that the role of the media in focusing attention on the problem and the salience of the problem to the state are crucial determinants of policy implementation. For example, for the Love Canal hazardous waste site, the media were crucial in getting the state of New York and the federal government involved in addressing the problem (Levine, 1982). This discussion leads to the proposition that the greater the salience of the problem and the greater the amount of media attention given to the problem in question, the greater the tendency to implement the program quickly, with fewer modifications.

Degree of Problem Severity   A number of studies have examined the effect of a state's context, especially in terms of severity or salience of the problem in the state. In general, the conclusions assert that states try harder if the problem appears to be worse in the state. For example, Lester et al. (1983) examined the effect of severity of the hazardous waste problem on state hazardous waste policy implementation in the fifty American states. Severity (as measured by industrialization, pollution potential, chemical waste generation, and the total number of hazardous waste sites in the state) was strongly related to the implementation of state hazardous waste policy.

Similarly, Bowman (1984) and Bowman and Lester (1985) again found severity of the hazardous waste problem to be related to hazardous waste policy implementation in the fifty states, while Rowland and Feiock (1983) found that states' regulatory efforts in this area were negatively related to their dependency on waste-generating industries. In other environmental policy research, Wassenberg (1986) found that severity of the target problem was related to state implementation of the Federal Water Pollution Control Act of 1972 (FWPCA). On the other hand, a very recent study of RCRA implementation by the fifty states found that severity (as measured by the amount of waste generated in a state) surprisingly unrelated to RCRA implementation (Lester and Bowman, 1989).

Studies of OSHA implementation yielded inconclusive findings regarding the role played by problem severity. As measured by occupational illness and injury rates, as well as complaints about occupational hazards, severity appeared to be strongly related to enforcement vigor (Thompson and Scicchitano, 1985). A later OSHA study suggested that problem severity was less important in explaining enforcement behavior. The researchers concluded that additional work was needed to account for unexplained state variance (Thompson and Scicchitano, 1987: 118).

Thus, the available evidence suggests that the role of severity of the problem is a potentially important predictor of the success of a state policy implementation. Future research is needed in additional areas, however, before any firm conclusions may be drawn with regard to the effects of severity level on state implementation.

Continued Attention to the Problem   Finally, the amount and continuity of media attention to the problem addressed by a statute are believed to be related to policy implementation (Sabatier and Mazmanian, 1980). Two recent studies have found that media attention given to the hazardous waste problem was a crucial determinant of policy activity (Levine, 1982; Kramer, 1983). Specifically, Levine suggests that media attention played a crucial role at Love Canal by pressuring key decision makers to formulate courses of action more rapidly than they would have without such pressure (1982: 191). Conversely, the absence of sustained media attention has been cited as a primary reason why state regulatory agencies and industrial groups in Texas operate in a political subsystem that works to prevent the enactment of more stringent hazardous waste policies (Kramer, 1983: 135).

The various works just cited support the argument that state ecological capacity variables strongly affect state policy implementation. The next section presents additional evidence in which we tested the plausibility of several hypothetical relationships between state ecological capacity variables, as well as other variables discussed in this book, and state policy implementation for hazardous waste programs.

PRELIMINARY FINDINGS ABOUT ECOLOGICAL CAPACITY

As a preliminary test of the role of state ecological capacity on state policy implementation, we gathered data from two sources. First, in July 1987, federal implementors were interviewed at the EPA in Washington, D.C. All the regional liaison staff in the Office of Solid Waste's

State Programs Branch were interviewed as well. These individuals over-see and coordinate federal-state relations in the area of hazardous waste (RCRA) policy implementation. The questions were open-ended and were designed to gather information relating to the factors that were believed to promote or inhibit RCRA implementation at the state level. Existing documents at EPA headquarters were reviewed to glean their evidence on the factors influencing the pace of RCRA implementation by the states.

The second source of data used to examine these propositions was a mail survey administered to all the fifty states' waste management pro-gram implementors. The survey was mailed to state implementors in mid-September 1987, and responses were received from forty-three of the fifty states (for an 86 percent response rate). One follow-up letter was mailed to the nonrespondents in late October 1987. The survey consisted of questions (both closed- and open-ended) directed to the following topics: the nature of the state's compliance; attitudes toward hazardous waste policy; perceptions of national policy; and state eco-logical capacity to implement RCRA.

Of the forty-three states responding to the survey, forty- two evalu-ated their implementation experiences with RCRA. Most of the states categorized their experience in implementing RCRA as strategic delay, with their delays used to enact modifications that help the state's chances of achieving goals under RCRA. Thirty percent (N = 13) reported that they promptly complied with RCRA and made no modifi-cations in the law's provisions.

A smaller group of states (N = 6) delayed implementation and made no modifications. One state (Wyoming) indicated that it did not intend to seek RCRA authorization, indicating "defiance." The styles of im-plementation indicated by state implementors were cross-checked with actual empirical data and found to be consistent with this behavior.[2] Thus, there was significant variation in terms of implementation styles across the fifty American states as far as RCRA was concerned.

Unexpected Results

The state ecological capacity portion of the questionnaire yielded some surprising findings. In earlier research, two of us found that state wealth (as measured by state spending for environmental programs) was significantly related to the speed of RCRA compliance (Lester and Bow-man, 1989). States that spent more on environmental quality control were more likely to have obtained authorization for their hazardous waste programs much sooner than those states that spent very little. We anticipated that the survey would reconfirm the significance of state ecological variables, including wealth.

Table 6.1   State Capacity and Implementation Style (Means)

Variables	Compliance	Strategic Delay	Delay	Defiance
Agency Consolidation*	2.92	2.68	3.00	3.00
FTEs (1984)	20.36	48.33	15.40	2.00
Budget Size (1984)	1.37‡	2.18	1.72	.10
Policy Analysis†	.23	.46	.17	.00
NPL Sites (1983)	4.60	13.90	8.20	1.00

*Respondents' indication that the state had a consolidated agency structure for managing hazardous waste.
†Percentage of respondents indicating that the state agency had a capability for conducting policy analysis for hazardous waste management.
‡In millions of dollars.

SOURCE: Survey by the authors.

Much to our surprise, the results indicated that state ecological capabilities were not important determinants of RCRA implementation during the 1984–1988 period. As Table 6.1 indicates, state personnel, fiscal resources, state organizational capability, and problem salience were not related to the style of implementation adopted by these forty-three states. These results are particularly surprising given the fact that the EPA has recently spent a great deal of time evaluating state capacity to implement RCRA. From the standpoint of these results, it appears that the nature of the relationship between federal and state implementors (especially the nature of the federal message) and state and local inducements and constraints (especially a supportive advocacy coalition) are more crucial to state policy implementation in the RCRA case than are state ecological capacity variables.

In comparing these findings with the personal interviews with EPA headquarters staff charged with oversight of the RCRA program, some interesting contrasts arise. The regional liaison staff in the Office of Solid Waste's State Programs Branch consistently stressed the capability of the states to implement RCRA as a crucial determinant of authorization. An area of concern for virtually all the staff was the ability of the states to retain qualified staff due to the low salary structure in the states. High turnover rates, "job burnout" due to stress, and inexperienced staff were often mentioned by EPA staff as key constraints at the state level. Another commonly reported constraint by the regional liaison staff was the scarcity of fiscal resources in the states to adequately fund the RCRA program.

Thus, taken together, the interviews with EPA regional liaison staff, the review of existing documents at EPA, and the mail surveys to state implementors suggest two very different perspectives on the RCRA authorization process and the role and influence of state ecological capacity. Federal EPA staff perceive that constraints such as state ecological capacity are a major hurdle to achieving state implementation. State implementors perceive the nature of the relationship between themselves and EPA (especially intergovernmental communications) as a primary constraint on state implementation.

Such divergent perspectives may have contributed in a very direct way to substantial delays in achieving RCRA implementation by the fifty states. In perceiving the problem very differently, each set of actors may have focused attention on entirely different aspects of RCRA implementation and simply miscommunicated in the process.

Limitations of the Results

A number of limitations associated with this analysis require elaboration. These findings may be limited by the manner in which implementation is measured. Implementation style is a useful measure, but other measures, such as "completeness" of implementation (Crotty, 1987) might have produced different findings, especially if a slower response to implementation is in fact a more "complete" or a qualitatively "better" response. Moreover, these results are limited to the time period under study (1984–1988). The usual constraints of cross-sectional analysis apply in this instance.

We probed the plausibility of our propositions with bivariate statistical techniques. Multivariate analysis might have produced very different results. Thus, until we are able to more systematically test the model of implementation presented in this book, it is difficult to ascertain whether these results are due to model misspecification or the absence of multivariate analysis.

Finally, the results just presented are limited to this policy area. The relative influence of state ecological capacity may well depend on the type of policy under investigation (Gormley, 1986; Lowi, 1964; Ripley and Franklin, 1982). That is, the process of distributive or redistributive policy implementation may be very different from that of regulatory policy implementation. Until other policy areas are explored systematically, the generalizability of these findings remains tentative.

To attempt to address this latter point, we also gathered data on waste-water treatment implementation. These results are also preliminary regarding several aspects of state ecological capacity. It appears that although economic and political capacity positively influence implementation style, state situational capacity is more problematic. States with more severe water problems (as indicated in Chapter 2) are not more likely to implement. Possibly, however, it is the *perception* of problem severity (influenced, in part, by media attention) that actually affects implementation. Data gathered at the local level suggest that in several cases efforts by local politicians and media outlets to dramatize water pollution problems are indeed related to the speed and extent of implementation efforts.

Focus of Future Research

Despite these mixed findings, we continue to expect state ecological capabilities (such as those discussed earlier) to be important determinants of state policy implementation. Our future work will examine the effects of state ecological capacity on state implementation of family planning services and on the implementation of municipal waste-water treatment facilities in greater depth and with the above considerations in mind. Chapter 8 outlines a proposed research plan that addresses the shortcomings of the plausibility probes that we initiated in this and previous chapters.

Future research that is longitudinal in nature, cross-policy in design, and based on rigorous statistical analysis should produce findings that are very different from those in this initial examination.[3] Nevertheless, the findings produced in this chapter (as well as the others in this book) are more important for what they have begun rather than what has been completed.

CONCLUSION

In combination, the work summarized in this chapter supports our hypothesized relationships between state ecological capacity and state policy implementation. Specifically, from a review of previous literature, we know that state policy implementation is related to four types of predictor variables: (1) state wealth; (2) severity of the problem; (3) political factors, such as partisanship, legislative professionalism, bureaucratic organization, or group pressures; and (4) political economy factors, such as business dominance of the economy or economic dependency of the state on the industry affected by the policy being implemented.

Our future research will examine the effects of state ecological capacity on the implementation of family planning services and municipal waste-water treatment services. Although the initial research results discussed in this chapter suggest the importance of state ecological capacity to state policy implementation, any firm conclusions must await additional investigation.

Nevertheless, future research in this area should address a number of questions. First, the research should determine which *category* of ecological variables has the most influence on policy implementation. Are contextual variables more important in explaining state policy implementation than variables concerned with wealth or politics? Second, studies should determine which *single* variables in a state's ecology are most important in affecting state policy implementation. Which variables are unimportant? Are important variables being omitted? Finally, research should identify the *interrelationships* between and among these variables. What are the interactive effects of these variables on policy implementation? These are the kinds of empirical questions that future research on state ecological capacity must address.

Notes for Chapter 6

1. In fact, some recent research (Lester, 1986; Davis and Lester, 1987) indicated that the states have not replaced federal grant-in-aid cuts with their own-source funds in the environmental area. See also Nathan et al. (1983; 1987).

2. That is, we compared their selected responses with extant data on exactly how long it has taken each state to receive primacy. These data are available from EPA's Office of Solid Waste, State Programs Branch.

3. Systematic, comparative, longitudinal analysis by Goggin (1987) suggests that state ecology factors are important determinants of the implementation of child health policy in the states.

CHAPTER SEVEN

Feedback and Policy Redesign

On April 22, 1988, the House Energy and Commerce Committee's Subcommittee on Health and the Environment held hearings on House Resolution (H.R.) 3769—the House bill to reauthorize the Title X family planning provisions of the Public Health Service Act. Each of three factions presented its view of what to do about the family planning program's reauthorization.

The first to be presented was the Reagan Administration view, articulated by Dr. Robert Windom, the assistant secretary of health at the Public Health Service. Based on the experiences of the Department of Health and Human Services (DH&HS) with administering the family planning program, Windom recommended recasting the current family planning project grant program into an authority for grants for state family planning programs. Although some of the existing law's provisions would remain intact in this new block grant, the prohibition on abortion and abortion-related activities contained in the current Title X would be clarified, presumably resulting in a more restrictive program.

A second view came from people who run family planning programs in the states. From their experiences with the program, family planning laws work, but they are underfunded. This group of providers essentially supported reauthorization of Title X, as laid out in H.R. 3769, and if anything, the group wished to see the authority expanded, not contracted.

A third perspective was expressed by what could be called a "pro-life" coalition, one member of which described the Title X program as unlawfully promoting abortion—"a program which rapes the mind of children, undermines family values, and operates without regard to community standards" (Gasper, 1988). Jo Ann Gasper, former Deputy Assistant Secretary for Population Affairs who was fired from her appointed position in 1988 for insubordination, wanted to see attached to the bill a pro-life amendment that would prohibit grantees from providing abortion counseling.

At least one of the others who testified on the "pro-life" panel also wanted to see program funding cut for fiscal year 1989, and the family planning services program eventually eliminated altogether (Schwartz, 1988). The arguments presented by members of this panel were also based on recent studies of the implementation of this program in various states.

In 1987, North Carolina passed a state siting law for the disposal of hazardous wastes that makes North Carolina more restrictive than the federal Resource Conservation and Recovery Act permits. By mid-1988, EPA had convened a task force to look into whether the North Carolina siting law was inconsistent with federal law and regulations. If inconsistent, federal rules would have to be changed, thus leading to a new interpretation of the law that would expand the scope of the program. If the rules were found to be inconsistent and the EPA decided to maintain the status quo, North Carolina and other states that have challenged the federal law by passing their own more restrictive laws would either have to rescind their laws or lose federal funding.

The family planning case is an example of policy redesign by amendment. The hazardous waste example is a case of redesign by rule change. Both cases illustrate an important nexus between policy implementation and policy redesign. That linkage suggests the need to examine closely the ways in which the various states' implementation experiences with existing policy are communicated to policymakers in Washington, and whether and how national political and administrative elites, or *sovereigns* (Downs, 1967; Mazmanian and Sabatier, 1983), act on that advice.

More importantly, the cases raise a number of important questions for examination in this chapter:

- Which particular implementation experiences in the states are communicated to policymakers and managers in Washington?
- How are these experiences communicated?
- How are error-detection messages or success stories received and acted on?
- To what extent do the states' implementation experiences inform policy redesign?
- How do policymakers and managers adapt to changing circumstances over time?
- How do they respond to unique circumstances in individual states?

This chapter develops a general theoretical argument that helps illuminate the patterns of influence between elites in the states that have already implemented a public policy and elites in Washington who have the authority to modify that policy, either by amending the existing statute or by changing rules and regulations. Variables about the communications system and the participants and collections of individuals in that system are specified to make empirically warrantable predictions relative to policy redesign, an important but understudied aspect of political and administrative behavior.

The chapter begins by clarifying the meaning of "policy redesign" and by discussing two aspects of responsiveness—listening and learning. The literature is reviewed for the purpose of developing a general theoretical argument consistent with our Communications Model of Intergovernmental Policy Implementation, culminating in an enumeration of a number of propositions. The final section of the chapter probes the plausibility of some of these connections, using the preliminary results of our study as well as the findings of others.

CONCEPTUAL CLARIFICATION

What is the meaning of "policy redesign," and what are its principal characteristics? Policy redesign is the process by which an existing policy is modified, either by amending an existing statute or by adopting new rules and regulations, or by both amendment and rule change (Brown, 1983; Goggin, 1988). For policy redesign to occur, there must be

1. an existing policy
2. some degree of dissatisfaction with that policy
3. communications from agents in the states—elected and appointed officials, often acting as intermediaries for organized interests, including clients and attentive publics who would be affected by either maintaining or changing the status quo—to principals in Washington
4. action in Congress and/or an executive branch agency in response to pressure from constituents in the states

At the core of the concept is a dynamic process much like the implementation process; and like the study of implementation, any study of the policy redesign process is essentially a study of communications—with one set of policymakers (or remakers in this case) at the center of a federal system either more or less responsive to the preferences of another set of actors at the periphery. The theoretical fountainhead is a theory of learning that is based on information processing, but because it is a theory of human behavior, the process is not orderly, boundless, or error-free.

In this chapter, the *degree* of responsiveness of national policymakers in the face of conflicting supports and demands from below is described and explained. The chapter's primary focus is on members of Congress and their attempts during 1988 to redesign the family planning provisions in Title X of the Public Health Service Act. Responsiveness, therefore, is described in terms of what a Congressional office does or does not do about family planning services information acquisition, processing, and use.

Listening and learning compose specific aspects of Congressional behavior that constitute responsiveness. In the context of listening, a lawmaker can

- give no weight to messages (not listen)
- give unequal weight to messages (listen selectively)
- give equal weight to all messages (listen attentively)

Apparently, *not* listening may have cost one U.S. senator his job. Near the end of his 1988 contest with liberal Democrat Mike Lowry to try to recapture the U.S. Senate seat that he lost to Brock Adams in 1986, former Republican Senator Slade Gordon admitted that he had made some mistakes on key votes. In his words, "I needed to listen more" (Egan, 1989).

A Congressperson can listen (even to all points of view) and still fail to learn. On the other hand, learning can take place and have one of at least two possible consequences. Learning can result in a change of position on an issue, or it can have a confirmatory effect, leading to even stronger convictions. In terms of learning, then, a member of Congress or her or his staff can

- fail to learn (no learning)
- learn and change position (called *disconfirming learning*)
- learn and maintain position (called *corroborative learning*)

The question remains: How can the degree of responsiveness of any one Congressperson or Congressional office best be determined?

Besides conducting a controlled experiment, perhaps the best way to tell whether a member of Congress is listening to or learning from all messages, just some of them, or no messages at all is to combine subjective evaluations based on face-to-face interviews with direct observations of his or her behavior. Here, subjective evaluation means asking the Congressperson questions about the two-way communications between the Congressional office and influential people and organizations, either in Washington or back home in the district or state.

For example, a few of the questions actually used in interviews with members of Congress and their staffs in our study were "When you considered possible changes in the current Title X family planning law, whose advice did you actively solicit to help you make a decision about policy redesign?" and "Which organizations and individuals are most active in providing you with unsolicited information and advice about redesigning family planning reauthorization legislation?" With respect to subjective assessments of the nature and scope of learning, Congresspersons and staff were asked, "Can you think of a report on family planning or abortion that you have seen lately that has really impressed you?" If the person being interviewed named a report, then he or she was asked, "What have you learned from this report?"

Direct observations might include a close examination of the record, for example, behavior of Congresspersons during the public hearings (Boynton and Kim, 1988) or during roll-call voting (Clausen, 1973). A shift in position—signaled by a change in the form and content of debates about provisions in various alternative amendments during committee hearings or by a change in vote—might indicate true learning. This is especially true if it could be established from a perusal of appointment calendars, interviews with lobbyists, or from other sources of new information to which the member was exposed just prior to the opinion conversion.[1] Stronger positions on abortion over a period of years, for example, could be gleaned from a close, systematic examination of changes in the language used by a Congressperson during Congressional debate or changes in the type of questions a committee member might use to query those testifying at committee hearings.

HOW MEMBERS OF CONGRESS BEHAVE: A REVIEW

Any understanding of policy redesign hinges on a grasp of the patterns of power and influence that characterize top-down and bottom-up communications in the U.S. federal government system, and how these communications patterns shape the decisions of Congresspersons. Recent literature on bureaucratic behavior suggests that national sovereigns—the legislative committees and the executive branch agencies who have jurisdiction over a particular policy—control people and organizations at the subnational level of government in the federal system (Bendor and Moe, 1985; Chubb, 1985; Moe, 1985; Wood, 1988). This principal-agent theory posits that control is hierarchical and predictable. Thomas Anton (1984) has even claimed that centralization at the federal level of government in recent years has allowed states and localities little initiative and virtually no control.

Principal-agent studies invariably take a top-down perspective and examine the effects of principal power over and influence on agents. This chapter, however, turns the relationship on its head by examining the ability of agents at the periphery of the federal system to influence national policymakers. Rather than looking for the conditions under which hierarchical control effectively shapes agency results in subnational units of government, we seek to identify the conditions under which those who implement public policy shape—through the policy redesign process—the form and content of a new, reformulated public policy. The emphasis in this chapter, then, is on the feedback loop that is an integral part of implementation explicated in the Communications Model shown in Figure 1.1.

With that feedback loop in mind, there are five conditions that theoretically favor responsiveness on the part of members of the House, Senators, and their staffs in Washington to agents' demands for the redesign of existing policy. The type and degree of principal responsiveness to pressure from agents varies systematically and predictably with these conditions. Before turning to a discussion of those five conditions, however, the chapter gives a brief overview of the nature of individuals and collections of individuals, and of the way these key actors and organizations process information to decide whether and how to redesign an existing policy.

Exerting Two-way Control Between Agents and Principals

First, principals in Washington not only control agents in the states from the top down, but are also influenced or controlled by these state agents from the bottom up (see Chapters 3 and 4; Scholz and Wei, 1986). In fact, decision makers are bombarded with a variety of opinions about the workings of an existing program, this variety reflecting a diversity of interests and motives not only across but also within Congressional districts and states. It is assumed, therefore, that the preferences of state and local elites vary among agents and agencies.

Furthermore, the goals of the national government and the goals of individual states often conflict. What is in the best interest of the nation is not always in the best interest of an individual state. As Chapter 4 revealed, when the DH&HS Office of Population Affairs administrators' goal of limiting the counseling activities of clinic workers conflicted with clinic workers' desire to maintain their autonomy, the preferences of national principals did not coincide with the preferences of state and local agents. Indeed, conflict of interest is one of the pathologies of principal-agent relations, a condition exacerbated by increases in bureaucratic discretion.

Assessing Information and Alternatives

Second, as an information-processing and problem-solving set of activities, the policy redesign process proceeds in three stages:

1. *searching* for information about the performance of an existing policy
2. *estimating* the expected consequences of alternative ways of redesigning the policy versus maintaining the status quo or terminating the policy altogether
3. *choosing* among competing alternatives (Braybrooke and Lindblom, 1963; Whiteman, 1985)

Role of Nonpolicy Factors

Third, despite the general pattern of search, estimation, and choice, the individuals and organizations in Washington who are the targets of influence from agents in the states do not always act rationally. The main reasons for this irrational action are that the individuals and organizations have merely human cognitive abilities, adapt and adjust to the changing political and economic environment, and act instrumentally in their own or their organization's self-interest (Braybrooke and Lindblom, 1963; Cyert and March, 1963; March and Simon, 1958; Simon, 1957).

Examining Alternatives

Fourth, individuals process information, evaluate choices, and make policy redesign decisions by relying on some combination of

- calculations of expected costs and benefits of alternative choices
- preferences of reference groups
- core values (Kuklinski, Metlay, and Kay, 1982)

Richard Smith (1984) describes the cost/benefit calculation as an interpretive process, where legislators simplify the decision task into two stages. First, they construct scenarios of the many ways in which alternatives may affect citizens, institutions, and their own chances of reelection. Second, members relate these interpretations to their own personal goals.

Some of the best empirical research on Congressional decision making has shown that lawmakers take their cues from reference groups that are both internal and external to Congress. These internal and external cue-givers include constituents, other Congresspersons, party leaders, interest groups, the president, and the executive branch agencies (Clausen, 1973; Kingdon, 1973; Matthews and Stimson, 1970).

The key questions, then, become, "To whom are elected and appointed officials responsive?" and "How representative are the choices of elites?" In the last analysis, most elites tend to listen to and speak for those who share their world views: core values—in the form of an operational code—tend to color the way a decision maker searches for and processes information (George, 1970).

Nevertheless, the nature of individuals and organizations and limits on their cognitive abilities are not the only factors affecting listening and learning behavior and, thus, responsiveness among policymakers in Washington. Theoretical and empirical research on the acquisition, communications, and use of knowledge suggests that policy redesign behavior also varies systematically and predictably with the

- reputation and status of the agents who are seeking to redesign the existing policy
- credibility of an agent's persuasive communications
- channels of communications that are used
- characteristics of individuals; constituent group; and, in the case of legislators, electorate of Congresspersons who are the targets of communications

Now the discussion turns to the expected relationships between the various components of an agent-principal model of policy redesign.

EXPLAINING RESPONSIVENESS

The policy redesign or feedback component of the Communications Model that is presented here posits that the degree of responsiveness on the part of the Congressperson and his or her staff varies systematically and predictably with both the nature of the political communications system, and characteristics of the individual decision maker and her or his environment. In the propositions that follow, the phenomenon to be explained is operationalized as the extent to which principals listen to and act on the communicated preferences of agents. Measures of responsiveness are determined by coding responses to items in an interview schedule used in face-to-face interviews with Congresspersons and their staffs and by observing their behavior. A more detailed discussion of operationalization, measurement, and sources of data can be found in Chapter 8.

The Role of Agents

Agents are political or administrative elites, for example, state governors and legislators, city mayors, or state and regional program managers who have experience with the implementation of an existing policy in at least one of the American states. They have either been asked or have voluntarily chosen to communicate that experiential knowledge to decision makers in Washington. Agents can also be the people (or their advocates) who are affected by program change, for example, program clients or service providers.

In the eyes of the targets of their communications, each agent has a degree of influence and control, the amount of influence being a function of his or her reputation and standing as a constituent. An agent's status depends on that agent's reputation, as perceived by the principals (sovereigns) (McGuire, 1973). An agent's importance as a constituent depends on the individual sovereign's assessment of the agent's capacity to advance the individual or organizational goals of the Congressperson in Washington who is the target of communications.

Hence, one expects policymakers in Washington to be much more likely to listen to and learn from agents in the states if these agents are perceived as legitimate and credible as well as capable of advancing the interests of the principal. The degree of responsiveness is influenced not only by the type of agent who makes contact with the policymaker in Washington, but also by the type of agency he or she represents.

The Role of Agencies

Agencies are the organizations with which agents are affiliated. For policy redesign, an agency can be a state political party, a committee in the state legislature, or a state bureaucracy such as California's Office of Family Planning, each acting on behalf of clients within the state. For family planning services, an agency could also be a national organization representing the interests of service providers, an advocate for poor women who are not being served by the Title X program, or a group of antiabortionists.

In the eyes of the targets of their communications, each agency has a degree of influence, the amount of influence being a function of the agency's reputation in the eyes of the recipients of agency communications. Reputation is a function of the collective expertise, skill, and capacity the agency possesses, the agency's ability to mobilize political support for or opposition to a policy, the organization's commitment to principals' goals, and the leadership of the organization (Kaufman, 1981). Thus, one expects to find that where, in the eyes of members of the Congressional office, the agency's collective expertise, skill, and capacity to advance the goals of the principal are high, the degree of principal responsiveness will also be high.

The Role of Messages

Messages are either written or verbal communications that express the sentiments of elites in the states. Such messages are directed to Congressional offices in Washington for the purpose of persuading decision makers to a point of view. These bottom-up communications occur for the express purpose of influencing the policymaker to do nothing, terminate a policy, or redesign it to correspond to the preferences of the sender of the message.

At the most fundamental level, messages must be received and understood (McGuire, 1973). Understanding is enhanced by a message's form—its clarity, internal consistency, and credibility as a politically, economically, and technically viable solution to a serious problem (Caplan, 1976). Moreover, the communications literature consistently shows that messages that conform to a recipient's preexisting positions are more easily accepted by the target of communications. Thus, assuming a convergence of interest between the sender and target of a message, clear, consistent, credible messages are much more likely to gain the attention of the recipients.

Studies of communications patterns also demonstrate that the channel selected to communicate messages is important. *Channels of communications* can be either formal or informal. Formal, bottom-up communications that can be used to get an individual or organizational point across include testimony at hearings and investigations, periodic program reviews and reports, letters and memoranda, and personal visits to Congressional offices.

One of the most effective means of communicating information to Washington is formal policy analysis and demonstration projects, both of which are aspects of the policy evaluation process. Besides formal channels, agents frequently employ informal means in order to get their points of view across. These communications include personal contacts, telephone calls, informal understandings and agreements, and comments during hearings.

An agent's views can also be channeled indirectly to decision makers, for example, through intermediaries such as fellow legislators, professional associations, lobbyists, or contacts in the White House and the agency. Committee staff or organizations such as the National Governors' Association or the Family Planning and Reproductive Health Association are also used as channels to transmit points of view to sovereigns. Most students of Congressional behavior point to personalized communications as the most effective way of getting a hearing.

One expects that the more personalized are the channels of communications used by agents, the more responsive will be the principal.

The Role of the Principal

Thus far, three components of the communications process—senders, their messages, and the channels they use to communicate their likes and dislikes—have been examined. But perhaps the most important element is the target of communications, in this case the principal. *Principals* are those elected officials in Washington (and their staffs) who are the object of all kinds of communications from their constituents. Communications originate with lobbyists; with political and administrative elites such as the governor, mayors of cities in the district, state legislators, and bureaucrats in the states; and with ordinary citizens. Each Congressional office has a set of individual-level and district-level attributes, some of which ought to influence the manner in which the Congressperson approaches the search, evaluation, and choice processes related to the redesign of an existing policy.

The individual-level variables that are likely to be important are

- prior position on the issue, as reflected in the representative's voting record
- core beliefs (ideological predisposition)
- political party affiliation
- extent of knowledge of and interest in the policy being redesigned
- number of years in a state- or local-level public office

Electoral factors affect listening and learning behavior as well (Caplan, 1976; Kovenoch, 1973; Webber, 1984). The most important such factor is the degree to which the district is competitive. Based on a number of studies, the expectation is that the most responsive principals are those, then, whose political party, ideology, and psychological predisposition toward redesigning the policy match the state governor's, whose expertise on the policy being reconsidered is limited, who have had experience as a state- or local-level elected or appointed official, and who are from competitive districts.

These propositions represent attempts to specify the circumstances under which members of Congress and their staffs are likely to act favorably on the preferences of people who matter at the subnational level of government in the U.S. federal system. In an ideal world, researchers could assign reliable values to the independent and dependent variables, and the policy redesign model could predict the degree of responsiveness on the part of principals. Although no attempt to discuss the specifics of testing the hypotheses derived from the model is made here, results of a recent ongoing study of the redesign of the Title X family planning services program does provide a basis for making judgments about the plausibility of some of the theoretical propositions. Such judgments encompass those that relate to *listening* on the part of Congresspersons and their staffs.[2] The results of a probe of the plausibility of propositions about the *learning* dimension of responsiveness are included in another report (Goggin, unpublished manuscript).

THE PRACTICE OF POLICY REDESIGN: THE FAMILY PLANNING CASE

The findings summarized in the following case are based on interviews with eight of the eighteen Congresspersons who sit on the House Energy and Commerce Committee's Subcommittee on Health and the Environment and sixteen staff members who specialize in family planning issues. These legislators and aides are from sixteen of the eighteen member offices (88.9 percent) represented on the subcommittee. For purposes of this study, the Congressional office is the unit of analysis. The data used to probe the plausibility of propositions about the *listening* aspects of responsiveness are drawn primarily from responses to both open-ended and structured questions on an interview schedule that was used during 1988 in face-to-face interviews with these twenty-four legislators and their staffs. Hearings transcripts and sources of biographical information such as *The Book of the States, Vital Statistics of Congress, 1987–88,* and *The Almanac of American Politics* were also consulted.

In general, one would expect to find a significant number of policymakers responsive to all points of view on any given issue, but in the case of family planning, Congresspersons or staff of only three Congressional offices represented on the Energy and Commerce Committee's Subcommittee on Health and the Environment listened attentively to every point of view. The vast majority of the people in subcommittee members' offices either ignored messages from agents from their states and districts or selectively perceived only those messages that conformed to the Congressperson's existing preferences. Table 7.1 summarizes the types of responses.

As Table 7.1 shows, nine of the sixteen subcommittee members' offices included in the study ignored what agents in their districts and states, as well as groups such as pro-life and pro-choice advocates based in Washington, had to say. Typically, members justified their listening behavior by referring to the issue as a matter of principle. As one aide put it, "He's against abortion on principle, and that's how he's going to vote, regardless of what his constituents want."

Table 7.1 Degree of Responsiveness Among
House Member Offices (In Percent)

Type	Percentage(N)
Ignores Messages	56.2(9)
Seletively Perceives Messages	25.0(4)
Listens to All Messages	18.7(3)
	100.0(16)

SOURCE: Face-to-face interviews with Congresspersons on the House Energy and Commerce Committee's Subcommittee on Health and the Environment and their aides.

Congresspersons or staffs of another four offices paid attention only to new information that fit with their current position on the issue. One influential Congressperson on the committee felt that responsiveness on this issue was tied less to the preferences of the people back home than to partisan party politics:

> The debate shifted when Republicans decided to embrace the pro-life position. What is different about Republicans is that they are much more loyal than Democrats to their party. The loyal Republicans have followed the party line and voted the pro-life position. So there are few Republicans on the committee—of course there are a few notable exceptions like Senator Weickert—who are willing to stand up and support the pro-choice position.

Thus, in more than eight out of every ten cases, a member's office failed to listen to all sides of the issue. This is because most of these members and their staffs had already made up their minds on the question of the need for family planning services and the related issue of abortion counseling. Moreover, although the facts were difficult to quantify, it was apparent from these and other interviews with members of the family planning establishment in Washington that in many cases lobbyists just quit contacting the offices of members who disagreed with them, as reflected in the members' voting records on family planning issues.

Indeed, there was little variance in listening patterns from one member office to the next: Most offices represented on the subcommittee either had no meaningful contact with outsiders or kept in close contact with only those people from the states or from Washington-based pro-choice or pro-life groups who shared their world view. Nevertheless, there were some exceptions. One of the mavericks on the committee, who is not considered one of the extremists on family planning matters, was described by his legislative assistant as a Congressperson who "starts with a moral position." Yet, according to his legislative assistant,

The Congressman's position is that the federal government should not restrict resources for family planning services. I talk with family planning advocates, with the people who provide family planning services in the state. If you look at the Congressman's voting record, you would say that he is pro-choice. But you will also see that he has not voted 100 percent pro-choice. Family planning and abortion are very difficult issues for him to talk about. We have come up with a standard letter to send to people when they ask about the issue, though. . . . His position hasn't influenced who comes to see him. For example, the liberal groups come in, and just last week the Students for Pro-Life were here to see him. . . . But we don't exclude any information or any point or view. Whoever wants to see him can get in to see him.

Using the propositions that are derived from our model of policy redesign as a guide, comparisons can be made of the listening practices of the typical subcommittee member or her or his staff (a nonlistener) with those of selective listeners and the handful of more open-minded Congresspersons and staff who tend to listen attentively to a full range of views on family planning and the related issue of abortion. The first issue to address is where most members of the House Energy and Commerce Committee's Subcommittee on Health and Environment and their aides turn for information and counsel when it comes to family planning and abortion-related issues.

Reputation of Agents and Agencies

Another way of posing this issue is to ask about the reputations of agents who have information on these issues that they would like to share with federal lawmakers. One way to infer reputation is to determine the extent to which the principal and his or her staff call upon that agent for advice. When members and legislative aides identified the people from whom they actively solicited advice on family planning matters, the most frequently mentioned (N = 15) source of information was "no one." This was followed by "lobbyists in Washington" (N = 9), and "service providers in the state" (N = 3).

These responses serve as an indicator of *active* listening, with most members of Congress apparently relying on their own resources for cues about how to vote on the reauthorization of funding for Title X, for example. But when advocates were asked to name the people and organizations who most frequently sought them out, which indicates *passive* listening on the part of the Congressperson, the advocates either for or against the reauthorization of Title X who were mentioned most often were not from the states at all. The most frequent response was "no one" (N = 17). Among the intermediaries—the pro-choice and pro-life organizations, for example—the ones who were apparently most active on Capitol Hill, at least among the staffs of subcommittee members' offices that were included in this study, were Planned Parenthood (N = 9), the Alan Guttmacher Institute (N = 5), the National Family Planning and Reproductive Health Association (N = 4), and The National Right to Life Committee (N = 2).

Members and their staffs were also asked to identify the sources of information that they considered *reliable*. Again, consistent with the findings already cited, most Congresspersons and their aides could not name a specific source of reliable information. The most frequently mentioned source of reliable information about family planning issues was the Congressional Research Service (CRS), which was mentioned by only six of the twenty-four people interviewed. Other sources that were also considered reliable for unbiased information about family planning and abortion questions are the Government Accounting Office (N = 5) and the Office of Technology Assessment (N = 3).

Those people in the Congressional offices who were classified as more open-minded on the basis of responses to items on the interview schedule tended to mention these information-generating agencies more often, compared to the offices with nonlisteners or selective listeners. But even these nonpartisan government agencies came under attack when their findings did not conform to the stated preferences of members of Congress. One member aide talked about the Office of Technology Assessment as "the devil's workshop," and a Congressperson characterized several sources of information on family planning issues as "biased."

What these findings on reputation show is that many Congresspersons and their aides are skeptical about the objectivity of informational material that is distributed by interest groups, whether the group supports or opposes continuation and expansion of the Title X family planning program. Although the most frequently mentioned interested parties were the intermediaries that make up the family planning establishment in Washington, the vast majority relied on no one but themselves (and in a few cases, close family members) for information and advice. As Table 7.2 shows, low prestige cuts across all types of subcommittee member offices, from offices where messages are ignored to offices that listen to all messages.

Table 7.2 relates agency and agent reputation in the eyes of Congresspersons and their aides to responsiveness. Only six of the sixteen subcommittee member offices portrayed all agents as highly reputable, with a majority of Congresspersons and staff in those offices characterizing at least some of the messengers in the states and localities or their agents in Washington as either not reliable or not credible as sources of information. The responses reported in Table 7.2 show that *credibility* is a term that is used sparingly with this issue, with only the most committed pro-choice or pro-life members willing to depend on

Table 7.2   Agent/Agency Reputation by Type of Member Office (In Percent)

Reputation	Type of Member Office		
	Ignores Messages	*Selectively Perceives Messages*	*Listens to All Messages*
High	33.3(3)	50.0(2)	33.3(1)
Low	66.7(6)	50.0(2)	66.7(2)
	100.0(9)	100.0(4)	100.0(3)

SOURCE: Face-to-face interviews with Congresspersons on the House Energy and Commerce Committee's Subcommittee on Health and the Environment and their aides.

agents for "reliable" information on the issues. As a result, many sub-committee member offices either turned to no one or relied on a single source for reliable information, usually a source that shared the member's view on the issue.

Channels of Communications

Because issues of family planning and abortion services—especially if discussed with teenagers in school-based clinics—are emotional, tend to be formed early in a Congressperson's career, and are firmly held, most Congresspersons and their professional staff do not have an open mind on these issues. Nonetheless, lobbyists use a variety of techniques to convince a member either to hold to her or his position (if in agreement with the lobby's position) or to change position (if not in agreement). But how do those who are interested in persuading a Congressperson to "vote their way" get their message across? What is the most effective channel of communications?

A variety of channels were used in contacting members of the Subcommittee on Health and the Environment and their staff. Methods included testimony at hearings, letters and phone calls, and personal visits to the district or Washington office. Most member offices reported that the personalized approach to communications works best; most emphasized the importance of appeals from individuals who reside in either the member's district or state. A few members or their aides mentioned the benefits of preparing a written "executive summary" of major points and key arguments to support the positions.

As a check on this, six lobbyists who are considered part of the family planning services establishment in the Washington, D.C. area were also interviewed. All agreed with what their targets of communications had to say about effective channels of communications; all agreed that there was no substitute for a personal office visit.

Table 7.3 Individual-Level and District-Level Attributes
by Type of Member Office (In Percent)

Attribute	Type of Member Office		
	Ignores Messages (N = 9)	Selectively Perceives Messages (N = 4)	Listens to All Messages (N = 3)
Ideology Agreement*	55.5(5)	50.0(2)	66.7(2)
Party Agreement*	55.5(5)	75.0(3)	66.7(2)
Expertise[†]	44.4(4)	75.0(3)	33.3(1)
Experience[‡]	66.7(6)	100.0(4)	33.3(1)
Safe Seat[‡]	22.2(2)	50.0(2)	66.7(2)

SOURCES
*For Governors, biographies in Michael Barone and Grant Ujifusa, *The Almanac of American Politics, 1988*. Washington, D.C.: National Journal Inc., 1987; for Congresspersons, ADA and ACU ratings for 1984, 1985, and 1986 in Alan Ehrenhalt, Renée Amrine, and Philip D. Duncan, eds., *Politics in America—The 100th Congress*. Washington, D.C.: Congressional Quarterly Inc., 1987.
[†]Based on opinion of a panel of experts.
[‡]Ehrenhalt, Amrine, Duncan, eds., *Politics in America—The 100th Congress*. Washington, D.C.: Congressional Quarterly Inc., 1987.

Table 7.3 summarizes the findings on the relationship between individual-level attributes and degree of responsiveness. At least in the case of family planning issues, a Congressional office's search, estimation, and choice behavior is apparently not affected by the degree of fit between the Congressperson's and the state governor's party identification or ideology. There were just about as many offices ignoring messages where there was no match (N = 4) as there were when there was a match (N = 5). Likewise, experts on family planning—those who were considered by a panel of experts to devote considerable attention to the issue and who considered it important—were just as likely to ignore messages as they were to either selectively perceive them or listen to all of them.

On the question of experience, we expected those with previous experience in state or local government to be more likely to listen to messages, but the opposite turned out to be the case. Of the eleven offices of Congresspersons who had previous experience in state government, only one person listened to all points of view; six ignored messages from states and districts and acted on their own strong feelings about family planning and abortion.

Table 7.3 also shows the relationship between the degree of competitiveness of a member's district and his or her degree of responsiveness to messages from the district or state. Our policy redesign model predicted that members who held safe seats would be more likely to ignore messages. The data show the contrary: Members with safe seats were *less,* not more, likely to ignore their constituents.

Six members of the subcommittee held safe seats; ten Congresspersons were from districts where the margin of victory in the last election had been less than 20 percent. Two of the six members who held safe seats (33.3 percent) ignored messages, whereas seven of the ten Congresspersons from competitive districts (70 percent) ignored messages from the state on this issue.

CONCLUSION

Theoretical and empirical research using principal-agent theory suggests that federal sovereigns control agents hierarchically, leaving states and localities little initiative and virtually no control. In this chapter, principal-agent theory has been turned on its head: The agent-principal approach taken in this chapter assumes that agents do have control—that principals are responsive to agents' demands and supports.

An argument was presented that specifies the conditions that favor responsiveness on the part of Congresspersons and agency officials in Washington to demands for the redesign of existing policy from elites in the states. It was thought that the degree of principal responsiveness to pressure from agents would vary systematically and predictably with (1) the reputation and status of the actors who are seeking to redesign the existing policy; (2) the form and content of these agents' communications; (3) the channels of communications; and (4) the interests, motives, experiences, attitudes, and beliefs, as well as individual-level, constituent, and electoral characteristics of the legislators and executives who are the target of communications.

The most striking finding is that in the case of family planning and abortion, Congresspersons and staffs of only three of sixteen offices of the House Energy and Commerce Committee's Subcommittee on Health and the Environment represented in this study listened to all points of view. Most Congresspersons and staffs interviewed either listened selectively or not at all. Moreover, the variables that were identified as capable of explaining differences in policy redesign behavior across subcommittee offices were not much help. Rather than responding to agents in the states who were trying to communicate their experiences with the family planning program, the vast majority of members were motivated by their own personal views on this emotional issue.

These findings may be peculiar to issues like family planning where personal conviction is paramount. Whether ignoring messages on the part of members and their staffs is common to other types of issues as well can only be determined by a comparative study of the redesign of policies of different types. One approach to answering this question might be to compare the listening behavior described above to the responsiveness of these same members to a fact-based issue like clean air, also an issue that has been recently considered as a candidate for redesign by members of the subcommittee.

For the most part, Congresspersons and staffs of most Congressional offices represented on the subcommittee neither found lobbyists to be reliable sources of information nor paid much attention to sources that espoused a point of view that was contrary to a Congressperson's prior voting record on family planning issues. Several interviewees challenged conventional wisdom that CRS, GAO, and OTA were credible sources of unbiased information, and many looked only to sources of information that would "bolster" a preconceived view of the success or failure of the program or the appropriate role of government in the provision of family planning services and abortion counseling. Finally, although a number of members of the subcommittee said they wished to avoid having to vote on Title X reauthorization or on the issues of school-based clinics or parental consent just prior to the 1988 election, even those subcommittee members from competitive districts ignored messages from their districts. They did so on the grounds that they had already made up their minds, and not much in the way of policy analysis was going to change their votes on this issue.

Notes to Chapter 7

1. There is a strong bias toward maintaining positions on key issues, however. Members of Congress who "flip-flop" on issues are subject to ridicule by opponents in the next election, a situation that is best illustrated by Republican candidate Ronald Reagan's attack on President Jimmy Carter in the 1980 presidential election campaign.

2. The paucity of cases makes even a tentative conclusion problematic. What is needed is a structured-focused comparison of cases; policy redesign permits an increase in the number of cases and a decrease in the number of variables. An author of this book is currently carrying out such a research project.

CHAPTER EIGHT

A Third-Generation Design for Research

As noted in previous chapters, first-generation research on policy implementation is concerned with detailed accounts of how a single authoritative decision was carried out, either at a single location or at multiple sites. Second-generation research is concerned with the development of analytical frameworks to guide research on implementation. The principal aim of third-generation research is to shed new light on implementation behavior by explaining why that behavior varies across time, across policies, and across units of government and by predicting the type of implementation behavior that is likely to occur in the future. In a word, the objective of third-generation research is simply to be more *scientific* in its approach to the study of why implementing actors make the decisions and take the actions they do.

If the study of policy implementation is to advance to this next generation, however, researchers must test theory as well as develop it. To do so requires that investigators have an explicit theoretical framework, that they generate hypotheses to be tested, that dependent and explanatory variables be operationalized, and that the necessary data be collected and carefully analyzed, both comparatively and longitudinally.

This chapter summarizes the hypotheses that are derived from the Communications Model of Intergovernmental Policy Implementation that was introduced in Chapter 1. The plausibility of the Communications Model was supported by the findings of others' studies as well as our own comparative research, as reported in Chapters 2 through 7. This chapter examines techniques for measuring the dependent and explanatory variables and explores possible sources of data and methods of data collection. Then the chapter describes some alternative techniques of analysis that could be employed in third-generation research. The chapter is meant primarily as a guide to those who are thinking about undertaking a third-generation research project. The suggestions about research design and the specific recommendations for executing such a design are only meant to illustrate this more scientific approach to the study of implementation.

THE COMMUNICATIONS MODEL AND ITS HYPOTHESES

The Communications Model presented in Figure 1.1 is conceptualized as a "candidate" theory (Eckstein, 1975) capable of predicting and explaining state-level implementation processes, outputs, and outcomes. The Communications Model is also capable of specifying the conditions under which various state implementation decisions and actions about the timing of implementation and change in program form and content during implementation are likely to occur. But before this discussion addresses the more specific issues of what precisely the nature of implementation behavior is and what "styles" apply to implementation, a more general approach to measuring implementation behavior longitudinally and comparatively needs to be outlined.

Two of the most confounding issues for those who study implementation are first, determining exactly when a policy can be considered implemented[1] and second, adopting a consistent strategy for measuring implementation variables in anticipation of testing hypotheses.[2] These issues are especially critical when researchers contemplate theory construction and validation. As a general rule, the manner in which variables are operationalized and the data collected is dictated by an investigator's research objectives and the theoretical perspective that she or he brings to the study.

The approach to measurement that is adopted here is deceptively simple: The concepts making up state implementation are operationalized using multiple, functionally specific indicators. Theoretically relevant categories are created for each variable, and both subjective and objective measures are used to assign values.

To arrive at more reliable measures and to minimize random measurement error, we recommend combining multiple indicators into a number of indexes.[3] For all indexes, the critical measurement issues are the actual assignment of values and the detection of changes in those values over time. Potential problems can be minimized by

- approaching measurement systematically
- using multiple, independent sources to achieve the least biased assignment of values to the components
- convening a panel of experts to aid in their construction
- being sensitive to the dynamics of political communications and state and local politics

These are the general guidelines that inform measurement of the three dependent variables outlined in the Communications Model and discussed in detail in this chapter. The same principle guides our discussion of other components of the model, as laid out in earlier chapters. Next, the specifics of the model are assessed.

Dependent Variables: Implementation Process, Outputs, and Outcomes

Recall that implementation is assumed to involve a number of related activities, such as

- passing state enabling legislation and administrative rules
- appropriating resources
- monitoring, enforcement, and redesign

All such activities are directed toward putting a policy in place at a number of sites over a period of time. Now one can visualize each of the related implementation activities as an occasion for delay and/or modification. Each provides a unique opportunity for elites to make known their views about what the state—or any other implementing unit—should do with regard to implementation. Given these attributes, variation in implementation is conceptualized along a two-dimensional continuum from outright defiance to compliance, with two types of delay—one simple and the other strategic—in the middle of the continuum. Because the model is dynamic, it is possible to track changes in the status of implementation from one time period to the next.

The fourteen- to twenty-year implementation period for the three policies examined in this book encompasses a set of discrete implementation activities that occur during the life of each program. At any time a number of factors combine to produce a specific implementation-related result. At its simplest, in any one year, implementation occurred (scored as a 1) or it did not (scored as a 0). If implementation were that simple, state implementation behavior could be described dichotomously. However, the implementation process is far more subtle. Examining each of the segments probably shows movement between the extremes of "no implementation" and "implementation."

A continuum is incorporated in our suggested measures of the dependent variables. On the basis of a historical reconstruction of what actually happened over the life of each program, an assessment is made at each stage of the process and a value is assigned based on the value of its elements. For example, on a four-point scale, a variable would be assigned a value of 0 (indicating defiance); 0.33 (indicating delay); 0.67 (indicating strategic delay); or 1 (indicating compliance) whenever any one of the implementation activities occurred. Such a measurement scheme tracks the ups and downs of the implementation process over time. If a researcher wishes, she or he can calculate a summary implementation score for each state over a ten- to twenty-year period.

It is vital to remember that implementation as a process must be distinguished from implementation as the results of that process. Following convention, implementation results are categorized as either outputs or outcomes, with measures peculiar to each policy. Because any investigator who is doing cross-policy research is unlikely to find identical measures for each policy, she or he must search for *functionally* equivalent measures for each.

Our comparative study employed annual state expenditures—in either absolute or per capita amounts—as the indicator of outputs. Chapter 2 examined these measures across policies, across states, and over time. As noted in that chapter, it is exceedingly difficult to define expected outcomes and find adequate measures, especially for hazardous waste management and clean water. In the case of waste-water treatment, some rough measures might be the percentage of river miles and lake acres that meet their designated use requirements.

For family planning, considerable controversy surrounds the issue of how desired programmatic outcomes should be defined and operationalized. Whether one sees the goal of the program as a reduction in the number of unplanned births or as a reduction in the rate of unplanned pregnancies dictates the choice of outcome measures. If the most desirable outcome is reduction in births, public health statistics on the number of live births apply; if a reduction in pregnancies is the principal goal, then the rate of abortion, or the number of pregnancies per 1000 "at-risk" women, might be the most appropriate indicator.

Independent Variables: Federal-Level Inducements and Constraints

The Communications Model suggests a number of hypotheses for testing. For simplicity, each hypothesis describes an implementation activity based on all other factors being equal and assumes implementation of a sound policy solution to a recognized problem. The first set of hypotheses (designated throughout the chapter by H and consecutive numbers) is drawn from Chapter 3 and concerns the role of messages and their senders in national government. Depending on their attributes, the messages and their senders can act as either a federal-level inducement or constraint on implementing behavior:

H1: If federally initiated messages are (a) accompanied by resources; (b) credible as a viable solution to a salient problem for that state; (c) clear; (d) consistent; (e) frequently repeated; and (f) actually received, the actors who make the joint decision for the state are more likely to opt for prompt implementation without modifications.

H2: The more legitimate and credible the federal senders of messages, or principals, in the eyes of state officials, the more likely the state's implementation is to proceed promptly and without modifications.

Measuring Policy Content Chapter 3 covered the aspects of message content that are important for purposes of the theory and summarized some of the evidence available on the issues. What remains is to discuss the matter of *measuring* policy content, which can be a difficult task.

Although policy content is a complicated affair, propositions that explain variation in implementation in terms of differences in policy content would seem amenable to testing. One could measure variations in content by constructing an index for messages at various points in time. Standardized scores for each of the components could be summed and then divided by the number of components.

Several of these elements of policy content, covered earlier, are difficult to tap in a reliable and valid fashion, each with a single indicator. Therefore, a strategy of using multiple measures for each element seems appropriate. Specifically, measures of policies' resources and credibility can be obtained by

- content analysis of each law and regulation
- judgments by panels of experts in each substantive area who sort and rank laws and regulations systematically
- categorizing and analyzing policy elites' responses to interview and mail questionnaire items regarding their subjective evaluations of messages' contents

Whereas this general strategy is sensible, some further measurement considerations and refinements provide additional guidance.

Take, for instance, the matter of financial resources—often a component of the content of many federal laws, or authorizing or reauthorizing amendments to them. Appropriate measures would be the dollar amount of appropriations for the program and/or the extent to which financial resources are provided for the implementation process itself (a line item to that effect or obvious discretion in the hands of the implementors in this regard).

Because the character of the implementation process is likely to be affected by the *perceptions* by state or local implementors about the resource question, two additional measures may be useful. First, implementors are likely to adapt dynamically to a policy if the rate of growth in resources devoted to it is relatively high. An additional measure thus would be the growth rate in the federal portion of the program budget over the implementation period being examined. Also, interview and mail questionnaire items can directly tap implementors' perceptions of federal generosity.

Another measurement issue arises from any analysis of certain aspects of policy credibility. As shown earlier, one feature of credible policy is efficacy. Of course, technical ease or difficulty may be an "objective" matter (at least within the context of a specific period, national culture, and so on), but it affects implementing actors through their perceptions. Measures of the ease of solving the substantive problem, then, should not only include judgment by a panel of experts who sort and rank laws and regulations systematically. They should also measure responses to interview and mail questionnaire items about the implementing elites' subjective evaluations of the ease of solving the substantive problem in question.

Likewise, certainty and perceived certainty of effects can be measured in parallel fashion. The best measure of certainty of effects is the set of judgments made by a panel of experts who have some knowledge of the substantive field and systematically examine the federal message(s). Perceptual measures are best tapped, in turn, by surveys and interviews with the implementors themselves.

The simplest measure of citizen participation requirements is via a panel of experts who examine the content of the federal message for this item. However, measuring policy type is best accomplished via the threefold strategy mentioned earlier: using content analysis of the message(s) itself (themselves), employing systematic examination by a panel of experts, and administering interviews and surveys among the implementing actors.

Measuring Policy Clarity   In the Communications Model, public laws and administrative rules and regulations are conceptualized as federal messages. There is a commonly held view that public laws are invariably vague in terms of either their goals or the means to achieve them. Yet clarity of legal or regulatory language clearly does vary from time to time and place to place; and variance in clarity over time or across messages can be detected. Clarity can be defined in terms of at least two elements: means and ends.

Using these two attributes, a clarity scale or index can be created. The scale might range among the following, ranked here from low to high degrees of clarity:

1. messages that merely prescribe in vague terms some desired future state of affairs or task (where a value of 1 is assigned)
2. messages that contain straightforward statements of their standards or targets (where a value of 2 is assigned)
3. messages that set forth specific procedures regarding issues like deadlines or formal relations—in the form of interagency agreements—with other implementors (where a value of 3 is assigned)
4. messages embracing clarity with respect to both means and ends (where a value of 4 is assigned).

The assignment of values to each message at each point in time can be determined both *objectively,* by coding the law for means and ends content, and *subjectively,* by asking implementors to rate the clarity of each message in terms of both means and ends.

Measuring Policy Consistency   Messages can be (individually or cumulatively) clear but inconsistent. For if policy is conceptualized as a message, as it is in this book, or as a stream of messages—perhaps emanating from several federal sources, perhaps flowing through time—one is alerted to the possibility, indeed the likelihood, that policy on any topic may not be completely coherent and consistent.

Measurement of consistency *over time* involves the systematic analysis of message content each time a major policy statement occurs—for example, each time an amendment passes Congress or a rule is changed. Measurement of *cross-message* consistency involves the same procedure for content analysis, but with a focus on differences between the content of one message, say a law, and another, for example, the regulations.

Measuring Policy Form   As outlined earlier in this chapter in the discussion of measures of policy content, an index can be constructed for policy message form by summing the standardized scores for each of the components and dividing the total by the total number of components. And as in the case of content, the elements of policy form each deserve brief elaboration.

Again, prudence dictates the adoption of a strategy involving multiple measures for many of these components of policy form. In particular, measures of message clarity, consistency, and frequency of transmission can be multiple, including

- content analysis of each law and regulation, over a considerable period of time
- judgment by a panel of experts who analyze the messages systematically and assess the issue of frequency
- perceptual data from the state and local levels through responses by elites in the policy sector to interview and mail questionnaire items

Investigating the subject of policy message receipt is a bit more ephemeral. The major measures here are perceptual and can be tapped through interviews and questionnaire responses from state and local officials. Records and correspondence from state and local agencies can also be a valuable source of data on the receipt of policy messages. It takes great ingenuity, persistence, and effort, however, to obtain systematic information like this from large numbers of implementing units. Without a major resource commitment to obtain such records, it would make most sense to conduct systematic research by using perceptual information on this subject.

The discussion thus far has focused primarily on characteristics of the federally propagated policy message, specifically various aspects of message content and form. However, as indicated earlier, the effect of such messages is influenced by characteristics of the sender as well. The discussion now turns briefly to this subject.

Measuring Perceptions About Federal Officials   Measures of the perceptual matters discussed in this section are best based on responses to interview and mail questionnaire items addressed to state and local elites in the policy field. This is true, for instance, regarding the subject of the legitimacy of federal principals. Some reliability problems occur in interviews and questionnaire responses, especially due to memory loss that prevents accurate reconstruction of perceptions retrospectively over a several-year period; but this approach is nevertheless probably the most feasible. In settings where a somewhat public contemporaneous record of events has been developed—for example, through minutes of meetings at the state or local level, regular newspaper coverage of events, or internal reports that program managers prepare periodically—these sources may improve efforts to systematize data collection.

Independent Variables: State and Local Inducements and Constraints

The second set of hypotheses is drawn from Chapter 4 and concerns the role and influence of state- and local-level actors, their reputations, and the form and content of their communications with decision makers, each acting as an inducement or a constraint on implementation:

H3: States with larger, stronger, and more cohesive supportive advocacy coalitions and supportive state legislatures are more likely to implement programs promptly and without modifications.

H4: If supportive messages initiated at state or local levels are (a) credible as a viable solution to a salient problem for that state; and are (b) clear, (c) consistent; (d) frequently repeated; and (e) actually received, then the actors who make the joint decision for the state are more likely to opt for prompt implementation without modifications.

H5: The more legitimate and credible the supportive state or local senders of messages in the eyes of state officials, the more likely the state's implementation is to proceed promptly and without modifications.

Measuring the Strength of an Advocacy Coalition   The Communications Model predicts that variations in subnational communications across states, across programs, or across time are systematically related to the manner or style in which implementation occurs in a number of ways. Besides elected and appointed officials, the Communications Model directs the researcher to examine the interests and motives of organized interests, again using multiple indicators and multiple sources of data. The propensity of a state to perform all five implementation functions (as discussed in Chapter 2) varies directly with the relative strength of state and local proponents and opponents, separated into advocacy coalitions.

Strength is a function of three characteristics of these senders of messages—skill, cohesiveness, and the level of resources. If strength lies with those whose preferences coincide with the positions of federal-level senders, cooperation is likely. If proponents are weaker than their opponents in any of the three characteristics, there is likely to be conflict, leading to delays and changes.

The relative strength of competing advocacy coalitions could be measured in three ways:

- a ratio of relative strength based on total membership of the competing interest groups in each policy area
- a comparison of total resources spent on lobbying by each advocacy coalition
- interviews with local officials and members of each advocacy coalition to obtain an indication of each coalition's degree of cohesiveness and skill

As previous chapters hypothesized, the higher the level of skill, cohesiveness, and resources, the greater the effect on policy implementation.

State and local politics are characterized by considerable interlocal diversity, especially with regard to interests, incentives, and motivations. At these levels of politics, the focus is on individual political and administrative elites—the elected and appointed officials who must make policy work—and their constituents, the leaders of organized policy opponents and proponents.

Measuring the Attributes of Elected and Appointed Officials
Knowing something about key legislators in the State Senate and House aids prediction and explanation of the course of implementation. To measure individual-level attributes, multiple indicators and several sources of data must be consulted. A telephone interview method, using an amply pretested interview protocol, is the most feasible way of eliciting information from elected officials. Two types of questions should be asked. One type deals with the legislator's role orientation (trustee, advocate, or delegate). Standard attitudinal items that have been developed by state legislative scholars would be appropriate. The other type of questioning addresses the legislator's predisposition toward the policy and his or her assessment of constituency preferences. Responses to these questions can be scaled and scored.

The public administrator and his or her bureaucratic organization are also crucial independent variables. Interviews with relevant bureaucratic actors (policy managers) are the mechanism for assessing how they will likely interpret and react to messages. The local orientation—a function of the bureaucrat's background (in-state or not), method of appointment (by a superior or a board), and career future (within the agency or outside)—should help explain the bureaucrat's behavior. These indicators would yield scalar values to which scores would be assigned accordingly.

Measuring Message Content and Form   A state's implementation style is also constrained by the content and form of the messages of state and local decision makers and members of the attentive public for each policy, as well as the standing of these subnational senders in the community. This variable in the Communications Model emphasizes the importance of state and local politics (for example, the organization of interests within the state) in understanding how and why implementation occurs the way that it does in the states.

State- and local-level messages and messengers can be subjected to the same kind of analysis that has been outlined here. Like the federal level, the messages and their senders vary across policies and time. The implementation terrain is further complicated, however, by *intrastate* variance. Depending on the issue, advocacy coalitions can vary from a simple structure to a complex, polynucleated structure. State implementors may be virtually bombarded with messages. As a result, making the local-level communications system operational and measuring its effectiveness are complex.

The *local message index* is a combination of a number of characteristics of each of three institutional clusters: interest groups, state and local elected officials, and the focal state agency. One way of making messages operational is through content analysis of each relevant state enabling law, policy statement, ordinance, and regulation. An index can be constructed by examining each major law, statement, ordinance, and regulation for content and form and by comparing message content for consistency across time as well as for consistency with the content of federal-level messages. These observations would be made at periodic intervals during the entire implementation period.

Another way of gauging message content and form is with elite interviews. Elites could be queried regarding their subjective evaluations of the messages' characteristics. Asking elites from each of these clusters to reconstruct the implementation process provides the nuances and subtleties that content analysis of documents cannot provide. Legitimate concerns over reliability can be lessened somewhat if researchers interview a sufficient number of elites. In addition, interviews should be supplemented by mail questionnaires to an even larger group of relevant actors.

The measurement of messages from the policy subsystem is produced by analyzing the substance of the message, its clarity, and its specificity. For example, is an interest group's message to implementors clear in its intent and consistent over time? Variations in message content and form can be assigned actual values at specific intervals for each of the components of the subnational level variables. It is imperative that measurements be recorded at intervals because messages may shift over time. Each policy is the subject of multiple messages. The multiple messages can be aggregated into separate indexes for interest groups and state and local elected officials. Certainly cost-bearing and beneficiary interest groups send completely different messages to implementors. The message that the legislature sends via its resource allocation choices may be at odds with its substantive message regarding policy implementation.

Measuring the Attributes of Senders   Like the measure of federal messengers' attributes, the *local sender index* is composed of measures of the legitimacy, popularity, and credibility of state sovereigns' and members of the state's attentive public. The circumstances surrounding periodic legislative, executive, or lobbying activities directed toward promoting or thwarting implementation should be taken into account. In examining documents in connection with these political activities, researchers must look not only for evidence of legitimacy, popularity, and credibility but also for indications of the nature, scope, and intensity of support or opposition of each state- and local-level sender.

Content analysis of appropriate documents is useful here, as well as objective data regarding a sender's attributes. Most important, however, is elite interviewing that evaluates each state sender's legitimacy, popularity, and credibility. The *perceptions and assessments* of key actors are what matter. Judgments about the coding of data from the documents can be cross-checked against the subjective assessments of relevant elites in the states. Values would be assigned categories of responses to arrive at an index score for each of the institutions at intervals during the entire implementation period.

Intervening Variable: Organizational Capacity

The next set of hypotheses is drawn from Chapter 5 and concerns the role and influence of state organizational capacities on state policy implementation.

H6: The greater the number of organizational units involved in the implementation process, the greater the likelihood of delay and modification during implementation.

H7: The more personnel a state devotes to implementing a program, the greater the likelihood of prompt implementation without modifications.

H8: The larger the program budget on a per capita basis, the greater the likelihood of prompt implementation without modifications.

Measuring Organizational Units   Organizational capacity here is treated as a function of the structure, personnel (that is, human resources), and financial characteristics of state agencies. The independent variable in the first hypothesis (H6), the number of organizational units, is fairly easy to measure. State-level officials can almost always provide formal structures of the implementation apparatus upon request. Organization charts can be obtained by written request, and more detailed information can be garnered from an analysis of responses to items on a questionnaire or from interviews.

Sometimes the state itself or the federal government has mandated certain elements of that structure. It is often useful to know about such aspects, because these are likely to be treated especially seriously by the participants. When local organizational units are also included in the structure, the elements at that level too should be included as a feature of the overall network. If the policy message clearly requires the inclusion of nongovernmental organizational units in the implementation apparatus, these units too should not be neglected.

In such cases, it can be difficult to develop an absolutely clear picture of the interorganizational arrangements. In these situations, it is wise to assess the reliability of any measure developed from the response of a state official by asking other officials about the program's organizational structure.

One final element of organizational structure is pertinent here. As described in Chapter 5, implementing organizations have goals, and the program being implemented may or may not fit neatly with these goals. Assessments of agency goals can easily be obtained through questionnaire and interview responses with agency personnel, as well as via official agency statements of purpose. Goals of programs under study may be measured by content analysis of policy messages, judgments rendered by panels of experts, and responses from policymakers and managers. Evidence on this notion is documented in a couple of second-generation studies of the implementation of some intergovernmental health programs (Goggin, 1986; 1987) and has long been a staple of the literature on policy and administration (Downs, 1967).

Another important element of organizational capacity has to do with human resources, or personnel. Earlier discussions indicated the expectation that the number of personnel devoted to a program's implementation is positively related to the timing of policy implementation. Number of personnel here means, as indicated earlier, the number of full-time equivalent personnel devoted per capita to the program.

An alternative measure, somewhat more sensitive to the quality as well as quantity of the entire mix of human resources targeted by a state at an implementation process, is the number of full-time equivalent professional staff per capita. Both figures can be obtained relatively easily from state agencies charged with implementation; often these data are compiled in annual budget documents as well. Due care should be taken to ensure, however, that all agencies tasked with implementation are included in the totals used.

Measuring Financial Resources   Financial resources, the third component of organizational capacity, comprise the funds budgeted for implementation, on a per capita basis, for the program in question. Such data are easily available from state agencies charged with implementation and/or from state budget documents.

Intervening Variable: Ecological Capacity

The fourth set of hypotheses is drawn from Chapter 6 and concerns the role and influence of state ecological capacity on state implementation.

H9: States with greater financial resources at their disposal are more likely to implement a program promptly and without modifications.

H10: The more conducive the state political environment to the program being implemented, the greater the tendency to implement a program promptly and without modifications.

H11: The greater the salience of the target problem to the state and the greater the state media attention given to the target problem, the greater the tendency to implement a program promptly and without modifications.

Measuring State Fiscal Capacity   The Communications Model relies on a category of intervening variables to explain and predict the processes, outputs, and outcomes associated with state implementation. One category of intervening variables is state ecological capacity as the concept was explored in Chapter 6. The hypotheses posed thus far seek to explain and predict state decisions, or predispositions to act. The Communications Model takes account of the important distinction between decisions and actions, suggesting that variations in the capacity to act across states, across programs, or across time also affect the manner or style in which implementation occurs in a number of ways. Thus, state actions regarding when and how to implement are constrained by the economic, political, and situational capacities of the states to act on those preferences.

As stated previously, generally the belief is that states with larger fiscal resources implement programs faster and with fewer modifications. To test the relationship between socioeconomic conditions and implementation, an *economic capacity index* may be constructed. This index is a profile of each state based on the state's overall economic characteristics. It may be operationalized annually and includes measures that gauge a state's socioeconomic environment, which affects a state's ability to perform all the tasks that lead to implementation. The most promising measures of this concept include the following per capita indicators:

- income
- tax capacity
- tax effort
- general expenditures

These data are readily available from the *Statistical Abstract* series and the Advisory Commission on Intergovernmental Relations (ACIR) *Tax Capacity* series.

Measuring State Political Capacity   State political capacity (or the political milieu) also makes the adoption of certain directives problematic. As noted in Chapter 6, in some instances an open, liberal, innovative, and progressive political milieu facilitates policy implementation; in other situations, the reverse is true—a closed, conservative, noninnovative, and nonprogressive political environment is more compatible with policy implementation. To examine the relationship between state politics and implementation, a *political capacity index* may be constructed. This is an indication of a state's political environment (or milieu) for implementation of the program under consideration.

Thus, this particular variable may be operationalized at several points in time and includes such measures as

- the liberalness (or conservativeness) of the state
- the "openness" of the state political system
- the "innovativeness" (or "noninnovativeness") of the state
- a state's political culture (such as moralistic versus traditionalistic)

To construct these indexes for each state at several points in time, a number of sources of data may be consulted and, where possible, annual scores should be calculated. The data employed by Wright, Erikson, and McIver (1985) may be used to construct a mean policy liberalism score for each state; the work of Herzik (1985) may be used for calculating the "openness" of the state political system; innovativeness may be measured by drawing on the approach used by Walker (1969) and Gray (1973) for each state; and the pioneering research of Elazar (1966) and Johnson (1976) may be used to construct a political culture index.

Measuring State Situational Capacity   A state's situational capacity also affects the state's ability to act. Two situational components are pertinent to state capacity: salience of the target problem to the state and media attention to the target problem in the state. Each component may be measured periodically, using primary data functionally related to the program being implemented and collected during the course of interviews and field work. A *problem saliency index* may be measured by specific indicators in each functional area. For example, the total number of Superfund sites on the National Priority List (NPL) would reflect problem severity in the state in the hazardous waste case, and the number of aborted pregnancies in the state would reflect problem severity in the family planning case.

A *media attention index* may be constructed by a content analysis of newspaper indexes and stories on the issue in the state where the policy is to be delivered. One would expect that greater media attention would be associated with prompt implementation without modifications (Levine, 1982). The attention level may also be measured by the number of times the issue is mentioned as a priority item by key decision makers in the state, using such sources as legislators' press releases, *State Government News,* and *Newsbank,* a reference service. In this manner, the support for the issue by key decision makers and members of the press and general public can be measured.

The measurement strategies and sources of data listed thus far have been described as they relate to the dependent, independent, and intervening variables of the Communications Model. The following discussion explores measures for the feedback variables that treat implementation as an *independent* variable to help explain the nature and extent of listening and learning by national and state policymakers as they go about the task of redesigning public policy.

Feedback and Policy Redesign

The final set of hypotheses—couched in the language of terms like *principals* and *agents* that were introduced in Chapter 7—is concerned with the role and influence of state- and local-level actors who are intimately involved with the implementation of an existing policy. The following hypotheses represent hunches about what accounts for differences in the degree of responsiveness among policymakers in Washington to the supports and demands of political and administrative elites in the states.

H12: The greater the agent's legitimacy, credibility, and capability of advancing the interests of the principal, the more responsive is the principal.

H13: The greater the agency's collective expertise, skill, and capacity to advance the interests of the principal, the more responsive is the principal.

H14: The greater the clarity, consistency, and credibility of the message, the more responsive is the principal.

H15: The more personalized the channels of communications used by agents, the more responsive is the principal.

H16: The better the fit between the principal's and the agent's political party, ideology, and psychological predisposition toward redesigning the policy, the more responsive the principal.

H17: The more a principal possesses policy expertise, the more experience he or she has as a state- or local-level elected or appointed official, and the more competitive a principal's district, the more responsive the principal.

Dependent Variables: Listening and Learning   In these hypotheses, the *degree* of responsiveness of national policymakers in the face of conflicting supports and demands from below is described and explained. Here, *responsiveness* connotes the action or inaction of a

Congressperson or bureau chief's office about the acquisition, processing, and use of feedback concerning existing policy performance.

Listening and learning constitute responsiveness. As discussed in Chapter 7, listening can take on one of three values:

- no listening
- selective listening
- attentive listening

The degree of learning can be categorized as

- no learning
- disconfirming learning
- corroborative learning

Given this conceptualization, perhaps the best way to measure the degree of responsiveness of any one political or administrative policymaker is to combine subjective evaluations based on face-to-face elite interviews with direct observations of elite behavior. For example, in the case of a legislator, researchers can conduct a close examination of a Congressperson's behavior during hearings or roll-call voting. Changes in position over time can be captured by a close examination of the form and content of debates about provisions in various alternative amendments during committee hearings or roll-call votes. A similar approach could be adopted to measuring changes in the manner in which bureaucrats in Washington listen and learn.

Independent Variables: Agents, Agencies, Messages, and Channels   The several hypotheses discussed earlier seek to identify the conditions under which those who implement public policy shape—through the policy redesign process—the form and content of a new, reformulated public policy. Again, the hypotheses draw heavily on theories of communications. Chapter 7 developed an argument that policy redesign behavior varies systematically and predictably with

- the reputation and status of the agents who are seeking to redesign the existing policy
- the credibility of agent communications
- the channels of communications used

A brief excursion into the nuances of measuring these communications variables might prove instructive.

Agents are elected politicians like the governor, or appointed administrative elites, such as the state program manager who has personal experience with the implementation of an existing policy in at least one of the American states. *Agencies* are the organizations with which agents are affiliated. The two independent variables in Hypotheses 12 and 13 are operationalized as national principals' perceptions of that agent's or agency's reputation. Reputations are assigned values based on coding of responses to items on an interview schedule used in face-to-face interviews.

Messages can be either written or verbal communications that express the sentiments of elites in the states. Values assigned to individual messages are determined by assessing the principals' perceptions of the message clarity, consistency, and credibility. These three attributes of messages are evaluated on the basis of coding responses to items on an interview schedule used in face-to-face interviews. The experience of those who send messages is also taken into account.

Channels of communications can be either formal or informal. Channels of communications that agents use are determined by examining the responses to items on an interview schedule used in face-to-face interviews. Indicators of the degree to which these agents personalize their messages include coded responses to questions addressed to both principals and agents. These elites' subjective assessments of various lobbying techniques are used to determine the degree of effectiveness for each channel used.

Independent Variable: Attributes of Principals   Hypothesis 17 posits that policy learning and listening behavior are systematically and predictably associated with individual-level, constituent, and—in the case of legislators—electoral characteristics.

Principals are elected and appointed officials in Washington (and their staffs) who are the targets of communications. Each principal's office has a set of individual-level and district-level attributes, each measured in a different manner.

Measuring Principal Characteristics   The principal's ideological predisposition is operationalized as the average ratings of conservative and liberal organizations, as reported annually in the *Congressional Quarterly Almanac*. Political party affiliation is self-explanatory. Extent of knowledge of and interest in the policy being redesigned is operationalized as the combined opinions of a panel of experts. Number of years in a state- or local-level public office is taken from biographical information listed in various sources. The competitiveness of a district variable is operationalized as the size of the margin of victory in the last contested election. Safe seats are those where the margin of victory was greater than 20 percent.

Summary of the Communications Model Hypotheses

To summarize, these seventeen hypotheses are based on the Communications Model that this book has explored throughout. The variables have been operationalized and indicators have been suggested. In the context of these variables, several possible sources of data have also been discussed. This section's discussion illustrated the way an investigator contemplating a third-generation research project on implementation might proceed. It is but one way—by no means the only way—to think about a broad range of conceptual and measurement issues when designing third-generation research.

METHODS OF ANALYSIS FOR IMPLEMENTATION

This chapter has argued that a new generation of research is emerging, one based on diachronic, comparative, and systematic methods of analysis that are designed to test, rather than to generate, hypotheses. This section highlights several ongoing empirical studies of the implementation process in which these various methods of analysis are used. Such a discussion is important in that it illustrates several available methods of analysis that are potentially useful in third-generation research on policy implementation.

Time Series Analysis

A study by B. Dan Wood (1988) analyzes the sequence, magnitude, and duration of changes in the implementation process across time. The method of analysis Wood used in this study is the time-series quasi experiment (Campbell and Stanley, 1966); that is, the response through time of a particular bureaucracy to a particular set of policy initiatives. Wood's focus is on the Environmental Protection Agency's clean-air policy and how this bureaucracy responded to policy initiatives from 1977 to 1985. Wood's research thus employs a longitudinal design with finely divided monthly intervals to capture an empirically rich and dynamic implementation process.

The specific technique used in Wood's analysis is *time series impact assessment* (Box and Tiao, 1975). This method requires the identification and estimation of mathematical components that separately describe the stochastic and deterministic variations in the series (Wood, 1988). According to Wood, modeling the series offers both an excellent way to control for the independent effects of series noise and an elegant description of the series' response to events of interest. The goal of Box-Tiao modeling is to produce a parsimonious yet theoretically complete explanation for the variance in the time series process.

Dynamic Modeling

An approach by John Chubb (1985) integrates the general insights of policy implementation research with the methods of public finance, using economic models of fiscal choice as a foundation. By using an econometric model, the effects of national policies on state and local decision making are estimated.

Chubb suggests that pure economic models are inadequate, because they ignore the "complicated hierarchy of political and administrative factors that implementation research has taught us are so critical" (Chubb, 1985: 995). His resulting political economy framework is then tested econometrically with an analysis of the performance of two major federal grants programs in the 50 states during the years 1965–1979.

This approach has certain advantages. First and foremost, it provides a framework for analyzing empirically important noneconomic, as well as economic, elements of policy implementation. Second, the framework permits an analysis of the political environment as a determinant of policy implementation. Typically, studies of policy implementation focus on the bargaining and interaction between the bureaucracy and its clientele. Finally, the approach permits the formal specification of hierarchical relationships across time and the rigorous derivation of positive and normative results (Chubb, 1985: 998–99).

The major disadvantage of this technique, however, is that it requires a certain familiarity with the methods of public finance. Unfortunately, few political scientists who study policy implementation are familiar with these econometric approaches.

Network Analysis

This approach was developed largely by Benny Hjern and his colleagues—David Porter, Ken Hanf, and Chris Hull. It begins by identifying the "network of actors" involved in service delivery in one or more local areas and asks them about their goals, strategies, resources, activities, and contacts. Essentially, the researcher sets out to reconstruct what actors are part of the implementation process, then describes and analyzes their patterns of social interaction (Hjern and Hull, 1983). This approach then uses the contacts as a vehicle for developing a network technique to identify the local, regional, and national actors involved in the planning, financing, and execution of relevant governmental and nongovernmental programs (Hjern and Porter, 1982).

As Sabatier (1986) notes, this approach has several strengths:

- It represents an explicit and reliable methodology for identifying a policy network, that is, an "implementation structure."
- The approach enables one to assess the relative importance of a variety of governmental programs by means of private organizations and market forces in solving these problems.
- It enables one to see all sorts of unintended consequences of governmental and private programs.
- It is an approach that can deal with a policy/problem area involving a multitude of public (and private) programs, none of which are preeminent.
- This approach is well-equipped to deal with strategic interactions over time (Sabatier, 1986: 33–34).

However, this approach has several limitations as well:

- It tends to overemphasize the ability of subnational implementors to frustrate the goals of national implementors.
- It accepts the participants in an "implementation structure" as given without examining the prior efforts of various individuals that might affect participation rates.
- It fails to start from an explicit theory of implementation to guide the inquiry. That is, this approach needs to be related to an explicit body of theory (composed of social, economic, and legal factors) that structures the perceptions, resources, motives, and participation of these actors (Sabatier, 1986: 34–35).

Discriminant Analysis

Studies by Wassenberg (1986) and Lester and Bowman (1989) use discriminant analysis to determine the "critical" variables affecting state policy implementation. Wassenberg sought to explain why some states have achieved primacy in the National Pollution Discharge Elimination System (NPDES) program during 1972–1984. Lester and Bowman sought to identify systematically the factors promoting or inhibiting state implementation of the Resource Conservation and Recovery Act (RCRA) of 1976 using the conceptual framework developed by Sabatier and Mazmanian (1979).

This particular technique provides a way of determining how selected independent variables work in combination with each other in explaining policy implementation. More specifically, the procedure involves identifying the set of discriminating variables that best describes the differences between groups represented by the dependent variable

(Klecka, 1980). Also, by using a stepwise procedure, redundant variables may be eliminated from the analysis. Discriminant analysis can also be used to classify cases. In this instance, if one were to discover states about which there was no information as to implementation status, discriminant analysis could assign the states to groups based on their values on the most salient variables (Aldrich and Cnudde, 1984).

Content Analysis

Although content analysis as a technique is not new, it was used in the mid-1980s by Paul Sabatier and his associates to explore the beliefs of relatively large numbers of policy elites over periods of a decade or more (Sabatier, Brasher, and Jenkins-Smith, 1987). These researchers used content analysis of public hearings, other government documents, and interest group publications to explore the determinants of policy change.

Such an approach has numerous advantages:

- It permits a much more detailed analysis of beliefs than can be captured by partisan affiliation and interest group scorecards.
- The content analysis of policy documents is better suited than attitudinal surveys to the examination of changes in beliefs of elites over time. It does not automatically limit analysis to the replication of previous work, nor does it require scholars to maintain an interest in a topic for an extended period of time. Public documents spanning an enormous range of topics and time periods are relatively easy to obtain, and coding several decades worth of records can be done in a year or so.
- The researcher is not limited to studying elites from legislatures or any other particular institution. In fact, most public hearings contain testimony from individuals representing a wide variety of interest groups, administrative agencies, legislative districts, research organizations, and so on (Sabatier, Brasher, and Jenkins-Smith, 1987: 3–4).

Content analysis also, of course, has limitations:

- Development of a coding frame that indicates the range of items to be coded is difficult.
- Validity of responses is a problem. How does the researcher know if actors are expressing their "true" opinions?
- Code reliability is another problem. For example, if one uses a "thematic statement"—a clause, sentence, or paragraph that expresses an opinion or belief—as the codable unit, one becomes

acutely aware of how easy it is for different coders to interpret a piece of testimony in quite different ways (Sabatier, Brasher, and Jenkins-Smith, 1987). Thus, there is no such thing as immaculate perception.

Nevertheless, preliminary findings from these scholars indicate that much can be learned about policy implementation and elite beliefs through the method of coding the content of policy changes (Jenkins-Smith, St. Clair, and Martin, 1987).

The Social Experiment

Recent studies by Richard Nathan and his associates (1983; 1987) use field network evaluation methods to evaluate the impact of the Reagan Administration's domestic programs on state and local government. The research approach has five key elements:

- In each jurisdiction, a field associate analyzes the effects of the federal policy or policies being studied. In preparing the analysis, an associate interviews officials of government and nonprofit agencies and examines both unpublished and published records and reports containing program and fiscal information and statistics.
- A central research staffperson, in consultation with all of the field associates, develops a common analytical and reporting format for the associates to use in developing and writing up their findings.
- Information is gathered at several times over a period of years to analyze the effects of federal policy changes on a longitudinal basis.
- The analysis focuses on the nature of the actual changes in federally aided programs in each local area, the effects of these changes, and how the grantee government responds to them.
- A central staffperson coordinates the research, prepares reports to summarize the field analyses, and presents generalizations across the states and over time (Nathan et al., 1983: 10–11).

The primary advantages of this approach are that it is diachronic in design, intensive in its analysis, and comprehensive. However, it is limited because substantial amounts of time and financial support are necessary to carry out this type of project.

Regression Techniques

A number of scholars have used multiple-regression analysis to assess the unique effects of several variables hypothesized to affect policy implementation in the fifty states (see, for example, Lester et al., 1983; Thompson and Scicchitano, 1985; 1987; and Crotty, 1987; 1988).

The technique of multiple-regression analysis is an important (and often used) tool for social scientists in the analysis of nonexperimental data. The technique has a number of assumptions:

- an absence of specification error and interval-level data
- no measurement error
- for each observation, a value of zero for the expected value of the error term
- additive effects of the independent variables
- linear relationships between X and Y
- uncorrelated and normally distributed error terms
- no perfect linear relation of an independent variable to one or more of the other independent variables in the model (Lewis-Beck, 1980)

When the assumptions of regression are met, the coefficient estimates derived for a random sample will have many desirable properties; however, when one or more of these assumptions are violated, the application of regression analysis may produce misleading or problematic coefficient estimates (Berry and Feldman, 1985).

A "MIXED-METHOD" APPROACH TO STUDYING IMPLEMENTATION

When, as we have suggested, the top-down and bottom-up approaches are synthesized into a single, parsimonious model, persuasive communications are *critical* to both explanation and prediction. To study communications requires multiple methods of *both* data collection (for example, surveys of attitudes, beliefs, and opinions; content analysis; and the use of panels of experts, documentary research) *and* data analysis, especially techniques that are longitudinal and comparative and that combine intensive with extensive analysis.

We have reviewed how a number of implementation scholars are presently approaching the study of the dynamics of policy implementation; many of these studies emphasize the importance of collecting data over time. Most of the studies just outlined examine implementation retrospectively. One approach, the naturally occurring experiment, has been successfully used by Richard Nathan and his associates (1983;

1987). It examines policy dynamics as the implementation unfolds. Whereas each method has its proponents and advantages, when researchers test the validity of a dynamic model of implementation, a combination of approaches is particularly useful (Diesing, 1971; Yin, 1982).

More specifically, it is preferable to combine the strengths of extensive, large N longitudinal techniques with the advantages of an intensive small N (case study) approach (Goggin, 1986). Case studies may be used to validate, invalidate, or interpret the findings of a large N study that uses statistical techniques.

One type of theory-confirming study is the "crucial case" (Eckstein, 1975: 116–17). The crucial case serves the same purpose as a well-constructed experiment: the investigator selects a case that possesses the specified characteristics under which a law must hold, and observations are compared with predicted results. If the case fits with the predictions, the case is theory confirming.

Equally useful is the deviant case. In this instance, relevant additional conditions that may not have been present in the other cases might be uncovered. This opens up the possibility of revising the theory in light of new findings, for example, adding new independent variables to the model. Thus, one may probe the plausibility of hypotheses (Eckstein, 1975: 79–139) with a small N comparison of cases to pave the way for the complementary pooled cross-sectional time series analysis that should follow (Plewis, 1985; Stimson, 1985). In other words, the first phase of one's research through an exploration of individual cases of policy implementation may be undertaken with a view toward fine-tuning the theory (or model) being used before committing oneself to the more costly and time-consuming task of statistical validation over time.

Although not strictly a study of public policy implementation, Paul Peterson's *City Limits* (1981) illustrates how regression analysis of the determinants of expenditure levels in many cities in general can be combined skillfully with an intensive case study of New York City to *enrich* a more general theory of urban public policy. The most common function of case studies, however, is to illustrate typical historical cases that have been identified in the larger diachronic (over time) study (Goggin, 1986).

THE CHALLENGE AHEAD

After passing through two stages or "generations," policy implementation research is changing focus from theory construction to theory testing. At center stage of this new "third-generation" scholarship is a set of analytical policy techniques that are both comparative and longitudinal in nature. This chapter drew from some of the latest scholarship to illustrate how these techniques have been used (together with their findings) and proposed a "mixed-method" approach to studying the dynamics of public policy implementation that combines both large N (quantitative) and small N (comparative case study) analyses. If the study of policy implementation is to achieve its full potential, the creative and sensitive development and application of methods for systematic empirical research must also be a top priority.

Thus, the challenge to implementation scholars that lies ahead is to devise research designs that are genuinely comparative, longitudinal, and systematic in their approach. Policymakers and managers should be able to use the knowledge generated from this third generation of implementation studies to design or redesign policies to make them work.

In the Conclusion of this book, we summarize our findings, list some caveats, and give some advice to students, colleagues, and practitioners. We hope that students of implementation find our Communications Model, our findings, our measures, and our suggested research designs useful in their own "third-generation" studies of public policy implementation.

Notes for Chapter 8

1. A *case* of implementation in this study is defined as all of the decisions and actions directed at either carrying out the intent of a policy or modifying policy to facilitate that end. Using this operational definition, there are a maximum of 150 cases (3 policies × 50 states). Another, disaggregated way of defining a *case* is as any occasion for delay. Using each of the five activities associated with the implementation process as an occasion for delay, there are a maximum of 750 cases (3 policies × 50 states × 5 activities). In either event, when an implementation activity occurs, implementation behavior is observed.

2. We approach measurement issues with the aim of ultimately going beyond previous efforts in this field of study by (1) classifying each of several hundred cases of implementation along a continuum of implementation styles, measuring the timing of implementation and the extent and direction of change in program form and content during implementation; (2) documenting the frequency with which each type of implementation occurs; (3) specifying the patterns of influence that lead to various outcomes; and (4) measuring the relative importance and the interactive effects of each of several possible influences on the political behavior both of individuals and of collections of individuals

(organizations and states), and of the consequences of those implementing decisions and actions.

3. Anyone engaged in empirical research on implementation must be sensitive to validity and reliability problems associated with the measurement strategy adopted. In fact, validity and reliability are two of the reasons why a multiple indicator strategy is recommended. We also recommend combining different variables to construct several indexes. There are sound theoretical reasons for believing that the individual components of an index tap a single underlying concept. Each component can also be treated as a variable and correlated with other variables (components and dependent variables) during the course of an investigation.

CONCLUSION

Findings, Caveats, and Practical Advice

❖
❖

We began this book by cautioning readers not to look for a definitive test of a general theory of implementation in these pages, yet we tempered this disclaimer with a trio of promises. First, we promised to lay out a dynamic model of how and why implementors behave as they do. In this regard, communications theory, as well as a number of other theories, was the thread used to sew disparate pieces into a coherent whole. The book's arguments synthesized the work of many first- and second-generation study scholars (including our own second-generation research) to lend credence to the theorizing. One of the unique contributions of the model is that it integrates the major concerns and variables of the top-down and bottom-up research traditions into a single framework.

Second, in anticipation of the costlier and more time-consuming task of validation that we hope will follow, we promised to probe the plausibility of our hunches about why implementation and its anticipated and unanticipated consequences might vary—from one time period to the next, from policy to policy, or across units of government. The book's approach to this plausibility probe has been to report on both the work of others in this field and some recent findings of our own, much of which is original research. In the integration of approaches, the cross-policy comparisons, the emphasis on the role of the states, and the reliance on systematic comparative and diachronic analysis, we believe our perspective is distinctive.

Third, we promised that there would be something in this book for students who are being introduced to the study of implementation for the first time, for scholars who are engaged in research on implementation, and for those who practice the craft of implementation. This Conclusion takes up each of these promises in turn. The chapter begins with a summary of findings as they relate to various components of the Communications Model of Intergovernmental Policy Implementation. Following this brief account, some caveats are listed for readers to ponder. And finally, the Conclusion offers some practical advice to students, scholars, and practitioners.

COMMUNICATIONS MODEL RESEARCH FINDINGS

Recall that the book began by identifying a number of problems that plagued earlier theoretical and empirical work on this subject, and the discussion urged readers to think beyond these constraints to new possibilities, including the possibility of testing—not merely generating—hypotheses. This book was intended to be viewed as a bridge between second- and third-generation implementation research. If the volume has adequately served its purposes, it not only provides an up-to-date assessment of the field but also acts as a catalyst to unleash a wide variety of more ambitious, more "scientific" third-generation type studies. Preceding chapters offered both a synthetic theory and an inventory of related propositions tied clearly to the overall perspective.

The book also supplied concrete evidence from all three policy cases that there are considerable variations in implementation processes, outputs, and, to a lesser degree, outcomes. Precisely how the variations that exist across settings, policies, and time might be linked to the independent and intervening variables that constitute the main components of our model is the question addressed next.

In general, research findings lend considerable support for most of the hypotheses listed in Chapter 8, but findings call other hypotheses into question. As such, the results of our research thus far can serve both as a guide for fine-tuning the Communications Model and as a manual for future hypothesis-testing. Two facts are obvious. The Communications Model is not deterministic. For example, implementation is not dictated entirely by the wealth or the political culture of a state. Nor do the findings indicate that there is a single cause that explains the varieties of implementation behaviors. Based on our observations of the implementation of these three policies, there is considerable causal complexity. But what seems to account for the observed variance?

Although patterns do emerge, it is clear from this comparative study that implementation is not a monolithic whole. Neither is it entirely idiosyncratic: There is not a completely unique experience attached to each instance of implementation. Findings suggest that although each case has its peculiarities, the experiences among various states and various implementors also have a number of things in common. Indeed, what has happened during the implementation of clean-water policy is quite different from what has occurred during the implementation of family planning services or hazardous waste management policies.

One implication of the findings given throughout the book is that no scientific principles apply under all circumstances. Yet from a comparison of these differences one might conclude that the type of policy determines, to a large extent, what is likely to happen during implementation. Of course, any meaningful general statement of this nature can only be made *with confidence* after the universe of cases has been carefully defined and a study designed and executed that includes a meaningful sample—both in terms of number and type—of cases.

Undoubtedly, in all three of the policy cases, what happened in Washington, D.C. during the life of the program—especially the manner in which federal messages such as laws, amendments to legislation, rules, regulations, procedures and policy directives were communicated as federal messages from the top down—markedly affected what happened in the 50 states and thousands of communities around the country. A direct correlation exists between the attributes of federal-level inducements and constraints and the styles of implementation, with the three cases arranged on a continuum.

At one end of the continuum is clean water, for which resources were heavily committed, efficiency of implementation was high, and messages were marked by considerable clarity. In the middle of the implementation spectrum is hazardous waste management—which prompted a more controversial, less credible mandate, and, consequently, had more mixed results. Family planning is on the other end of the continuum: Its implementation got off to a relatively fast start in many states—before the 1973 *Roe v. Wade* Supreme Court decision legalizing abortion—but then, in recent years, the program became mixed up with abortion and the conservative tide against it. The Reagan years ushered in an antiabortion firestorm that has led to conflict and stalemate—a classic example of ideological bargaining, with the sovereigns in Washington locked in a zero-sum game where if either the pro-life or pro-choice faction wins, the other must necessarily lose.

What happens at the subnational level of government in the federal system also matters. Even the best of policies can go awry if there is resistance at the level of impact—where plans have to be converted into action. The critical factor here seems to be the type and configuration of the individuals and organizations actively involved in implementation struggles. The wider the advocacy coalition supporting the goals of the program, the more straightforward the implementation.

In the case of hazardous waste management, a centralized management process might be more efficient in the short run, but such centralization might be perceived as illegitimate and therefore lead to resistance to change in the long run. Findings here also support a direct connection between size and strength of the supportive advocacy coalition and the speed of implementation. For example, our research shows that in defiant states, there was no consensus among important actors, and, thus, no supporting advocacy coalition. The opposite was true for compliant states.

For family planning services, the policy experiences of the early 1970s in California revealed a willingness to compromise—to strike a political bargain. Local family planning officials were able to convince state legislators of the practicality of providing family planning services to poor women. But in the 1980s, and now the 1990s, no such pragmatic compromise seems imminent over the issue of building a wall of separation between abortion and family planning. In the late 1980s ideological antiabortionists turned up the heat by demonstrating at local abortion clinics and by civil disobedience; and abortion turned out to be a major issue in the 1988 presidential campaign. The July 1989 *Webster v. Reproductive Health Services* Supreme Court decision strengthening the states' rights to restrict abortion was a harbinger of things to come.

Waste-water treatment, a much more intergovernmental program than Title X family planning, prompted a correspondingly higher degree of discretion in hands of local officials. Unlike the Resource Conservation and Recovery Act (RCRA) case, pressure from the bottom up did not come from environmentalists, but rather from developers, real estate interests, and chambers of commerce. Again, their success at influencing implementation can be tied to superior communications and their ability and willingness to mobilize resources to put policies in place.

Some evidence supports the proposition that fragmentation of organizational structures adversely affects implementation. Yet other evidence from our research shows that under some conditions, complicated, multiunit structures may encourage implementation. Personal will and skill of program managers also matters, with the evidence here supporting the proposition that tight, centralized structures encourage compliance. These types of structures may not, however, assist in achieving policy goals, because actual results tend to depend on the nature of the policy tasks themselves.

In handling of hazardous waste, the presence of a single designated toxics agent in a state—a move toward consolidation of environmental organizations—facilitated timely implementation. Regarding the linkages between number of personnel and implementation style, the results are mixed: States moving in the direction of compliance had more full-time employees (FTEs) than states that were defying the federal mandate; however, strategic delayers had even more FTEs. One plausible explanation is that "strategic delayers" were more interested in what

Crotty (1988) calls "completeness" of implementation—more interested in outcomes than style.

There are a number of alternative explanations that can be teased from the data, however. If one listens to the EPA managers in the regions, then the explanation lies more with the quality than the quantity of human resources; high turnover rates, job burnout, and inexperienced staff were key constraints at the state level, as was scarcity of fiscal resources. From the standpoint of the local implementors, however, communications patterns, especially between their offices and regional EPA headquarters, turned out to be significant.

Reducing the number of waste-water treatment units (an observation made over time), without sacrificing clean-water outputs in the process, seems to be systematically related to speed of implementation; and recent attempts at privatisation have also resulted in more integrated structures. When it comes to clean-water personnel, most of the evidence here is anecdotal.

With family planning programs, at least in the early years of Title X implementation, states that used state health departments and county clinics got services into the hands of clients more quickly. Moreover, in times of cutbacks and retrenchment, as was the case beginning in fiscal year (FY) 1982, consolidation seemed to have had positive effects upon implementation.

Measuring ecological capacity, our results cast doubt on the proposition that the wealthiest states are the first to implement a policy; nor are they always the ones to get the best results. Regarding whether state policy liberalism has an effect on implementation, our findings indicate that the degree of the effect depends on the issue. Conservative states are more likely to resist aggressive marketing of family planning services, but they are also more likely to work with federal officials to see that waste-water treatment plants are put on line.

The findings from our research on hazardous waste undermines conventional wisdom about the linear relationship between state wealth and innovation. State ecological variables were apparently not that important. Results from the other cases are not systematic enough to shed light on the veracity of the state ecology hypothesis.

Finally, we have marshaled evidence about what happens during the feedback process, as policymakers redesign policies on the basis of information and advice received from the states and from elsewhere in the federal system. Although the feedback mechanism is apparently working, in the case of family planning, it is working very poorly. At least on this issue, most members of Congress are close-minded or seek information selectively, drawing primarily on those sources that confirm their established positions.

Poor responsiveness on the part of members of Congress may be due to the fact that of the three policies chosen for comparison, Title

X is the least intergovernmental. There is less discretion associated with the project grant. It may also be that during the period under investigation, pressure from organized interests and the attention of administrative and political elites in the states focused on the executive branch, evidenced by the 75,000 letters and postcards sent to the Office of Population Affairs during the "gag rule" public comment period. Indeed, as a general rule, most feedback on the workings of existing policies is probably directed to the executive branch agencies at the *program* level, rather than to the Congress at the *policy* level.

Probably, however, poor responsiveness and virtually nonexistent policy learning during the legislative redesign process is due to the nature of the policy at stake. In other words, family planning may be a deviant case. On issues that are less emotionally charged, there is reason to believe that policymakers are much more likely to listen to and learn from the experiences of the states. One of this book's authors is investigating this question.

CAVEATS

These, then, are the highlights from our research on the implementation of three policies of national importance. Readers should not read too much into the results of our research. We see them as a starting point for further research rather than a set of verified conclusions. In reporting our findings, recall that we approached the task of explanation and prediction comparatively and to some extent longitudinally. These findings share the validity and reliability shortcomings of previous research as well. Whereas the cases selected to investigate in this study are analyzed systematically, and in some respects the approaches to measurement and data collection and analysis described in Chapter 8 are employed, we have *not* applied all the methods described in our discussion of how a "third-generation" research project might be designed and conducted. As the subtitle of this book implies, this effort must be viewed as a halfway house between second- and third-generation scholarship.

Some readers might consider the testable hypotheses that are derived from the model to be, on their face, quite obvious. To some extent this is true, but most of the existing first- and second-generation literature on implementation has not been organized in a manner that allows for consideration of even these basic hypotheses. Below the surface, however, one can see that results summarized in this book go beyond the expression of purely bivariate propositions; in some instances the hypotheses are conditional, and in other cases relationships among hypotheses are specified. Consider the earlier discussions of three key variables.

First, regarding the dependent variables in this study, we noted that whether prompt implementation meant success or failure depended upon a number of factors, not the least of which was the soundness of the underlying theory. In that connection, we were careful to note that some actions taken by the states could lead to compliance with the law but could also eventually lead to poor programmatic performance, as measured by levels of expenditure or by changes in objective conditions.

Second, we noted that the relationships between organizational structure and implementation are more subtle and complex than a simple bivariate hypothesis implies. For example, simple and integrated structures could lead to prompt program implementation but could also create unanticipated negative consequences for day-to-day administration of the program.

Third, the relationship between message clarity and implementation is not that straightforward. For one thing, measuring messages for clarity objectively, for example, by using a panel of experts or by using coders to analyze the content of laws and regulations, could provide one picture of message clarity, but asking implementors their opinions about their *perceptions* of message clarity may give quite different results. For another, a law or regulation that is clear and consistent even in the eyes of the person who has to implement it—with clearly targeted goals and specific strategies for achieving them—can lead to compliance if the goals are consistent with those of the implementing agency but can lead to defiance if the goals are antithetical to the organization's mission or beyond the organization's capabilities. These are some of the conceptualization and measurement issues so often ignored or treated superficially in much of the implementation literature of the first two generations.

SOME PRACTICAL ADVICE

The opening paragraphs of the Preface described this book as one that is about both knowing and doing. It claimed that there is something in the book to appeal to students who knew little of public policy implementation before reading it, to colleagues who have made research on implementation their scholarly focus, and to implementors in the field. At the risk of offending all three, we have taken the bold step of closing this Conclusion with a bit of advice for each.

We admonish students to take our claims about why implementation occurs the way that it does and test them in the real world. Rather than accepting what we say about why implementation varies, be skeptical! If the opportunity to test hypotheses presents itself, take it.

We urge our colleagues who are actively engaged in theoretical or empirical research on implementation also to be skeptical. Think seriously about pursuing a research plan that shares the basic elements of "third-generation" research. Recognize that what has been outlined in the preceding chapters is only one way of looking at implementation—by no means the only model of implementation processes, outputs, and outcomes. In taking up this challenge to approach the study of implementation more scientifically, be prepared to undertake costly and time-consuming research projects, many of which will require collaboration and outside funding.

The people who are charged with the responsibility of transforming plans into action—of operationalizing and interpreting what others have decided should be accomplished—should be alert to the fact that our model is not deterministic, that implementation is not bound to fail, regardless of the circumstances. Implementors need to recognize that they have the ability to manipulate many of the variables that we suggest will impact upon implementation. Organizational structure, the quality and number of personnel assigned to implementation, and the patterns of communications adopted are just a few key factors that may come under implementor scrutiny and control.

The book has combined an up-to-date review of the implementation literature with a report of our own original research in order to posit a set of testable hypotheses. To this a number of concrete suggestions were added about how to go about combining the elements of third-generation research, namely conceptualizing, operationalizing, measuring, and testing. For the average reader, there may be widespread pessimism about the value of social science research, especially academic or basic research carried out for the primary purpose of shedding light on a general theory of implementation. Of these readers, be they practitioners, students, or colleagues, we ask that you reflect upon the long-run contributions that this more scientific approach to the study of implementation, one that stresses validation of hypotheses leading to broad generalization about implementation and its causal complexities, might offer.

Chronology of Important Developments in the Implementation of Hazardous Waste Management, Clean-Water, and Family Planning Programs

❖
❖

LEGISLATIVE HISTORY OF THE RESOURCE CONSERVATION AND RECOVERY ACT OF 1976

1976   Congress passed RCRA, the major federal legislation for controlling and managing hazardous waste.

1980   EPA finalized regulations for Subtitle C of RCRA.

1980   Congress passed Superfund legislation for cleanup of abandoned hazardous waste sites (not covered under RCRA).

1984   First state (Mississippi) received RCRA final authorization.

1984   EPA issued Enforcement Response Policy to bring uniformity to RCRA enforcement efforts.

1984   Congress passed the Hazardous and Solid Waste Amendments, designed to speed up and improve regulatory performance under RCRA.

LEGISLATIVE HISTORY OF CLEAN WATER ACT OF 1972

1972   Congress enacted revisions in Federal Water Pollution Control Act, commonly known as the Clean Water Act of 1972, provided for creation of effluent limitations on discharge of point-source water pollutants into all waterways in the United States, and offered states opportunity to assume responsibility. Construction grants were set at 75 percent federal share.

1977   Original deadline for compliance for municipal waste-water treatment plants was extended for some types of cases.

1981   Regulations were relaxed for certain treatment requirements. Federal match was reduced to between 33 percent and 55 percent.

1981–82   National tax legislation indirectly encourages privatisation of infrastructure provision, including waste-water plants.

1983   Deadline was extended again, until July 1, 1988.

1986   Tax reform weakened incentives for privatisation.

1987   Clean Water Act revisions tightened regulatory standards, also eliminated grant program in favor of gradual replacement with state-run revolving loan programs.

LEGISLATIVE HISTORY OF FAMILY PLANNING SERVICES AND POPULATION RESEARCH ACT OF 1970

1970   Congress passed Family Planning Services and Population Research Act of 1970.

1975   Congress added provisions relating to the scope of family planning projects to be offered and direct grants and contracts.
          Federal share of funding for project costs was increased from 75 percent to 90 percent.

1978   Congress added provisions relating to infertility services and services for adolescents; placed increased emphasis on contraceptive research, family planning counseling, and SIDS research; and prohibited the use of public funds for programs where abortion is used as a method of family planning.

1981   Congress added a provision relating to family participation in projects.

1980s   The Reagan Administration attempted to fold family planning services into a state-administered block grant.

1988   Department of Health and Human Services announced a final "gag" rule that would prevent family planning clinics that receive federal funds from giving advice about the availability of abortion services.

1989   In *Webster v. Reproductive Health Services,* the U.S. Supreme Court upheld a woman's right to choose to have an abortion but gave states authority to place further restrictions on abortion.

References

Abney, Glenn and Thomas P. Lauth. 1986. *The Politics of State and City Administrators.* Albany, N.Y.: State University of New York Press.

_____. 1987. "Perceptions of the Impact of Governors and Legislatures in the State Appropriations Process." *Western Political Quarterly* 40: 335–42.

"Abortion Decision Will Be Overturned, President Predicts." 1989. *Houston Chronicle* January 14: 14A.

ACIR [Advisory Commission on Intergovernmental Relations]. 1979. *Citizen Participation in the Federal System.* Washington, D.C.: U.S. Government Printing Office.

_____. 1980. *The Federal Role in the Federal System.* Washington, D.C.: U.S. Government Printing Office.

_____. 1984. *Regulatory Federalism: Policy, Process, Impact and Reform.* Washington, D.C.: U.S. Government Printing Office.

_____. 1985. *The Question of State Government Capability.* Washington, D.C.: U.S. Government Printing Office.

AGI [The Alan Guttmacher Institute]. 1979. *Family Planning, Contraception, Voluntary Sterilization, and Abortion: An Analysis of Laws and Policies in the United States, Each State and Jurisdiction* (as of October 1, 1976, with 1978 Addenda)(pp. 37–42). Rockville, Md.: Department of Health, Education, and Welfare (DHEW Publication No. [HSA]79–5623).

_____. 1976. "Organized Family Planning Services in the United States: FY 1975." *Family Planning Perspectives* 8: 269–74.

_____. 1984. *Organized Family Planning Services in the United States, 1981–1983.* New York: The Alan Guttmacher Institute.

Aldrich, John and Charles F. Cnudde. 1984. "Probing the Bounds of Conventional Wisdom: A Comparison of Regression, Probit, and Discriminant Analysis." In Herbert Asher et al., eds. *Theory Building and Data Analysis in the Social Sciences.* Knoxville, Tenn.: University of Tennessee Press.

Allison, Graham T. 1971. *Essence of Decision.* Boston: Little, Brown.

Anderson, John E. and Lisa G. Cope. 1987. "The Impact of Family Planning Program Activity on Fertility." *Family Planning Perspectives* 19: 152–57.

Anton, Thomas J. 1989. *American Federalism and Public Policy: How the System Works.* New York: Random House.

_____. 1983. "Decay and Reconstruction in the Study of American Inter-governmental Relations." Paper presented at the 1983 Annual Meeting of the American Political Science Association. Chicago.

_____. 1984. *Intergovernmental Change in the United States: Myth and Reality.* Ann Arbor, Mich.: University of Michigan Institute of Public Policy Studies.

Aron, Joan. 1979. "Intergovernmental Politics of Energy." *Policy Analysis* 5: 451–71.

Bailey, Stephen and Edith Mosher. 1968. *ESEA: The Office of Education Administers a Law.* Syracuse, N.Y.: Syracuse University Press.

Ball, Bruce P. 1976. "Water Pollution and Compliance Decision Making." In Charles Jones and Robert Thomas, eds. *Public Policy Making in the Federal System.* Beverly Hills, Calif.: Sage.

Ball, Howard, Dale Krane, and Thomas P. Lauth. 1982. *Compromised Compliance: Implementation of the 1965 Voting Rights Act.* Westport, Conn.: Greenwood Press.

Bardach, Eugene. 1977. *The Implementation Game: What Happens After a Bill Becomes a Law.* Cambridge, Mass.: MIT Press.

Barrett, Susan and Colin Fudge, eds. 1981. *Policy and Action: Essays on the Implementation of Public Policy.* London and New York: Methuen.

Baum, Lawrence. 1981. "Comparing the Implementation of Legislative and Judicial Policies." In Daniel A. Mazmanian and Paul A. Sabatier, eds. *Effective Policy Implementation.* Lexington, Mass.: Lexington Books.

Bender, Lewis G. and James A. Stever, eds. 1986. *Administering the New Federalism.* Boulder, Colo.: Westview Press.

Bendor, Jonathan. 1985. *Parallel Systems: Redundancy in Government.* Berkeley, Calif.: University of California Press.

Bendor, Jonathan and Terry Moe. 1985. "An Adaptive Model of Bureaucratic Politics." *American Political Science Review* 79: 755–74.

Berman, Paul. 1978. "The Study of Macro- and Micro-Implementation." *Public Policy* 26: 157–84.

_____. 1980. "Thinking About Programmed and Adaptive Implementation: Matching Strategies to Situations." In Helen M. Ingram and Dean E. Mann, eds. *Why Policies Succeed or Fail.* Beverly Hills, Calif.: Sage.

Berman, Paul and Milbrey McLaughlin. 1978. *Federal Programs Supporting Educational Change.* Santa Monica, Calif.: Rand Corporation.

Berry, William D. and Stanley Feldman. 1985. *Multiple Regression in Practice.* Beverly Hills, Calif.: Sage.

Blalock, H. M, Jr. 1971. *Causal Models in the Social Sciences.* Chicago: Aldine.

Bowen, Elinor. 1982. "The Pressman-Wildavsky Paradox: Four Addenda on Why Models Based on Probability Theory Can Predict Implementation Success and Suggest Useful Tactical Advice for Implementers." *Journal of Public Policy* 2: 1–21.

Bowman, Ann O'M. 1983. "The Politics of Hazardous Waste Regulation: Theoretical and Practical Implications." In James P. Lester and Ann O'M. Bowman, eds. *The Politics of Hazardous Waste Management.* Durham, N.C.: Duke University Press.

_____. 1984. "Explaining State Response to the Hazardous Waste Problem." *Hazardous Waste* 1: 301–8.

_____. 1985. "Hazardous Waste Management: State Government Activity or Passivity." *State and Local Government Review* 17: 155–61.

Bowman, Ann O'M., Malcolm L. Goggin, James P. Lester, and Laurence J. O'Toole, Jr. 1987. "Third-Generation Implementation Studies: Conceptual and Methodological Issues." Paper presented at the Annual Meeting of the Midwest Political Science Association. Chicago.

Bowman, Ann O'M. and Richard C. Kearney. 1986. *The Resurgence of the States.* Englewood Cliffs, N.J.: Prentice-Hall.

Bowman, Ann O'M. and James P. Lester. 1985. "Hazardous Waste Management: State Government Activity or Passivity?" *State and Local Government Review* 17: 155–61.

_____. 1987. "Implementing Intergovernmental Policy: The Resource Conservation and Recovery Act of 1976." Paper presented at the Annual Meeting of the Southern Political Science Association. Charlotte, N.C.

Box, George E. P. and G. C. Tiao. 1975. "Intervention Analysis with Applications to Economic and Environmental Problems." *Journal of the American Statistical Association* 70: 70–79.

Boynton, G. R. and Chong Lim Kim. 1988. "Legislative Representation as Parallel Processing and Problem Solving." Paper presented at the 1988 Annual Meeting of the International Studies Association. St. Louis.

Braybrooke, David and Charles Lindblom. 1963. *A Strategy of Decision: The Cognitive Maps of Political Elites.* New York: Free Press.

Brewer, Garry D. 1974. "The Policy Sciences Emerge to Nurture and Structure a Discipline." *Policy Sciences* 5: 239–44.

Brown, Lawrence D. 1983. *New Policies, New Politics.* Washington, D.C.: The Brookings Institution.

Browne, Angela and Aaron Wildavsky. 1984. "Implementation as Mutual Adaptation." In Jeffrey L. Pressman and Aaron Wildavsky. *Implementation* 3d ed. Berkeley, Calif.: University of California Press.

Browning, Rufus P. and Dales Rogers Marshall. 1976. "Implementation of Model Cities and Revenue Sharing in Ten Bay Area Cities: Design and First Findings." In Charles Jones and Robert Thomas, eds. *Public Policy-Making in the Federal System.* Beverly Hills, Calif.: Sage.

Brudney, Jeffrey L. and F. Ted Hebert. 1987. "State Agencies and Their Environments: Examining the Influence of Important External Actors." *Journal of Politics* 49: 186–206.

Bullock, Charles S., III. 1980. "Implementation of Equal Education Opportunity Programs: A Comparative Analysis." In Daniel A. Mazmanian and Paul A. Sabatier, eds. *Effective Policy Implementation.* Lexington, Mass.: Lexington Books.

Campbell, Donald T. and Julian C. Stanley. 1966. *Experimental and Quasi-Experimental Designs for Research.* Chicago: Rand McNally.

Caplan, Nathan. 1976. "Factors Associated with Knowledge Use Among Federal Executives." *Policy Studies Journal* 4: 229–34.

Chubb, John E. 1983. *Interest Groups and the Bureaucracy.* Stanford, Calif.: Stanford University Press.

_____. 1985. "The Political Economy of Federalism." *American Political Science Review* 79: 994–1015.

Clausen, Aage. 1973. *How Congressmen Decide: A Policy Focus.* New York: St. Martin's.

Cobb, Roger W. and Charles D. Elder. 1981. "Communications and Public Policy." In Dan D. Nimmo and Keith R. Sanders, eds. *Handbook of Political Communications.* Beverly Hills, Calif.: Sage.

Cohen, William S. and George J. Mitchell. 1989. *Men of Zeal: A Candid Inside Story of the Iran-Contra Hearings.* New York: Penguin.

Conlan, Timothy, with Introduction by Samuel H. Beer. 1988. *New Federalism: Intergovernmental Reform from Nixon to Reagan.* Washington, D.C.: The Brookings Institution.

"Court's Move Heartens Anti-Abortion Forces." 1989. *Congressional Quarterly Weekly Report.* January 14: 87.

Crotty, Patricia McGee. 1987. "The New Federalism Game: Primacy Implementation of Environmental Policy." *Publius* 17: 53–67.

_____. 1988. "Assessing the Role of Federal Administrative Regions: An Exploratory Analysis." *Public Administration Review* 48: 642–48.

Cyert, Richard and James G. March. 1963. *A Behavioral Theory of the Firm.* Englewood Cliffs, N.J.: Prentice-Hall.

D'Amato, Alfonse. 1988. *Congressional Record.* 134 (May 17): §5986–87.

Davis, Charles E. and James P. Lester. 1987. "Decentralizing Federal Environmental Policy." *Western Political Quarterly* 40: 555–65.

Dawson, Richard E. and James A. Robinson. 1963. "Inter-Party Competition, Economic Variables and Welfare Policies in the American States." *Journal of Politics* 25: 265–89.

Derthick, Martha. 1972. *New Towns In-Town.* Washington, D.C.: Urban Institute.

Diesing, Paul. 1971. *Patterns of Discovery in the Social Sciences.* Chicago and New York: Aldine-Atherton.

Donovan, Patricia. 1984. "The Adolescent Family Life Act and the Promotion of Religious Doctrine." *Family Planning Perspectives* 16: 222–28.

Downs, Anthony. 1967. *Inside Bureaucracy.* Boston: Little, Brown.

Durant, Robert F. 1984. "EPA, TVA, and Pollution Control: Implications for a Theory of Regulatory Policy Implementation." *Public Administration Review* 44: 305–15.

_____. 1987. "Toward Assessing the Administrative Presidency: Public Lands, the BLM, and the Reagan Administration." *Public Administration Review* 47: 180–89.

Dye, Thomas R. 1966. *Politics, Economics, and Public Policy: Outcomes in the American States.* Chicago: Rand McNally.

_____. 1988. *Politics in States and Communities* 6th ed. Englewood Cliffs, N.J.: Prentice-Hall.

Easton, David. 1969. "The New Revolution in Political Science." *American Political Science Review* 63: 1051–61.

Eckstein, Harry. 1975. "Case Studies and Theory in Political Science." In Fred I. Greenstein and Nelson W. Polsby, eds. *Handbook of Political Science,* Vol. VII. Reading, Mass.: Addison-Wesley.

Economic Report of the President. 1988. Washington, D.C.: U.S. Government Printing Office.

Edwards, George C., III. 1980. *Implementing Public Policy*. Washington, D.C.: C. Q. Press.

Egan, Timothy. 1989. "Washington State Foes in Close Senate Contest." *The New York Times National Edition* November 1: 17.

Elazar, Daniel J. 1966. *American Federalism: A View from the States*. New York: Crowell.

_____. 1984. *American Federalism: A View from the States* 3d ed. New York: Harper & Row.

Elmore, Richard F. 1979. "Backward Mapping: Implementation Research and Policy Decisions." *Political Science Quarterly* 94: 601–16.

_____. 1987a. "Implementation." *Journal of Policy Analysis and Management* 6: 278–79.

_____. 1987b. "Instruments and Strategy for Public Policy." Paper presented at the 1987 Annual Meeting of the Midwest Political Science Association. Chicago.

EPA [U.S. Environmental Protection Agency]. 1987. *EPA Needs Survey Report to Congress*. Washington, D.C.: U.S. Environmental Protection Agency.

_____. 1985. *EPA Construction Grants*. Washington, D.C.: U.S. Environmental Protection Agency.

Erikson, Robert, Norman Luttbeg, and William Holloway. 1975. "Knowing One's District: How Legislators Predict Referendum Voting." *American Journal of Political Science* 19: 231–46.

Ethridge, Marcus E., III. 1981. "Legislative-Administrative Interaction as 'Intrusive Access': An Empirical Analysis." *Journal of Politics* 43: 473–92.

Federal Register. 1987. 52 (September 2): 33210–15.

Federal Register. 1988. 53 (February 2): 2922–46.

Fenno, Richard F., Jr. 1973. *Congressmen and Committees*. Boston: Little, Brown.

Fenton, John H. and D. Chamberlayne. 1969. "The Literature Dealing with Relationships Between Political Processes, Socioeconomic Conditions and Public Policies in the American States: A Bibliographic Essay." *Polity* 1: 388–404.

Fiorina, Morris and Roger Noll. 1978a. "Voters, Legislators, and Bureaucracy: Institutional Design in the Public Sector." *American Economic Review* 68: 256–60.

_____. 1978b. "Voters, Bureaucrats, and Legislators: A Rational Choice Perspective on the Growth of Bureaucracy." *Journal of Public Economics* 9: 239–53.

Friend, J. K., J. M. Power, and C. J. L. Yewlett. 1974. *Public Planning: The Inter-Corporate Dimension*. London: Tavistock.

Fund [Fund for Renewable Energy and the Environment]. 1988. *The State of the States*. Washington, D.C.: Fund.

Game, Kingsley W. 1979. "Controlling Air Pollution: Why Some States Try Harder." *Policy Studies Journal* 7: 728–38.

GAO [U.S. General Accounting Office]. 1976. "Little Accomplished in Insuring that Proper Rents Are Charged Under the Section 236 Rental Assistance Housing Program." October 5 (CED 76-146).

_____. 1987. "Surface Mining: Interior Department and States Could Improve Inspection Programs." December (RCED 87-40).

_____. 1988. "Water Pollution: Efforts to Clean Up Michigan's Rouge River." August (RCED 88–164).

Gasper, Jo Ann. 1988. "Testimony of Jo Ann Gasper, Hearing on Title X of the Public Health Services." April 22 (mimeo).

George, Alexander L. 1979. "Case Studies and Theory Development: The Method of Structured-Focused Comparison." In Paul Gordon Lauren, ed. *Diplomacy: New Approaches in History, Theory, and Policy.* New York: Free Press.

Glazer, Amihai and Marc Robbins. 1983. "Voters and Roll-Call Voting: The Effect on Congressional Elections." *Political Behavior* 2: 91–106.

Glazer, William A. 1955. "The Type and Uses of Political Theory." *Social Research* 22: 275–96.

Goggin, Malcolm L. 1986. "The 'Too Few Cases/Too Many Variables' Problem in Implementation Research." *Western Political Quarterly* 38: 328–47.

_____. 1987. *Policy Design and the Politics of Implementation: The Case of Child Health Policy in the American States.* Knoxville, Tenn.: University of Tennessee Press.

_____. 1988. "Policy Redesign: A Concept and Its Empirical Referents." Paper presented at the Annual Meeting of the Western Political Science Association. San Francisco.

_____. Unpublished manuscript. *Policy Makers, Listening, and Learning: A Comparative Analysis of Policy Redesign.*

Goggin, Malcolm L., Ann O'M. Bowman, James P. Lester, and Laurence J. O'Toole, Jr. 1990. "A Third-generation Design for Studying the Dynamics of Policy Implementation." In Dennis Palumbo and Donald Calista, eds. *Implementation and the Policy Process.* New York: Greenwood Press.

Goggin, Malcolm L., David Cownie, David Romero, Larry Gonzalez, and Susan Williams. 1985. "Block Grants and the New Federalism: Theory and Practice." Paper presented at the 1985 Annual Meeting of the Southwestern Social Science Association. Houston.

Goggin, Malcolm L. and Steven Laubacher. 1990. "Administrative Discretion in Policy Implementation: MHMR Deinstitutionalization Policy in Texas." Paper presented at the 1990 Annual Meeting of the Midwest Political Science Association. Chicago.

Gold, Rachel Benson and Jennifer Macias. 1986. "Public Funding of Contraceptive, Sterilization and Abortion Services, 1985." *Family Planning Perspectives* 18: 259–64.

Gold, Rachel Benson and Barry Nestor. 1985. "Public Funding of Contraceptive, Sterilization and Abortion Services, 1983." *Family Planning Perspectives* 17: 25–30.

Gormley, William T. 1986. "Regulatory Issue Networks in a Federal System." *Polity* 18: 595–620.

Gray, Virginia. 1973. "Innovation in the States: A Diffusion Study." *American Political Science Review* 67: 1174–85.

Greenhouse, Linda. 1989. "Supreme Court to Hear Argument on Law Limiting Abortion Access." *The New York Times National Edition* January 10: 1, 9.

Greenstone, J. D. and Paul Peterson. 1976. *Race and Authority in Urban Politics.* Phoenix edition. Chicago: University of Chicago Press.

Gunn, Lewis. 1978. "Why Is Implementation So Difficult?" *Management Services in Government* 33: 169–76.

Gurr, Ted Robert and Desmond S. King. 1987. *The State and the City.* Chicago: University of Chicago Press.

Hambleton, Robin. 1983. "Planning Systems and Policy Implementation." *Journal of Public Policy* 3: 397–418.

Hanf, Kenneth, Benny Hjern, and David O. Porter. 1978. "Local Networks of Manpower Training in the Federal Republic of Germany and Sweden." In Kenneth Hanf and Fritz W. Scharpf, eds. *Interorganizational Policy Making.* Beverly Hills, Calif.: Sage.

Hanson, Russell L. 1983. "The Intergovernmental Setting of State Politics." In Virginia Gray, Herbert Jacobs, and Kenneth N. Vines, eds. *Politics in the American States* 4th ed. Boston: Little, Brown.

Hargrove, Irwin C. 1980. "The Search for Implementation Theory." Paper presented at the Annual Meeting of the Association for Public Policy Analysis and Management.

Harrigan, John J. 1988. *Politics and Policy in States and Communities* 4th ed. Glenview, Ill.: Scott, Foresman/Little, Brown.

Hays, R. Allen. 1988. "State-Local Relations in Policy Implementation: The Case of Highway Transportation in Iowa." *Publius* 18: 79–95.

Hebert, Ted, Jeffrey Brudney and Deil S. Wright. 1983. "Gubernatorial Influence and State Bureaucracy." *American Politics Quarterly* 11: 243–64.

Heilman, John and Gerald W. Johnson. 1989. "Assessing Capital-Intensive Privatisation: The Role of System and Process." *Policy Studies Review* 8: 549–72.

Henig, Jeffrey R. 1985. *Public Policy and Federalism.* New York: St. Martin's.

Herzik, Erik B. 1985. "The Legal-Formal Structuring of State Politics: A Cultural Explanation." *Western Political Quarterly* 38: 413–24.

Hindera, John and Malcolm L. Goggin. 1990. "Is Bureaucratic Policy Making Compatible with Democracy?" Paper presented at the 1990 Annual Meeting of the Southwestern Social Science Association. Fort Worth.

Hjern, Benny. 1982. "Implementation Research—The Link Gone Missing." *Journal of Public Policy* 2: 301–8.

—————. 1987. "Policy Analysis: An Implementation Approach." Paper presented at the 1987 Annual Meeting of the American Political Science Association, Chicago.

Hjern, Benny and Chris Hull. 1983. "Going Interorganizational: Weber Meets Durkheim." Paper presented at the Annual Meeting of the American Political Science Association, Washington, D.C.

—————. 1982. "Implementation Research as Empirical Constitutionalism." *European Journal of Political Research* 10: 105–15.

—————. 1985. "Small Firm Employment Creation: An Assistance Structure Explanation." In Kenneth Hanf and Theo A. J. Toonen, eds. *Policy Implementation in Federal and Unitary Systems: Questions of Analysis and Design.* Dordrecht, Netherlands: Martinus Nijhoff.

Hjern, Benny and David O. Porter. 1982. "Implementation Structures: A New Unit for Administrative Analysis." *Organization Studies* 2: 211–37.

Hofferbert, Richard I. 1972. "State and Community Policy Studies: A Review of Comparative Input-Output Analyses." *Political Science Annual* 3: 3–72.

Hogwood, Brian W. and Lewis A. Gunn. 1984. *Policy Analysis for the Real World.* Oxford, England: Oxford University Press.

Holtman, Robert B. 1967. *The Napoleonic Revolution.* Philadelphia: J. B. Lippincott Company.

Hull, Christopher J. with Benny Hjern. 1987. *Helping Small Firms Grow: An Implementation Approach.* London: Croom Helm.

Ingram, Helen. 1978. "Future Policy Directions: Challenges for the States." *American Behavioral Scientist* 22: 311–20.

Ingram, Helen and Dean E. Mann. 1980. "Policy Failure: An Issue Deserving Analysis." In Helen Ingram and Dean Mann, eds. *Why Policies Succeed or Fail.* Beverly Hills, Calif.: Sage.

Jacob, Herbert and Michael Lipsky. 1968. "Outputs, Structure, and Power: An Assessment of Changes in the Study of State and Local Politics." In M. D. Irish, ed. *Political Science: Advance of the Discipline.* Englewood Cliffs, N.J.: Prentice-Hall.

Jenkins-Smith, Hank C., Gilbert St. Clair, and D. Bruce Martin. 1987. "Change and Continuity in Elite Belief Systems: The 1973–1979 OCS Leasing Debate." Paper presented at the Annual Meeting of the Midwest Political Science Association. Chicago.

Jewell, Malcolm E. 1982. "The Neglected World of State Politics." *Journal of Politics* 44: 638–57.

Johannes, John and John McAdams. 1981. "The Congressional Incumbency Effect: Is It Casework, Policy Compatibility, or Something Else?" *American Journal of Political Science* 25: 512–31.

Johnson, Charles A. 1976. "Political Culture in the American States: Elazar's Formulation Examined." *American Journal of Political Science* 20: 491–509.

Johnson, David. 1989. "North Trial Opens After Long Delay." *The New York Times National Edition* February 22: 12.

Johnson, Gerald W. and John Heilman. 1987. "Metapolicy Transition and Policy Implementation: New Federalism and Privatisation." *Public Administration Review* 47: 468–78.

Johnson, Julie. 1989. "Reagan Urges Abortion Fight." *The New York Times National Edition* January 14: 7.

Jones, Charles. *Clean Air.* 1975. Pittsburgh: University of Pittsburgh Press.

_____. 1976. "Why Congress Can't Do Policy Analysis (Or Words to That Effect)." *Policy Analysis* 2: 251–64.

_____. 1988. *The Reagan Legacy: Promise and Performance.* Chatham, N.J.: Chatham House.

Kau, James, Donald Keenan, and Paul Rubin. 1982. "A General Equilibrium Model of Congressional Voting." *Quarterly Journal of Economics* 97: 271–93.

Kaufman, Herbert. 1978. "Reflections on Administrative Organizations." In Joseph Pechman, ed. *Setting National Priorities: The 1978 Budget.* Washington, D.C.: The Brookings Institution.

_____. 1981. *The Administrative Behavior of Federal Bureau Chiefs.* Washington, D.C.: The Brookings Institution.

Kelman, Steven. 1984. "Using Implementation Research to Solve Implementation Problems: The Case of Energy Emergency Assistance." *Journal of Policy Analysis and Management* 4: 75–91.

Kessler, Mark. 1987. "Intergovernmental Environments, Attitudes, and the Policy Outputs of Public Agencies." *Administration and Society* 19: 48–73.

Kincaid, John. 1980. "Political Culture of the American Compound Republic." *Publius* 10: 1–15.

Kingdon, John W. 1973. *Congressmen's Voting Decisions.* New York: Harper & Row.

_____. 1984. *Agendas, Alternatives, and Public Policies.* Boston: Little, Brown.

Klecka, William R. 1980. *Discriminant Analysis.* Beverly Hills, Calif.: Sage.

Kovenock, David. 1973. "Influence in the U.S. House of Representatives: A Statistical Analysis of Communications." *American Politics Quarterly* 4: 407–64.

Kraft, Michael E. and Ruth Kraut. 1985. "The Impact of Citizen Participation on Hazardous Waste Policy Implementation: The Case of Clermont County, Ohio." *Policy Studies Journal* 14: 52–61.

Kramer, Kenneth W. 1983. "Institutional Fragmentation and Hazardous Waste Policy: The Case of Texas." In James P. Lester and Ann O'M. Bowman, eds. *The Politics of Hazardous Waste Management.* Durham, N.C.: Duke University Press.

Kuklinski, James H., Daniel S. Metlay, and W. D. Kay. 1982. "Citizen Knowledge and Choices on the Complex Issue of Nuclear Energy." *American Journal of Political Science* 26: 615–42.

Kuklinski, James and Donald McCrone. 1980. "Policy Salience and the Causal Structure of Representation." *American Politics Quarterly* 8: 139–64.

Labaton, Stephen. 1989. "States March into the Breach." *The New York Times National Edition* December 18: 1; 26.

Lasswell, Harold D. 1956. *The Decision Process.* College Park, Md.: The University of Maryland Press.

Lester, James P. 1985. "Hazardous Waste and Policy Implementation: The Subnational Role." *Hazardous Waste and Hazardous Materials* 2: 381–97.

_____. 1986. "New Federalism and Environmental Policy." *Publius* 16: 149–65.

_____. 1988. "Superfund Implementation: Exploring the Conditions of Environmental Gridlock." *Environmental Impact Assessment Review* 8: 63–70.

Lester, James P. and Ann O'M. Bowman. 1986. "Subnational Hazardous Waste Policy Implementation: A Test of the Sabatier-Mazmanian Model." Paper presented at the 1986 Annual Meeting of the American Political Science Association. Washington, D.C.

_____. 1989. "Implementing Intergovernmental Policy: A Test of the Sabatier-Mazmanian Model." *Polity* 21: 731–53.

Lester, James P., Ann O'M. Bowman, Malcolm L. Goggin, and Laurence J. O'Toole, Jr. 1987. "Public Policy Implementation: Evolution of the Field and Agenda for Future Research." *Policy Studies Review* 7: 200–216.

Lester, James P., James Franke, Ann O'M. Bowman, and Kenneth Kramer. 1983. "Hazardous Wastes, Politics, and Public Policy: A Comparative State Analysis." *Western Political Quarterly* 36: 258–85.

Lester, James P. and Emmett N. Lombard. 1987. "Comparative State Environmental Policy: Toward an Intergovernmental Analysis." Paper presented at the 1987 Annual Meeting of the Southwestern Social Sciences Association. Dallas.

Lester, James P. and Patrick Keptner. 1984. "State Budgetary Commitments to Environmental Quality Under Austerity." In John G. Francis and Richard Ganzel, eds. *Western Public Lands*. Totawa, N.J.: Rowman and Allanheld.

Levin, Martin and Barbara Ferman. 1986. "The Political Hand: Policy Implementation and Youth Employment Programs." *Journal of Policy Analysis and Management* 5: 311–25.

Levine, Adeline G. 1982. *Love Canal: Science, Politics, and People*. Lexington, Mass.: Lexington Books.

Lewin, Tamar. 1988. "Abortion Foes Switch Tactics—and Prepare for a New Day." *The New York Times National Edition* November 27: D5.

_____. 1989a. "Views on Abortion Remain Divided." *The New York Times National Edition* January 23: 14.

_____. 1989b. "Lawsuit Tests Michigan Ban on Public Funds for Abortion." *The New York Times National Edition* March 3: 12.

Lewis, Deborah, Joan MacKenzie, R. Barry Nestor, and Barbara Shprecher. 1976. "Expenditures for Organized Family Planning Services in the United States: 1974." *Family Planning Perspectives* 8: 39–42.

Lewis-Beck, Michael S. 1977. "The Relative Importance of Socioeconomic and Political Variables for Public Policy." *American Political Science Review* 71: 559–66.

_____. 1980. *Applied Regression: An Introduction*. Beverly Hills, Calif.: Sage.

Lijphart, Arend. 1971. "Comparative Politics and the Comparative Method." *American Political Science Review* 65: 682–93.

Lindblom, Charles E. 1980. *The Policy-Making Process* 2d ed. Englewood Cliffs, N.J.: Prentice-Hall.

Linder, Stephen H. and B. Guy Peters. 1987. "A Design Perspective on Policy Implementation: The Fallacies of Misplaced Prescription." *Policy Studies Review* 6: 459–75.

Lipsky, Michael. 1971. "Street Level Bureaucracy and the Analysis of Urban Reform." *Urban Affairs Quarterly* 6: 391–409.

Long, Norton. 1949. "Power and Administration." *Public Administration Review* 9: 257–64.

Love, Janice and Peter C. Sederberg. 1987. "Euphony and Cacophony in Policy Implementation: SCF and the Somali Refugee Problem." *Policy Studies Review* 7: 155–73.

Lowery, David and Lee Sigelman. 1982. "Political Culture and State Public Policy: The Missing Link." *Western Political Quarterly* 35: 376–84.

Lowi, Theodore J. 1964. "American Business and Public Policy, Case Studies and Political Theory." *World Politics* 16: 677–715.

_____. 1972. "Four Systems of Policy, Politics, and Choice." *Public Administration Review* 32: 298–310.

_____. 1979. *The End of Liberalism* 2d ed. New York: Norton.

McFarlane, Deborah R. 1989. "Testing the Statutory Coherence Hypothesis: Implementation of Family Planning Policy in the States." *Administration and Society* 20: 395–422.

McGuire, William J. 1973. "Persuasion, Resistance, and Attitude Change." In I. deSola Pool, W. Schramm, F. Frey, N. Macoby, and E. B. Parker, eds. *Handbook of Communication.* Chicago: Rand McNally.

March, James and Hebert Simon. 1958. *Organizations.* New York: Wiley.

Marvel, Mary K. 1982. "Implementation and Safety Regulation: Variation in Federal and State Administration Under OSHA." *Administration and Society* 14: 15–33.

Matthews, Donald R. and James A. Stimson. 1970. *Yeas and Nays: Normal Decision-Making in the U.S. House of Representatives.* New York: Wiley.

Mayhew, David R. 1974. *Congress: The Electoral Connection.* New Haven: Yale University Press.

Mazmanian, Daniel A. and Paul A. Sabatier, eds. 1980. *Successful Policy Implementation.* Policy Studies Organization.

_____, eds. 1981. *Effective Policy Implementation.* Lexington, Mass.: Lexington Books.

_____. 1983. *Implementation and Public Policy.* Glenview, Ill.: Scott, Foresman.

Mazmanian, Daniel A., Michael Stanley-Jones, and Miriam J. Green. 1988. *Breaking Political Gridlock.* Claremont, Calif.: California Institute of Public Affairs.

Mead, Lawrence M. 1977. *Institutional Analysis: An Approach to Implementation Problems in Medicaid.* Washington, D.C.: Urban Institute.

Meier, Kenneth. 1987. *Politics and the Bureaucracy* 2d ed. Monterey, Calif.: Brooks/Cole.

Merton, Robert. 1949. *Social Theory and Social Structure.* Glencoe, Ill.: Free Press.

Miller, G. J. and Terry M. Moe. 1983. "Bureaucrats, Legislators, and the Size of Government." *American Political Science Review* 77: 297–329.

Miller, Warren and Donald Stokes. 1963. "Constituency Influence in Congress." *American Political Science Review* 57: 45–56.

Moe, Terry M. 1985. "Control and Feedback in Economic Regulation: The Case of the NLRB." *American Political Science Review* 79: 1094–116.

Montjoy, Robert S. and Laurence J. O'Toole, Jr. 1979. "Toward a Theory of Policy Implementation: An Organizational Perspective." *Public Administration Review* 39: 465–76.

Moynihan, Daniel P. 1969. *Maximum Feasible Misunderstanding: Community Action and the War on Poverty.* New York: Basic Books.

Mueller, Keith J. 1984. "Local Government Implementation of National Inspired Programs: A Comparative Analysis." *Journal of Urban Affairs* 6: 166–78.

Nakamura, Robert T. and Frank Smallwood. 1980. *The Politics of Policy Implementation.* New York: St. Martin's Press.

Nathan, Richard P., Fred C. Doolittle, and Associates. 1983. *The Consequences of Cuts: The Effects of the Reagan Domestic Program on State and Local Governments.* Princeton, N.J.: Princeton University Press.

_____. 1987. *Reagan and the States.* Princeton, N.J.: Princeton University Press.

National Wildlife Federation. 1979. *Toxic Substances Programs in the U.S. States and Territories: How Well Do They Work?* Washington, D.C.: National Wildlife Federation.

"The Need for Family Planning Services in the United States, 1974." 1974. *Family Planning Perspectives* 6: 27–29.

Nestor, Barry. 1982. "Public Funding of Contraceptive Services, 1980–1982." *Family Planning Perspectives* 14: 198–203.

Nestor, Barry and Rachel Benson Gold. 1984. "Public Funding of Contraceptive, Sterilization, and Abortion Services, 1982." *Family Planning Perspectives* 16: 128–33.

The Office of Population Affairs. *The Adolescent Family Life Demonstration Projects: Program and Evaluation Summaries.* 1987 Update. Washington, D.C.: Office of Population Affairs.

Olsen, Joseph A. and Stan E. Weed. 1986. "Effects of Family-Planning Programs for Teenagers on Adolescent Birth and Pregnancy Rates." *Family Perspective* 20: 153–70.

Orr, Margaret Terry. 1983. "The Impact on State Management of Family Planning Funds." *Family Planning Perspectives* 15: 176–84.

Ostrom, Elinor. 1985. "Racial Inequities in Low-Income Central City and Suburban Communities: The Case of Public Services." In Kenneth Hanf and Theo A. J. Toonen, eds. *Policy Implementation in Federal and Unitary Systems: Questions of Analysis and Design.* Dordrecht, Netherlands: Martinus Nijhoff.

O'Toole, Laurence J., Jr. 1983. "Interorganizational Cooperation and the Implementation of Labour Market Training Policies: Sweden and the Federal Republic of Germany." *Organizational Studies* 4: 129–50.

_____. 1986. "Policy Recommendations for Multi-Actor Implementation: An Assessment of the Field." *Journal of Public Policy* 6: 181–210.

_____. 1988. "Strategies for Intergovernmental Management: Implementing Programs in Interorganizational Networks." *International Journal of Public Administration* 11: 417–41.

_____. 1989a. "Alternative Mechanisms for Multiorganizational Implementation: The Case of Wastewater Management." *Administration & Society* 21: 313–39.

_____. 1989b. "Goal Multiplicity in the Implementation Setting: Subtle Impacts and the Case of Wastewater Treatment Privatisation." *Policy Studies Journal.*

O'Toole, Laurence J., Jr. and Robert S. Montjoy. 1984. "Interorganizational Policy Implementation: A Theoretical Perspective." *Public Administration Review* 44: 491–503.

Palumbo, Dennis. 1986. "Privatization and Corrective Policy." *Policy Studies Review* 5: 598–605.

_____. 1987. "Introduction." *Policy Studies Review* 7: 91–102.

Panel on Adolescent Pregnancy and Childbearing. National Research Council. 1987. *Risking the Future: Adolescent Sexuality, Pregnancy, and Childbearing.* Washington, D.C.: National Academy Press.

Parks, Roger B. 1985. "Metropolitan Structure and Systemic Performance: The Case of Policy Service Delivery." In Kenneth Hanf and Theo A. J. Toonen, eds. *Policy Implementation in Federal and Unitary Systems: Questions of Analysis and Design.* Dordrecht, Netherlands: Martinus Nijhoff.

Perrow, Charles. 1972. *Complex Organizations: A Critical Essay.* Glenview, Ill.: Scott, Foresman.

Peters, B. Guy. 1986. *American Public Policy: Promise and Performance* 2d ed. Chatham, N.J.: Chatham House.

Peterson, Paul E. 1976. *School Politics Chicago Style.* Chicago: University of Chicago Press.

_____. 1981. *City Limits.* Chicago: University of Chicago Press.

Peterson, Paul E., Barry G. Rabe, and Kenneth K. Wong. 1986. *When Federalism Works.* Washington, D.C.: The Brookings Institution.

Pfeffer, Jeffrey and Gerald R. Salancik. 1978. *The External Control of Organizations: A Resource Dependence Perspective.* New York: Harper and Row.

Plewis, Ian. 1985. *Analyzing Change: Measurement and Explanation Using Longitudinal Data.* New York: Wiley.

Porter, David O. 1976. "Federalism, Revenue Sharing and Local Government." In Charles Jones and Robert Thomas, eds. *Public Policy-Making in the Federal System.* Beverly Hills, Calif.: Sage.

Powell, John Duncan. 1985. "Assault on a Precious Commodity: The Local Struggle to Protect Groundwater." *Policy Studies Journal* 14: 62–69.

Pressman, Jeffrey and Aaron Wildavsky. 1973. *Implementation.* Berkeley, Calif.: University of California Press.

_____. 1984. *Implementation* 3d ed. Berkeley, Calif.: University of California Press.

Prezeworski, Adam and Henry Teune. 1970. *The Logic of Comparative Social Inquiry.* New York: Wiley-Interscience.

Rawson, George E. 1981. "Organizational Goals and Their Impact on the Policy Implementation Process." In Dennis J. Palumbo and Marvin A. Harder, eds. *Implementing Public Policy.* Lexington, Mass.: D. C. Heath.

Reagan, Ronald. 1981. *Annual Budget Message to Congress.*

_____. 1986. "Reagan, Meese on Iran-Nicaragua Deals." In *C. Q. Almanac.* Washington, D.C.: Congressional Quarterly: 38D–39D.

_____. 1989. *Annual Budget Message to Congress.*

Reinhold, Robert. "Sweeping Changes Weighed to Reduce Los Angeles Smog." 1988. *The New York Times National Edition* December 19: 1, 12.

Riggs, Fred W. 1975. "Organizational Structures and Contexts." *Administration & Society* 7: 150–88.

_____. 1980. "The Ecology and Context of Public Administration." *Public Administration Review* 40: 107–15.

Ripley, Randall B. and Grace A. Franklin. 1982. *Bureaucracy and Policy Implementation.* Homewood, Ill.: Dorsey Press.

Rose, Douglas. 1973. "National and Local Forces in State Politics: The Implications of Multi-Level Policy Analysis." *American Political Science Review* 67: 1162–73.

Rosenbaum, David E. 1988. "Emotional Issues Are the 1988 Battleground." *The New York Times National Edition* November 4: 1, 9.

Rosenbaum, Nelson. 1980. "Statutory Structure and Policy Implementation: The Case of Wetlands Regulation." In Daniel A. Mazmanian and Paul A. Sabatier, eds. *Effective Policy Implementation*. Lexington, Mass.: Lexington Books.

Rosenbaum, Walter A. 1983. "The Politics of Public Participation in Hazardous Waste Management." In James P. Lester and Ann O'M. Bowman, eds. *The Politics of Hazardous Waste Management*. Durham, N.C.: Duke University Press.

Rosoff, Jeannie I. and Asta M. Kenney. 1984. "Title X and Its Critics." *Family Planning Perspectives* 16: 111–19.

Ross, Lester. 1984. "The Implementation of Environmental Policy in China: A Comparative Perspective." *Administration & Society* 15, 489–516.

Rowland, C. K. and Richard Feiock. 1983. "Political and Economic Correlates of Regulatory Commitment: Interstate Variance in Hazardous Waste Regulation." Unpublished manuscript.

Sabatier, Paul A. 1986. "Top-down and Bottom-up Approaches to Implementation Research: A Critical Analysis and Suggested Synthesis." *Journal of Public Policy* 6: 21–48.

_____. 1987. "Knowledge, Policy-Oriented Learning, and Policy Change: An Advocacy Coalition Framework." *Knowledge: Creation, Diffusion, Utilization* 8: 649–92.

Sabatier, Paul A. and Anne Brasher. 1986. "An Advocacy Coalition Framework of Policy Change Within Subsystems: Preliminary Results from Lake Tahoe." Paper presented at the 1986 Annual Meeting of the American Political Science Association. Washington, D.C.

Sabatier, Paul A., Anne Brasher, and Hank Jenkins-Smith. 1987. "Measuring Change over Time in Elite Beliefs and Public Policy: Content Analysis of Public Documents." Paper presented at the Annual Meeting of the Midwest Political Science Association. Chicago.

Sabatier, Paul A. and Daniel A. Mazmanian. 1979. "The Conditions of Effective Implementation: A Guide to Accomplishing Policy Objectives." *Policy Analysis* 5: 481–504.

_____. 1980. "The Implementation of Public Policy: A Framework of Analysis." *Policy Studies Journal* 8 (Special Issue 2): 538–60.

Sapolsky, Harvey. 1972. *The Polaris Missile System: Bureaucratic and Programmatic Success in Government*. Cambridge, Mass.: Harvard University Press.

Savage, Robert L. 1976. *The Literature of Systematic Quantitative Comparison in American State Politics*. Unpublished manuscript.

_____. 1981. "Looking for Political Subcultures: A Critique of the Rummage Sale Approach." *Western Political Quarterly* 34: 331–36.

Scharpf, Fritz W. 1976. "Does Organization Matter? Task Structure and Interaction in the Ministerial Bureaucracy." *Organization and Administrative Studies*. Berlin: International Institute of Management.

Schlitz, Timothy and R. Lee Rainey. 1978. "The Geographic Distribution of Elazar's Political Subcultures Among the Mass Population: A Research Note." *Western Political Quarterly* 31: 450–60.

Schlozman, Kay Lehman. 1984. "What Accent the Heavenly Chorus? Political Equality and the American Pressure System." *Journal of Politics* 46: 1006–32.

Schneider, Anne and Helen Ingram. 1988. "Filling Empty Boxes: A Framework for the Comparative Analysis of Policy Designs." Paper presented at the 1988 Meeting of the Western Political Science Association. San Francisco.

Schneider, Keith. 1984. "Ocean Incineration: The Public Fumes While EPA Fiddles." *Sierra* 73: 23–26.

Schneider, Saundra K. 1988. "Intergovernmental Influences on Medicaid Program Expenditures." *Public Administration Review* 48: 756–63.

Scholz, John T. and Feng Hung Wei. 1986. "Regulatory Enforcement in a Federalist System." *American Political Science Review* 80: 1249–70.

Schwartz, Michael. 1988. "Testimony of Michael Schwartz, Resident Fellow in Social Policy, The Free Congress Foundation, House Subcommittee on Health and Environment." April 22 (mimeo).

Shapiro, Martin M. 1988. *Who Guards the Guardians? Judicial Control of Administration.* Athens, Ga.: University of Georgia Press.

Sharkansky, Ira. 1968. "Regionalism, Economic Status and Public Policies of the American States." *Social Science Quarterly* 49: 9–26.

Sieber, Sam D. 1973. "The Integration of Fieldwork and Survey Methods." *American Journal of Sociology* 78: 1335–59.

Simon, Herbert A. 1957. *Administrative Behavior; A Study of Decision-Making Processes in Administrative Organization* 2d ed. New York: Free Press.

Simon, Herbert A. and DeWitt C. Dearborn. 1958. "Selective Perception: The Identification of Executives." *Sociometry* 21: 140–44.

Singh, Susheela. 1986. "Adolescent Pregnancy in the United States: An Interstate Analysis." *Family Planning Perspectives* 18: 210–20.

Smith, Richard A. 1984. "Advocacy, Interpretation, and Influence in the U.S. Congress." *American Political Science Review* 78: 44–63.

Smith, Susan J. 1989. "Governments Are Searching for Cost-Effective Care for AIDS Patients." *Governing* 2: 52–56.

Stewart, Joseph, Jr. and Charles S. Bullock III. 1981. "Implementing Equal Education Opportunity Policy." *Administration & Society* 12: 427–46.

Stimson, James A. 1985. "Regression in Space and Time: A Statistical Essay." *American Journal of Political Science* 29: 914–47.

Strouse J. C. and P. Jones. 1974. "Federal Aid: The Forgotten Variable in State Policy Research." *Journal of Politics* 36: 200–207.

Stuart, Reginald. 1983. "Plan for Big Dump Stirs Tampa Fight." *The New York Times* December 12: A24.

Thomas, Clive S. and Ronald J. Hrebnar. 1988. "Changes in the Number and Types of Interest Groups Active in the States." *Comparative State Politics Newsletter* 9: 28–36.

Thomas, Robert D. 1981. "Targeting and Federalism: Components of a Policy Dilemma." *Urban Interest* 3: 10–21.

Thompson, Frank. 1982. "Bureaucratic Discretion and the National Health Service Corps." *Political Science Quarterly* 94: 419–35.

Thompson, Frank and Michael J. Scicchitano. 1985. "State Implementation Effort and Federal Regulatory Policy: The Case of Occupational Safety and Health." *Journal of Politics* 47: 686–703.

_____. 1987. "State Implementation and Federal Enforcement Priorities." *Administration & Society* 19: 95–124.

Thompson, James D. 1967. *Organizations in Action: Social Science Basis of Administrative Theory.* New York: McGraw-Hill.

Tolchin, Martin. 1989. "'87 Law to Benefit the Mentally Ill May Instead Pose Threat to Them." *The New York Times National Edition* February 2: 1, 8.

Torres, Aida. 1978. "Organized Family Planning Services in the United States, 1968-1976." *Family Planning Perspectives* 10: 83-88.

_____. 1979. "Organized Family Planning Services in the United States, 1976-1977." *Family Planning Perspectives* 11: 342-47.

_____. 1984. "The Effects of Federal Funding Cuts on Family Planning Services, 1980-1983." *Family Planning Perspectives* 16: 134-38.

Torres, Aida, Patricia Donovan, Nancy Dittes, and Jacqueline Darroch Forrest. 1986. "Public Benefits and Cost of Government Funding for Abortion." *Family Planning Perspectives* 18: 111-18.

Torres, Aida and Jacqueline Darroch Forrest. 1985. "Family Planning Clinic Services in the United States, 1983." *Family Planning Perspectives* 17: 30-35.

Treadway, Jack M. 1985. *Public Policymaking in the American States.* New York: Praeger.

Tucker, Harvey J. 1982. "Interparty Competition in the American States: One More Time." *American Politics Quarterly* 10: 93-116.

Tucker, Harvey J. and Eric B. Herzik. 1986. "The Persisting Problem of Region in American State Policy Research." *Social Science Quarterly* 67: 84-97.

U.S. Department of Health & Human Services. Public Health Service. The Office of Population Affairs. 1987. *The Adolescent Family Life Demonstration Projects: Program and Evaluation Summaries.* (1987 Update). Washington, D.C.: The Office of Population Affairs.

Van Horn, Carl E. 1979a. "Evaluating the New Federalism: National Goals and Local Implementors." *Public Administration Review* 39: 17-22.

_____. 1979b. *Policy Implementation in the Federal System: National Goals and Local Implementors.* Lexington, Mass.: D. C. Heath.

_____. 1987. "Applied Implementation Research." Paper presented at the 1987 Annual Meeting of the Midwest Political Science Association. Chicago.

Van Horn, Carl E. and Donald S. Van Meter. 1976. "The Implementation of Intergovernmental Policy." In Donald S. Van Meter and Carl E. Van Horn, eds. *Public Policy in the Federal System.* Lexington, Mass.: Lexington Books.

Van Meter, Donald S. and Carl E. Van Horn. 1975. "The Policy Implementation Process: A Conceptual Framework." *Administration & Society* 6: 445-88.

Wagner, Kathryn D. 1986. "The Implementation Gap: Congress, EPA, and the Development of Environmental Politics." Paper presented at the 1986 Annual Meeting of the American Political Science Association. Washington, D.C.

Walker, David B. 1988. "American Federalism: Its Conditioners and Current Condition." Paper presented at the 1988 Annual Meeting of the Western Political Science Association. San Francisco.

Walker, Jack L. 1969. "The Diffusion of Innovation Among the American States." *American Political Science Review* 63: 886-99.

Wassenberg, Pinky S. 1986. "Implementation of Intergovernmental Regulatory Programs: A Cost-Benefit Perspective." In J. Edwin Benton and David R. Morgan. *Intergovernmental Relations and Public Policy.* Westport, Conn.: Greenwood Press.

Weatherley, Richard and Michael Lipsky. 1977. "Street-Level Bureaucrats and Institutional Innovation: Implementing Special Education Reform." *Harvard Educational Review* 47: 171–97.

Webber, David. 1984. "Political Conditions Motivating Legislator Use of Policy Information." *Policy Studies Review* 8: 110–18.

Weed, Stan E. and Joseph A. Olsen. 1986. "Effects of Family-Planning Programs on Teenage Pregnancy—Replication and Extension." *Family Perspective* 20: 173–95.

Weintraub, Bernard. 1989. "Quayle, on a Bush Mission, to Meet Foes of Abortion." *The New York Times National Edition* January 22: 16.

Whiteman, David. 1985. "The Fate of Policy Analysis in Congressional Decision Making: Three Types of Use in Committees." *Western Political Quarterly* 38: 294–311.

Wildavsky, Aaron. 1962. "Analysis of Issue Contexts in the Study of Decision Making." *Journal of Politics* 24: 717–32.

Williams, Bruce A. and Albert R. Matheny. 1984. "Testing Theories of Social Regulation: Hazardous Waste Regulation in the American States." *Journal of Politics* 46: 428–58.

Williams, Walter. 1980. *The Implementation Perspective.* Berkeley, Calif.: University of California Press.

Williams, Walter and associates, eds. 1982. *Studying Implementation: Methodological and Administrative Issues.* Chatham, N.J.: Chatham.

Williams, Walter and Richard F. Elmore, eds. 1976. *Social Program Implementation.* New York: Academic Press.

Wittrock, Bjorn and Peter DeLeon. 1986. "Policy as a Moving Target: A Call for Conceptual Realism." *Policy Studies Review* 6: 44–60.

Wood, B. Dan. 1988. "Principals, Bureaucrats, and Responsiveness in Clean Air Enforcements." *American Political Science Review* 82: 213–34.

Wright, Deil. 1967. "Executive Leadership in State Administration." *Midwest Journal of Political Science* 11: 1–26.

Wright, Gerald C., Robert S. Erikson, and John McIver. 1985. "Measuring State Partisanship and Ideology of Survey Data." *Journal of Politics* 47: 469–89.

Yewlett, Christopher J. L. 1985. "Comments on Benson and Weitzel: Interorganizational Analysis: A Field for Social Praxis Based on Social Structure, or Strategic Choice and Reticulist Judgment." In Kenneth Hanf and Theo A. J. Toonen, eds. *Policy Implementation in Federal and Unitary Systems: Questions of Analysis and Design.* Dordrecht, Netherlands: Martinus Nijhoff.

Yin, Robert K. 1982. "Studying the Implementation of Public Programs." In Walter Williams and associates, eds. *Studying Implementation: Methodological and Administrative Issues.* Chatham, N.J.: Chatham.

Index